"I love Paul Revere, whether he rode or not"
WARREN HARDING

ALSO BY RICHARD SHENKMAN

Legends, Lies & Cherished Myths of American History
One-Night Stands with American History, co-authored with Kurt Reiger

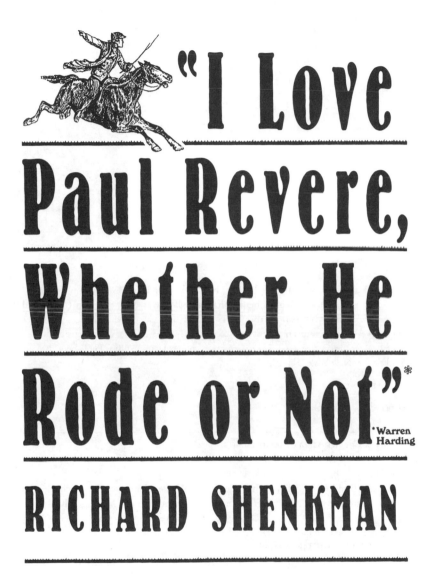

"I Love Paul Revere, Whether He Rode or Not"*

*Warren Harding

RICHARD SHENKMAN

HarperPerennial

A Division of HarperCollins*Publishers*

FIRST EDITION

Designed by Joan Greenfield

Library of Congress Cataloging-in-Publication Data

Shenkman, Richard.
    I love Paul Revere, whether he rode or not, Warren Harding : a new collection by the author of Legends, lies, & cherished myths of American history / Richard Shenkman.
       p.   cm.
    Includes bibliographical references (p.   ) and index.
    ISBN 0–06–016346–1 (cloth)
    1. United States—History—Errors, inventions, etc. 2. United States—History—Anecdotes. 3. Legends—United States. I. Title.
E178.6.S46   1991
973—dc20   91–55105

91 92 93 94 95 DT/RRD 10 9 8 7 6 5 4 3 2

For my father and my sister

Only a few days ago an iconoclastic American said there never was a ride by Paul Revere; that he started out with Colonel Dawes, an ancestor of the recent Director of the Budget, to give the warning to "every Middlesex village and farm," but was arrested, so it is said by a British sentry, and never made the ride. Suppose he did not; somebody made the ride and stirred the minutemen in the colonies to fight the battle of Lexington, which was the beginning of independence in the new Republic in America. I love the story of Paul Revere, whether he rode or not.

WARREN HARDING, 1923

Contents

PREFACE   xi

1   Patriotism   1

2   Religion   16

3   Work and Play   34

4   Business   52

5   Literature   76

6   Politics   98

7   Alcohol and Drugs   114

8   Women   130

9   Freedom and Democracy   140

10 Saints and Scalawags   165

11 History   182

12 So Many Myths   192

ACKNOWLEDGMENTS   201
NOTES   203
INDEX   221

Preface

Something which everybody accepts as the gospel truth is inevitably false.

H. L. Mencken

Imagine for a moment it is 1923. Al Capone is assembling an army of gun-toting henchmen in Chicago. (They will number 700 before he is through.) Cotton farmers in the South are sunk in depression. The Ku Klux Klan is on the rise. Newspaper headlines tell of corruption in the Veterans Bureau (the director has had to resign). Rumors in the capital hint of the coming Teapot Dome Scandal. (Eventually two secretaries in the cabinet will go to jail, convicted of corruption.)

But these are not the things that concern the president of the United States. What worries Warren Harding—touring the country on a campaign swing that will prove to be his last—is a recent attack on the legend of Paul Revere. An iconoclast had noted that Revere never completed the ride made famous by Longfellow. Before giving warning to Concord, Revere was discovered by the British and captured. Harding, however, told the crowd he didn't care. "I love the story of Paul Revere," the president intoned in his most presidential-sounding voice, "whether he rode or not."

Americans today are less scandalized by iconoclasm than Harding was. But we are less cynical than we think we are. Indeed, the evidence suggests we are just as susceptible to mythology as Americans in the past.

The danger is not that we have myths. They tell us who we are and what we cherish and all people have them. The danger is hiding from the fact that they are myths.

1
Patriotism

In Dr. Johnson's famous dictionary patriotism is defined as the last resort of a scoundrel. With all due respect to an enlightened but inferior lexicographer I beg to submit that it is the first.
AMBROSE BIERCE

Nothing seems more natural to an American than to venerate the patriotic symbols that represent America. They are virtually sacred. Scornful as we are of the candidate who wraps himself in the flag, it is often the candidate who fails to do so who loses.

But if Americans cherish their symbols of patriotism, they haven't always loved them. It used to be good enough just to respect them.

Take Old Glory, that "emblem of unity, of loyalty to home and to kindred, and to all that is sacred in life." The early adoption of the flag by the United States has been considered proof of its early acceptance as a sacred symbol of the United States. But that seems not to have been the case. Milo Quaife, in his exhaustive history of the flag, concluded that the generation that gave us the national flag remained astonishingly indifferent to it.

From early congressional debates, for instance, it is quite clear that the only reason the founders adopted a national flag was for the practical reason that the navy needed one for identification when sailing into foreign ports. The bill providing for the establishment of the flag consisted of a single sentence, just twenty-nine words long.* The preamble to the Constitution was longer (fifty-two words). When in 1794 someone introduced a bill to add two stars to the flag to take into account the admission into the union of Vermont and Kentucky, many members objected that the matter wasn't worthy of their attention. It is "a trifling business," said one, "which ought not to engross the attention of the House, when it was their duty to discuss matters of infinitely greater importance." The Vermont representative agreed. In the end, says Quaife, the members approved the bill "as the quickest way of terminating" debate about it.

The existence of great varieties of flag designs demonstrates the profound carelessness with which it was treated. Some stars came with five points. Some stars came with six. Some stars came in white. Some came in silver. Because Congress never specified if the stars should be arranged in a circle or in rows, flag makers stitched them both ways. On the eve of the Civil War it became fashionable to put them in an oval. Even the number of stripes seems to have varied by whim, though it was established by law. At one point the flag over the capitol had eighteen stripes, while the flag over the New York Navy Yard had only nine.

The flag is a particularly poor example of an early sacred symbol, as many Americans—including top government officials—were unsure of its appearance. More than a year after its adoption by Congress, Benjamin Franklin and John Adams, in a joint letter to the king of Naples, said it "consists of thirteen stripes, alternately red, white and blue."

They may be forgiven for their ignorance. For Americans in our early history seldom got the chance to see the flag. It did not fly from buildings. It was not put in the schools. It was never reproduced in the newspapers. And painters did not make pictures of it.

---

* "*Resolved,* That the flag of the [thirteen] United States be thirteen stripes, alternate red and white: that the union be thirteen stars, white in a blue field, representing a new constellation." June 14, 1777 (*Journal of the Continental Congress: 1774–1789* [1907], VIII, 464).

Wilbur Zelinsky, reporting on a search of major catalogs of art from the Revolutionary War, says he could not find a single depiction of the American flag.

The erroneous impression that Old Glory was ubiquitous in the Revolution is due to the fact that it is ubiquitous in the paintings of the Revolution done in the nineteenth century. But the fact is, not a single land battle in the Revolution was fought under the Stars and Stripes. There was no American flag at Bunker Hill, at Trenton, or even at Yorktown. Indeed, not until the Mexican-American War did American soldiers fight under Old Glory. Even then the use of the flag in battle was limited. The marines did not adopt the flag until 1876; the U.S. Cavalry not until 1887. Forget those pictures of George Custer and the Stars and Stripes. His men never carried it.

Soldiers did not go flagless, of course. They had battle flags to keep up their spirits. But nobody cares about those old battle flags. What we want is Washington crossing the Delaware with the Stars and Stripes. And what we want the artists in the nineteenth century gave us; pictures with flags sell.

Pictures counting more than words, it is likely we will forever think of the "boys on Bunker Hill" fighting under the flag John Trumbull put there in his famous painting of the battle. When we imagine stereotypical revolutionary soldiers, it is Archibald Willard's depiction in The Spirit of '76 that we think of. It features the flag and three haggard patriots, one playing a fife, the others beating drums. It is part of the myth of America and no more could be eliminated from our national memory than the Revolution it honors so sentimentally.

Of America's Revolutionary War heroes, only one fought under the Stars and Stripes, John Paul Jones, who has been the subject of endlessly silly stories. Biographer Augustus C. Buell, for example, claimed Jones's flag aboard the Bonhomme Richard* was sewn by a band of "dainty" girls "from slices of their best silk gowns"; one of

---

* Named in honor of Ben Franklin's Poor Richard.

the girls, Helen Seavey, was even said to have sacrificed her bridal dress to provide material for the stars. Actually, the story is as fanciful as Jones's famous sea-battle boast that he had "not begun to fight" (more on that later). And Helen Seavey never existed.

Better yet is the story of the flag's eventual disposal. After disappearing from sight for some eighty years, late in the nineteenth century it was said to have suddenly resurfaced. Through a chain of miracles, it was said, the very flag that had flown over the *Bonhomme Richard* had survived and survived largely intact despite its use during several fierce battles. The only thing missing from the flag was a piece that supposedly had been given to Abraham Lincoln during the Civil War. The family that produced the flag—the Staffords—had an elaborate story to explain how they came into possession of it. In brief, they said it had been awarded by Congress to one of their ancestors, who had bravely served under Jones on the *Bonhomme Richard* and who saved the flag from destruction when the ship sank. And they had an affidavit to prove it. The affidavit, signed by the secretary of the Marine Committee of Congress, dated 1784, confirmed that one James Stafford had been given "Paul Jones' Starry Flag of the Bon Homme Rich^d." It was considered authentic for a long time. The Smithsonian Institution even put the flag on display. (It remained on display through the 1920s.)

That was a mistake. By Jones's own statement, we now know that the flag that flew over his ship was destroyed in the battle in which he lost the ship; a cannon blew it up. We also know that the Stafford affidavit was a hoax. James Stafford never served on the *Bonhomme Richard,* and the committee that supposedly awarded him possession of the flag in 1784 had ceased to exist five years earlier.[1]

No doubt the founders would be pleased to see that the flag is respected today. But they would not understand it being worshiped. Worship of the flag is strictly a modern development. A hundred years or so ago only a few self-appointed flag defenders conceived of it as a sacred object. Schools were not required to fly the flag until 1890. Americans did not begin pledging allegiance to the flag until 1892. They did not begin saluting the flag until around the Spanish-

American War in 1898. * Flag Day was not nationally observed until 1916. The flag code, prescribing the proper way to treat a flag and dispose of it, was not approved by Congress until 1942 and did not become part of federal law until 1976.

The interesting thing is not that the rituals of flag worship go back only as far as the late nineteenth century but that Americans think they go back further. We have become so used to the idea that the flag is a sacred object that we cannot imagine a time when it was not considered one. However, there was a time when patriotism needed no such artificial braces. During the Revolution, when men were fighting and dying on the battlefield to establish a new nation, saluting the flag would have been regarded as an empty gesture. The thing to do was to go out and join the fighting. That was patriotism.

If Americans did not embrace flag rituals early on, once they did, they embraced the practice enthusiastically. There seemed to be plenty of reason. With the invasion of the "hordes" of immigrants from Europe, hordes with strange names and exotic accents, it was believed that flag rituals were needed to ensure the newcomers' loyalty.† Fear, then, was behind the movement to adopt flag rituals, but nobody ever remembers that. Today it is the descendants of those "hordes" of immigrants who often seem the most offended by violators of the rituals. It is interesting to speculate what "the ethnics" (as the politicians refer to them) might think if

---

* Americans were taught to salute by extending their right hand, "palm up and slightly raised." This proved embarrassingly similar to the Nazi salute, however, and during World War II was dropped. By order of Congress, Americans then began "saluting" the flag by crossing their right hand over their heart. (David R. Manwaring, *Render unto Caesar: The Flag-Salute Controversy* [1962], pp. 2–3.)

† Members of patriotic groups such as the Daughters of the American Revolution so feared the immigrants that they began to embrace the British against whom their ancestors had once fought. One proposed making "an alliance of hearts if not of hands with our kinsmen over the sea." After all, "We are of one tongue, one blood, one purpose." (Quoted in Wallace E. Davies, *Patriotism on Parade* [1955], p. 316.)

they discovered those rituals had been adopted to curb their ancestors.

Once the immigrants had been absorbed into the culture there should not have been much reason for retaining the rituals designed to Americanize the immigrants. But once invented, the rituals could not be eliminated. Every few years there seemed yet another compelling reason for keeping them. In World War I, they proved useful, as historian Bernard Weisberger has pointed out, in promoting "unity in the fight against the Kaiser." Later, says Weisberger, they were used "to inoculate against Bolshevism." [2]

(One cannot mention the flag, of course, without making reference to the story that it was Betsy Ross who stitched the first one. She did not, unfortunately. The whole story was made up by her grandson. Nor did she have anything to do with the selection of the flag's design or its colors. If anybody was responsible for designing the flag it was probably Francis Hopkinson, who was given credit by Congress for having done so. But no one individual actually designed the flag. Our flag came about through two modifications of the British Union flag, which included a red, white, and blue cross in the corner square and a solid red field. Our first flag, commissioned for the navy in 1776, was simply the basic British Union flag divided by white stripes. Our second flag, the Stars and Stripes, substituted stars for the cross in the corner square. The red, white, and blue colors were derivative. They did not, as some allege, come out of Washington's family crest. And they do not mean anything. Contrary to the Boy Scout *Handbook*, the blue in the flag does not represent justice, the white is not for purity, and the red is not for bravery.) [3]

If Americans were slow to revere the flag, they were also slow to sanctify the Fourth of July.* Boston did not celebrate the Glorious

---

* Of course, it is the second of July that should be celebrated; that's when independence was declared. Nothing happened on the fourth except the approval of the Declaration of Independence. See the author's *Legends, Lies & Cherished Myths of American History* (1988), pp. 138–39.

Fourth until the end of the Revolution, preferring instead to honor the Boston Massacre. Congress sometimes did and sometimes didn't declare the Fourth of July an official holiday. The holiday was overlooked by Congress in 1787, for instance, though that was the very year the Constitution was drafted.

Pride in the Fourth of July was clearly very great. On no other day of the year did Americans celebrate their country with such fervor. But it had not become a holiday of national unity. If anything, the holiday exacerbated divisions among Americans. On no other day of the year were patriots as likely to come to blows over politics as on the fourth. Michael Kammen reports that in most cities in the 1790s the political parties held separate celebrations of the holiday: "They held separate processions, separate dinners, and heard separate orations." Toasts reflected the fierce divisions, for example, "John Adams, may he like Sampson slay thousands of Frenchmen, with the jawbone of Jefferson." Not until the Federalist Party disappeared after the War of 1812 did Americans finally use the holiday to glorify the country instead of their own partisan cause.[4]

Jefferson in particular was often subject to attack on the fourth, for great as he seems to us, he was regarded in his own day as a politician, not a founding father, and by many as a particularly disagreeable politician. When it was disclosed after the Revolution that it was Jefferson who had primarily written the Declaration of Independence, Federalists scoffed that he had plagiarized it from John Locke. Many refused to mention it in their patriotic orations. Federalists considered it a "Philippic against Great Britain and her King," a king with whom they increasingly identified. If they associated it with revolution, it was the hated French Revolution they had in mind. Not until the so-called Era of Good Feelings—three decades after the end of the Revolution—did the Declaration finally become a sacred text.[5]

Much is often made of the fact that Jefferson and Adams died on the Fourth of July in 1826—exactly fifty years after the adoption of the Declaration of Independence. It is said that by then they had become good friends. Adams is supposed to have remarked, just before he expired, "Jefferson still survives." But if they ended life friends, they weren't quite as good friends as they've been made out to be. Just five years before their deaths, Adams accused Jefferson of plagiarizing the Declaration of Independence from a North Carolina declaration of independence—just then publicly released—that had supposedly been approved a full year before Jefferson's. * "Mr. Jefferson," he wrote a friend, "must have seen it, in the time of it, for he has copied the spirit, the sense, and the expressions of it verbatim, into his Declaration of the 4th of July, 1776." Actually, Jefferson had not copied the North Carolinians. But Adams, of course, had been ready to believe the worst.[6]

The popularity of the "Star-Spangled Banner"—if it can still be said to be popular—is due as much to the fabulous circumstances under which it was written as to the appeal of its lyrics. Probably not one American in a hundred can recite the words to the song but almost everybody remembers how it came to be composed. Most of the story has been independently confirmed. Francis Scott Key actually was fortunate enough to watch the bombardment of Fort McHenry (which guarded Baltimore), and he actually waited through the night to see if "our flag was still there."

But did the flag he saw at "dawn's early light" fly through the night? As anyone can testify who has seen the flag, which is on display at the Smithsonian, it is huge: 30 feet by 42 feet. The stars alone measure 2 feet across, point to point. For this flag to have survived the night the fort was under attack—a stormy, rainy, windy night—is almost inconceivable. Walter Lord, who wrote an acclaimed book on the War of 1812, is of the opinion that it probably did not fly all night. If there was a flag on the pole in the morning, as there undoubtedly was, it was probably hoisted up the

---

* This was the so-called Mecklenburg Declaration that supposedly dated back to 1775 and that North Carolinians long considered the first declaration of independence. It wasn't. It was a hoax. See *Legends, Lies, & Cherished Myths of American History*, p. 140.

pole that morning. And that is precisely what an eyewitness says happened. According to the testimony of Midshipman Robert J. Barrett, as the British fleet sailed away after the battle, the Americans "hoisted a most superb and splendid ensign on their battery." This, says Lord, is "most likely" the flag Key saw. If there was a flag that flew all night it would have to have been the fort's so-called "storm flag," a small flag designed expressly for bad weather. But how Key could have seen it is a mystery. He was 8 miles away—possibly near enough to see the big flag, but not the smaller one.[7]

That Francis Scott Key is associated in the American mind with the War of 1812, and is thought of in connection with one of the great battles of the war, is ironic because Key hated the war. He told his mother he thought the United States was to blame for the conflict and deserved to lose it. In letters home to friends and neighbors Key condemned "this abominable war" as a "lump of wickedness."

Key volunteered to defend the capital but according to his biographer his service as a soldier was brief and uneventful, and when the war was over he confessed he was glad. His most thrilling moment had occurred when he was knocked off his horse by a "bone of bacon" and landed in a river.

About the song itself there are several myths. It was not immediately popular and it was not adopted as the national anthem until 1931. Army and navy bands did not begin playing it on a regular basis until the 1890s. Everyone knows it is sung to the tune of an old English drinking song, but few realize it was a song that celebrated not only wine but love. If Key ever felt any embarrassment over that, he never said so, but it's interesting that the fact is not more widely known.[8]

The surprising thing about some of the most famous paintings, poems, and stories that have been used to promote patriotism is that they really were not intended to do so. The Betsy Ross story was conceived by her descendants to make themselves seem more important. Emanuel Leutze's painting of Washington crossing the

Delaware was painted to give liberals in his native Germany encouragement to follow Washington's lead and revolt. Henry Wadsworth Longfellow's poem about Paul Revere, published in 1861, was written to impress northerners during the Civil War of the necessity of fighting for liberty:

> One, if by land, and two, if by sea;
> And I on the opposite shore will be,
> Ready to ride and spread the alarm
> Through every Middlesex village and farm
> For the country folk to be up and to arm.[9]

Few ideas are as fixed in peoples' minds as the belief that patriotism formerly was stronger in America than it is now. It is widely believed, for instance, that cupidity was unknown in the Revolution. Then there were giants among us! Then virtue reigned!

Actually, under the strain of the war, Americans often seemed to have acted rather worse than they otherwise would have. Certainly, they don't seem to have behaved better. Washington was of the opinion that a "dirty, mercenary spirit" pervaded society. Norman Gelb, in his book *Less Than Glory*, recounts in shocking detail innumerable instances of greed and corruption, including the sale to the army of rotten meat, tattered clothing, shoes that fell apart, half-empty flour barrels, and defective gunpowder. Professor Robert Shalhope writes that farmers "demanded usurious prices for their crops," and that merchants "engaged in a lucrative trade with the enemy." "Public officials and governmental contractors," he says, "indulged in widespread corruption."

Nor did the American taxpayer evince much enthusiasm for the cause. It had been thought Americans didn't like paying taxes without representation. But it turned out they just didn't like paying taxes, period. This may be considered a perfectly natural and healthy instinct. But it went unappreciated by the army, which suffered because of it. "I despise my countrymen," an army colonel wrote at one point.

I wish I could say I was not born in America. . . . The rascally stupidity which prevails, the insults and neglects which the army have met with, beggars all description. It must go no further. They can endure it no longer. I am in rags, have lain in the rain on the ground for forty hours past, and only a junk of fresh beef and that without salt to dine on this day, rec'd no pay since December, and all this for my cowardly countrymen who flinch at the very time when exertions are wanted, and hold their purse strings as tho they would damn the world, rather than part with a dollar to their army.

Pride in the army is surely defensible. Through seven long years of war—the longest war the United States ever fought until Vietnam—the army under Washington remained true to the cause. But the spirit of sacrifice even among army men wasn't universal. Desertions became so common that some scheduled attacks had to be canceled for lack of men to fight them; Gelb tells of a general in the South who discovered in the midst of a major assault that the seven thousand troops under his command had dwindled to only three thousand, resulting in a disastrous rout. It's estimated that up to a third of the soldiers in the Revolutionary army deserted. Some left to return home to their families or to join their state militias, but probably most got tired of the war or were scared of dying.

People who speak confidently of the Revolutionary soldier's patriotism often seem to think that from morning until night they dreamed patriotic thoughts and only such thoughts. In reality, says historian Merle Curti, "most of the time" the American soldier was preoccupied with the thoughts that preoccupy most soldiers: "thoughts of food, drink, mud, lice, and sex." We know from their letters that they only rarely seemed to have written of their patriotic feelings. It was enough that they made the decision to risk life and limb for their country. They did not have to write or talk or think about it. Much of the time, for instance, they appeared more interested in the cook's plans for breakfast than in Washington's plan of war. A popular chant went:

"What have you for your Dinners, Boys?"
"Nothing but Fire Cake and Water, Sir!"
"Gentlemen, the Supper is ready."
"What is your Supper, Lads?"
"Fire Cake and Water, Sir."
"What have you got for Breakfast, Lads?"
"Fire Cake and Water, Sir."

Washington's views on patriotism are interesting to consider. Burdened with the command of the soldiers, he had to learn what motivated them. His finding: They were motivated by self-interest. He observed in 1778:

Men may speculate all they will. They may talk of patriotism; they may draw a few examples from ancient story, of great achievements performed by its influence; but whosoever builds upon it, as a sufficient Basis for conducting this Bloody war, will find themselves deceived in the end. We must take the passions of Men as Nature has given them. . . . I do not mean to exclude altogether the Idea of Patriotism. I know it exists, and I know it has done much in the present Contest. But I venture to assert, that a great and lasting War can never be supported on this principle alone.[10]

If Americans have partly overestimated the extent of patriotism in the Revolution, they have ludicrously overestimated it in the Civil War. If the Minuteman is sentimentalized, the sentimentalism has by now become rather stale. But Billy Yank and Johnny Reb remain the romantic figures they always have been: Boy Scouts in blue and gray.

But it is worth remembering that many of the ones who fought for the North fought partly because they were paid to. More than a hundred thousand soldiers were hired to fight for the North. Many of these were immigrants, expressly brought over, says Shelby Foote, "by companies newly formed to supply the demand."

And in focusing on the people who decided to fight, we overlook the huge numbers of civilians who paid others to do their fighting for them. More than eighty-five thousand Americans who were drafted in the war got out of going by paying a $300 commutation fee. Among these were banker J. P. Morgan and Theodore Roosevelt, Sr., father of President Theodore Roosevelt. So many young men with means remained civilians that northern universities were able to enroll about as many students from the North during the war as they had before. No doubt the people who stayed home later suffered guilt feelings, but the fact is they did stay home. And more than two hundred thousand Americans who joined the Union army subsequently deserted.[11]

Sayings are often quoted to bolster American patriotism, but many are dubious in origin or misunderstood. Of these several deserve special consideration.

The delight in recalling Patrick Henry's most famous line—"Give me liberty or give me death"—is offset by the knowledge that there's no proof he said it. Or if he said it, he may not have been the first one to do so. It possibly was made up by William Wirt, Henry's first biographer, who made up so many "facts" in his book that historians reportedly find themselves asking "Is it fact or is it Wirt?" What is hard to understand is how, if Henry actually uttered such a thing, his contemporaries could have failed to record it. But then, they failed to write down any of his speeches in full, apparently not knowing—or caring?—that the speeches would still be considered noteworthy generations later. "Socrates himself," one contemporary lamented, "would pass unnoticed and forgotten in Virginia."

We know from a contemporary journal that Henry did utter the famous remark "Caesar had his Brutus; Charles the First his Cromwell; and George the Third may profit by their example." And we know that he responded, when a speaker interrupted and accused him of treason, "If this is treason, make the most of it." The speech caused a sensation, being bolder than any speech given that year. (It was in 1765, in response to the hated Stamp Act tax.) But the memory of the speech is spoiled by the fact that afterward Henry apologized for it.[12]

The boast that America would spend "millions for defense, but not one cent for tribute" (attributed to diplomat Charles Pinckney but actually spoken by legislator Robert Goodloe Harper), is also spoiled. For we did pay tribute. We just prefer not to remember we did. In 1795, in a treaty with Algiers, the United States agreed to pay the Barbary Pirates nearly $1 million in tribute to win the release of American citizens held in captivity. It was in disgust at our paying tribute that Harper laid down the principle that we shouldn't. Paying tribute proved to be folly, for eventually we had to pay millions for defense anyway. To stop the Barbary States from continued depredations, the United States had to go to war against them twice: between 1803 and 1805, and again in 1815.[13]

Nothing is as stirring as John Paul Jones's bravely defiant boast "I have not begun to fight." And the fact is, at the time he supposedly uttered the remark he had refused to surrender. Ultimately, it was the British who surrendered. But the fine remark that attaches to the victory of his ship, the *Bonhomme Richard*, over the British vessel, the *Serapis*, was apparently made up by a worshipful subordinate forty years later. The only contemporaneous record that survives is the report of the British commander of the *Serapis*. He merely noted that when Jones was asked if he'd surrender, Jones answered "in the most determined negative."[14]

Stephen Decatur's famous accomplishments as a courageous naval officer have been overshadowed by his even more famous toast, which is correctly rendered: "Our Country! In her intercourse with foreign nations may she always be in the *right* and always *successful, right or wrong.*" No other toast in American history has attracted such notice, or such criticism. To foreigners like G. K. Chesterton, it has seemed the epitome of American mindlessness. " 'My country, right or wrong,' [wrote Chesterton] is like saying, 'My mother, drunk or sober.' "

It's forgotten, however, to Decatur's unending misfortune, that it was a toast and only a toast, and like most toasts, hardly worth debating. It came near the end of a long night of heavy drinking and boisterous laughter, and if it was clearly extravagant, it was less so than many other toasts given that night by other dinner guests: "The Mediterranean [went one such toast]! The sea not more of Greek and Roman than of American glory!" "National glory [went another]! A gem above all price, and worthy every hazard to sustain its splendor." But the toast that "brought them to their feet with a roar" was Decatur's.[15]

2
Religion

Rellijon is a quare thing. Be itself it's all right. But sprinkle a little pollyticks into it an' dinnymit is bran flour compared with it.
"Mr. Dooley" (Finley Peter Dunne)

About their religious past Americans know little, and much of what little they know is comprised of stereotypes. From colonial history there are the "revered" and persecuted Pilgrim fathers, dressed in their somber black steeple hats and dark cloaks, who landed on a rock and lived in log cabins. They are succeeded by the exceptionally devout Puritans who, before they mysteriously disappear from history, establish an oppressive theocracy and burn some witches. The Puritans in turn are followed by the pious founding fathers, who are credited with building a Christian nation based on the idea of religious freedom. Little is believed to have happened in the nineteenth century. But in the twentieth, southern yokels put a professor on trial for teaching the novel theory that men come from monkeys.

The Pilgrims might not have objected to being called somber for they were a serious people. However, they certainly didn't look the way we think they did. They didn't wear ridiculous tall hats with shiny buckles, they weren't partial to black, and they didn't forsake jewelry. The one Pilgrim portrait that survives shows a man in a natty Elizabethan doublet featuring gold buttons, a starched white collar, and a braided gold tassel.[1]

Neither did they live in log cabins. The log cabin didn't arrive in America until the end of the seventeenth century. The Pilgrims lived in primitive clapboard houses with thatched roofs. (They made the boards by splitting logs with an ax.) [2]

Nor were they always revered. Until the nineteenth century, scarcely anyone paid them, their Mayflower Compact, or their Plymouth Rock much mind.

Even to hint that the Pilgrims once were ignored is, of course, to court controversy. One may as well say the Pilgrims never landed on Plymouth Rock (which, incidentally, they didn't—see below). And yet the evidence clearly shows that for the first 150 years after their arrival little mention was made of them. Attention was paid not to the Pilgrims but to their more successful cousins, the Puritans of Massachusetts Bay, who subsequently absorbed them. By the middle of the eighteenth century, people in Plymouth began touting the Pilgrims' achievements, but the movement to turn them into American heroes subsequently faltered when the leaders of the effort made the mistake of backing the British in the Revolution. Not until after the war did anyone think to give them a holiday, [*] and as late as 1789 they remained inconsequential enough that the Plymouth town clergyman thought nothing of running his field horses through the founder's graveyard, crashing tombstones along the way. And if that's not humiliating enough, there are reliable reports that some Plymouth residents used Pilgrim tombstones to cover open sewer holes.

As late as the nineteenth century, Americans hadn't even settled on the date of the Pilgrims' arrival in Plymouth. Some said they arrived December 21, others December 22. The confusion arose because of the difficulty of translating dates from the Old Style calendar—in use in the Pilgrims' era—to the New Style calendar that was adopted in the 1700s. Throughout the nineteenth century their arrival was celebrated alternately on one date one year, another date the next. Not until Massachusetts

[*] Forefathers' Day, celebrated in New England.

made December 21 a legal holiday in 1895 was the matter finally settled. *

There is really so little tradition behind the Pilgrim tradition that until the 1840s the Pilgrims weren't even known as "Pilgrims." They were called the "Old Comers" or the "Forefathers." Although they had been called Pilgrims by William Bradford in his history of Plymouth two hundred years earlier, Bradford's manuscript had been lost and with it the name. So much for hoary tradition.

The Pilgrims, in fact, weren't celebrated at all as national figures until the 1820s, after a landmark speech by a youthful Daniel Webster. And they did not become firmly entrenched in the popular imagination until the Victorians turned a Pilgrim secular festival into our Thanksgiving. Thanksgiving, indeed, tells us a lot more about the Victorians than it does about the Pilgrims. If the Pilgrims seem prim and proper, it is because the Victorians made them seem that way. It was the Victorians who made the holiday a religious and family event.

The Mayflower Compact, like the Pilgrims who wrote it, was similarly ignored. Not until the Revolution did the compact attract much attention. And when it did, it was the Tories who brought it to the public's notice. Patriots didn't get around to celebrating the document until after the Revolution.†³

It may seem inconceivable to think that Plymouth Rock was ever ignored, but it was. Until the middle of the eighteenth cen-

---

* The usual procedure in bringing a date under the old calendar into conformity with the new was to add eleven days to it. Thus, since the Pilgrims had landed in Plymouth on December 11, Old Style, the new date of their arrival was fixed on December 22. But upon further reflection it was decided that the date was really December 21 because the event took place in the 1600s when there was only a ten-day difference between the two calendars. (George Willison, *Saints and Strangers* [1945], p. 166.)

† Naturally, few mythmakers mention the Tories' involvement, it being rather inconvenient for a document with democratic pretensions to be the pride and joy of monarchists, but more on that later (see page 142).

tury, according to historian George Willison, the rock was considered "just another gray granite boulder." Local entrepreneurs had even tried to destroy it to make way for a new wharf. Indeed, the legend of Plymouth Rock did not surface until the 1740s and its origins are so suspicious that no reliable historian thinks the story is trustworthy. It's based on what one old man says he was told as a boy by another old man who had related what he had heard as a boy. Of such rock-hard evidence are myths made. *

To this day the Pilgrims' identity remains somewhat vague. Americans really don't even know who the Pilgrims are and in their ignorance mistakenly identify them with the Puritans. Even presidents get this wrong. In his farewell address, Ronald Reagan—twice in one paragraph—referred to the Puritan John Winthrop as a Pilgrim. † Actually, the Pilgrims and the Puritans were two different

---

* One would have thought, given all the fuss that's been made over Plymouth Rock, that efforts would have been made over the years to protect it. And they have! But in trying to save the rock, the mythmakers have nearly succeeded in destroying it. The effort began when town boosters moved the rock inland in the late eighteenth century, presumably the better to preserve it. But in moving it inland they split it in two, leaving half of it on the beach. The half on the beach subsequently was lost while the half moved inward became overgrown with weeds. Eventually, the beach half was found as the doorstep of an old warehouse, and the rock that was inland was given renewed care. But that left the town—to the everlasting consternation of the tourists —with two Plymouth Rocks. In 1880, to end the confusion, the rock that was inland was dragged down to the beach and attached to the other one. But to many the rock now seemed too far from shore for the Pilgrims to have landed on it. This necessitated yet another move, this time to a position closer to shore. In this move the rock was broken yet again. Since the 1920s it has remained embedded in the sand beneath a towering stone temple built of no fewer than sixteen columns, but the temple is built so high and the rock is so small that from where visitors stand above the rock it looks strikingly silly. (Willison, *Saints and Strangers*, p. 433.)
† Reagan, in 1969: "John Winthrop gathered the little band of Pilgrims together and spoke of the life they would have in that land they had never seen." Reagan, in 1986: "A little group of Puritans huddled on the deck [of the

groups. The Pilgrims came over on the *Mayflower*; the Puritans, arriving ten years later, settled the Massachusetts Bay Colony.[4]

Unlike the Puritans, the Pilgrims were a heterogeneous group, divided, as they put it, between saints and strangers. The saints journeyed to America for religious reasons, the strangers in hopes of improving their fortunes. Of the two groups, the saints were in the minority, forming only about a third of the *Mayflower*'s passengers and crew.*

That the Saints among the Pilgrims sought religious liberty is true, but the impression has been given that they were seeking it here because it had been denied them in Europe. This is untrue. While the Saints had been persecuted in England, they hadn't lived in England for a dozen years. They had been living in Holland, and

---

Arabella in 1630]. And then John Winthrop, who would later become the first governor of Massachusetts, reminded his fellow Puritans there on that tiny deck that they must keep faith with their God." Several paragraphs later: "Well, this is the common thread that binds us to those Quakers on the tiny deck of the *Arabella.*" Reagan, in 1989: "He [Winthrop] journeyed here on what today we'd call a little wooden boat; and like the other Pilgrims, he was looking for a home that would be free."

Actually, Winthrop would have been incensed had he known someday he would be called a Pilgrim. Winthrop held the Pilgrims in contempt. (He objected to their naive believe in utopianism.) He never had a chance to form an opinion about the Quakers. By the time the Quakers finally appeared in Massachusetts, Winthrop was dead. But he probably wouldn't have liked them any better than he had the Pilgrims. His political heirs persecuted the Quakers as Winthrop had once badgered other dissenters. (Ronald Reagan, *Speaking My Mind* [1989], pp. 44, 299–300, 417; Michael Wallace, "Ronald Reagan and the Politics of History," *Tikkun*, 2, No. 1 [1987], 17.)

* One can make the argument, and many do, that the Pilgrim Saints should be considered Puritans. And in a sense they were; both believed the Church of England had become corrupt and needed purifying. But the Pilgrims believed the Church of England had become so corrupt that they had to form their own church; they became known as Separatists. The Puritans continued to hope that the church could still be reformed from within. The Pilgrims, therefore, were far more radical in their approach than the Puritans, and deserve to be remembered as radicals.

in Holland they enjoyed complete freedom of worship. They left Holland not because they couldn't pray as they wished but because they wanted a place of their own in which to pray. Holland had proved so tolerant of the Pilgrims that their children had begun to adopt Dutch manners and ideas. If they remained, the Pilgrims feared, their children would stray.

In the popular imagination, next to the Pilgrims in importance are the Puritans, who are regarded as the most devoted churchgoers in American history, which is really saying something, because everybody knows Americans generally were always great church-goers—until recently, that is.

Or so we've all been led to believe. Actually, the Puritans weren't nearly as devoted churchgoers as they've been made out to be. While there aren't any hard statistics on church attendance in seventeenth-century America, through the tax rolls one can com-pute the number of people who belonged to a church, and the tax rolls show that theirs was often an exceedingly small group. In Boston, for instance, in 1649 better than half the adult males didn't belong to any local church. In Salem, which would become famous for its witches, church membership declined by the 1680s to barely 17 percent of the adult males. In four Connecticut towns studied by historians—four good Calvinist enclaves: New Haven, New London, Stonington, and Woodbury—only 15 percent of the adult males joined the local church in the 1670s.

That there was a great deal of piousness (not to mention self-righteousness) among the Puritans, no one would deny. Certainly few seemed to doubt the divinity of Christ or the existence of God; one historian is of the opinion that no one in seventeenth-century New England was an atheist. But among the Puritans themselves, there was the deep dark suspicion that faithlessness was dangerously on the rise, and it may very well have been so. For really it was only the first generation of Puritans who expressed the kind of devotion to God that made Puritanism synonymous with godliness. Probably by the second generation, and certainly by the third, many Puritans had lost the pioneers' extreme sense of devotion. And if they didn't exactly develop into hellions, they had strayed enough from the faith of their forefathers that many felt they could not, in good conscience, claim to have undergone an inner revelation of grace. Indeed, so many Puritans acknowledged that they had never established a personal relationship with God that by the end of the seventeenth century church membership standards had to be drastically loosened.[5]

Indeed, nowhere in seventeenth-century America were people as religious as we imagine. Yale University's Jon Butler, in his magisterial history of Christianity in America, reports that the stereotype we carry around in our heads of great religiosity was a myth of the nineteenth century. It was created, he says, as a warning to Americans that they would "reap dire consequences if they trod paths different from those supposedly followed by their colonial predecessors."[6]

The disillusioning truth seems to be that Americans in general in the seventeenth century were far too busy breaking land and building homes to worry much about religion. Butler reports that Virginia was "known for irreligion and indifference," that Maryland was famous for its "stunning secularity," that South Carolina built only a few churches, and that North Carolina built none. Further, few children seem to have been baptized, and ministers often were in short supply. Virginia made do with the same number of ministers in 1670 as in 1640, though its population had swelled from four thousand to thirty thousand.

Such are the facts that our own age, in comparison, looks more religious than critics normally concede. Consider church membership totals. Statistics indicate that proportionately more Americans belong to a church now than did so in the seventeenth, eighteenth, or nineteenth centuries. "Between 1650 and 1950," says Butler, "church adherence or membership rose rather than declined." Summarizing Butler's statistics, roughly 60 percent of Americans regularly attended church in the 1960s (according to the polls), 34 percent in the 1840s (according to the census), and between 15 and 75 percent in the 1600s and 1700s, with the lower numbers being far more typical by the middle of the seventeenth century. In colonial times, as now, rural areas usually had higher church attendance than urban ones, and female worshipers generally far outnumbered the males. If at all, men in the seventeenth century usually didn't join a church until they reached their forties.

Troubling, too, to those who like their Puritans simple and straitlaced, is that they had a weird fascination for folk magic and the occult. Shocking as it may seem to us, theirs was the age of heightened supernatural wonders, both godly and devilish—women under curses so they couldn't urinate, mysterious deaths, children awakened in the night by witches perched over their beds, dreams in which the identities of murderers were revealed, egg and glass experiments used to divine the future career of a woman's husband, little girls with swelling stomachs and strange voices, children who couldn't read the Bible without succumbing to "terrible agonies," levitations, strange fits, sex with the devil, "charms muttered over nail-parings," numerous cases of fortune telling. These and other paganish practices and beliefs filled the daily lives of the Puritans.[7]

If by chance the magicians or sorcerers or fortune-tellers happened to slip into inactivity, there were always the astrologers. Every community had its own astrologer, and every astrologer had a bagful of predictions based on the signs of the zodiac. In the event that an astrologer wasn't available, there was always the farmer's almanac, which included the latest astrological advice on when to reap, when to sow, when to get married, and when to breed.

Everybody knows Salem seemed to have a terrible problem with witches, and one would be loathe to deprive the town of its richly deserved notoriety in this regard. By the time the madness had ended there, 165 people had been accused of withcraft, 150 had been imprisoned, 55 had confessed to witchcraft, and 20 had been executed. But few realize Salem was hardly the only place bewitched by witches. Witches seemed to have been terribly fond of New Englanders in the Puritan era, and they surfaced repeatedly to display their charms. There were more than 200 incidents involving witches in New England before Salem, ending in the deaths of more than 25 victims. *

None of this suggests that the Puritans were fundamentally heathenish. But neither can it be claimed that they were conventionally pious. While many Puritans attributed the feats of supernatural wonders to God, their fascination with astrology and the occult suggest at the least that they remained wedded to paganish practices.[8]

Whatever their level of devotion, there would seem to be little reason to doubt the old image of Massachusetts as a church state, and an especially intolerant one at that. And yet there are doubts. Clifford Shipton, one of the most highly esteemed scholars in colonial history, says flatly that "there was no established church in Massachusetts." Shipton's position is that you can't say the Puritans created a church state since there was no single church to which they all belonged; every town had its own church.

More important, between the towns and the churches, the towns exercised nearly all of the traditional functions of government. They controlled taxes, services, and the elections. True, towns were required to select and support a minister, but many frequently refused to do so. If a town chose, for whatever reason, not to appoint a minister, none was appointed for it. Records show some towns went for years without a clergyman. Further, the Puritans expressly prohibited clergymen from sitting in the colonial legislature and discouraged their involvement in politics. The sep-

---

* No doubt people will continue to believe witches were burned to death, and probably some were somewhere. But in America the customary practice was to kill them by hanging. Of the 20 "witches" executed in Salem, 19 were hanged and 1 was pressed to death. Further, the image of the witch as a haggard old woman is in need of revision. Some of the Salem witches were young, and 42 of those accused were male. In addition, 2 dogs were put to death. (John Demos, "Underlying Themes in the Witchcraft of Seventeenth Century New England," *Religion in American History,* eds. John Mulder and John Wilson [1978], p. 90.)

aration was so well established that when Massachusetts asked a minister to negotiate a treaty with some Indians, the Indian chief pointed out that the clergyman, by tradition, ought not to comply. After consideration, the clergyman apparently agreed and withdrew.[9]

Skeptics may doubt whether government officials actually resisted the powerful influence of the churches. Certainly it would be naive to think the churches exercised no power at all. After all, until late in the seventeenth century only church members could vote. And Massachusetts quite clearly can be said to have had an established religion, if not a single established church. Revisionism can be carried only so far!

However, government officials not only repeatedly refused to be swayed by church opinion but they frequently directly challenged the right of clergymen to interfere in secular affairs. When the pastor in Sudbury, Massachusetts, intervened in a controversy considered entirely secular in nature he was bluntly told not to "meddle." When some ministers intervened in a dispute between several towns and Boston, Governor John Winthrop rebuked the clergymen for interfering in matters "which did not belong to their calling." (Similarly, when government leaders tried to intervene in church matters, *they* were rebuffed. In 1639 the Massachusetts General Court—the colony's legislature—suggested that the churches were holding too many meetings and that the meetings were lasting too long. Church ministers, in response, told the court to mind its own business.)[10]

But if people have overestimated the power of churches in Puritan Massachusetts, they have underestimated the influence of other churches in the rest of the colonies. Indeed, most people would be hard-pressed to name a single other colony in which the churches were supported by the government. Vague as people are about New England's religious history, they know virtually nothing at all about religion's role in society anywhere else. Thus, it would undoubtedly come as a shock to most Americans to learn that there was another established church in America, the Anglican church, and that it dominated most of the southern colonies and played a minor role in several of the middle colonies. Not a word is ever said about this church, however, undoubtedly because it was run by the Church of England and tied to the crown, and in the Revolution it died an unholy death. Not even the Episcopalians care to remember the church, though they are its direct heirs. (What American, after the Revolution, would want to be associated with a church tied to England?)

Speaking of the deaths of churches, it is almost universally believed that Puritanism died sometime back in the 1600s. Not one American in a million probably has any true idea of what happened to Puritanism. Mysteriously, it just seems to have disappeared. Actually, it continued to thrive in New England through the beginning of the nineteenth century. The reason for the confusion is that the Puritans stopped calling themselves that. Instead, they referred to themselves as Congregationalists, a name that bespeaks the importance of the churches' local control.

An interesting though minor matter worth noting is the idea that the Puritans settled exclusively in New England and that they settled there because they liked the cold weather, presumably since it gave them pleasure to endure it. Actually, most of the seventy-five thousand English men and women who came over during the Great Puritan Migration from 1629 to 1640 settled in warm-weather climates. Eight thousand went to Virginia, three thousand to Bermuda, and more than thirty-five thousand to the West Indies. Only fourteen thousand went to Massachusetts.[11]

Also worth noting is the Great Awakening, which is regarded by many as a great "event" in the history of colonial religion. In reality, it is more of an event to us than to the people who lived through it. The idea that Americans suddenly became gripped by evangelical fervor in the 1730s is the work of a nineteenth-century historian named Joseph Tracy, who coined the term in an effort to justify his own generation's revivals. There actually were no revivals in most of the colonies, and in any case, revivals didn't suddenly erupt in the 1730s. Mass revivals occurred as early as the 1690s and lasted well into the 1740s.[12]

No one denies revivals became especially popular in New England in the 1730s, but New England wasn't America, though New Englanders often forgot that, and it was New Englanders, for the most part, who wrote the history books.

If, however, the Great Awakening wasn't so great, it was certainly emotional, and emotional in a stereotypical way, people literally falling into the aisles in paroxysms of joy. But it did not, interestingly, lead to intolerance, which is where emotional religious revivals are often thought to lead. History often makes a mockery of our expectations, and the Great Awakening is a great example of this. Instead of intolerance it led to diversity and pluralism. By the time revivalism had peaked, some two hundred new churches had been established, giving worshipers more choices in the selection of a denomination.[13]

The belief that the United States was founded as a Christian nation is held by those who think it's in danger of coming under the influence of non-Christians. But the fact is it never was a "Christian nation," except in the most literal sense that most of the people in it were Christian. Not a word is said about Christianity in the Constitution. Nor is it mentioned in the Declaration of Independence. The Declaration refers only to "nature's God."

As for the beliefs of the founding fathers, the remarkable thing is not that so many believed in Christianity but that so many expressed doubts about it. Alfred Aldridge has shown that Ben Franklin never believed in the divinity of Christ and as a young man he toyed with polytheism. Frank Manuel reports that as an old man John Adams became fascinated with paganism, and spent the better part of a year slugging through the twelve volumes of Charles François Dupuis's history of the origins of religion, which advanced the heretical idea that Christianity and paganism stem from common fertility myths. Adams never abandoned his faith in Christianity, but was troubled enough by Dupuis's account to suggest that a reward "in medals of diamonds" should be offered to anybody able to refute him.

Thomas Jefferson believed in God and considered himself a Christian, but he seemed to reject the divinity of Christ and considered Calvin's sermons blasphemous. Alexander Hamilton, both at the beginning of his life and near the end, expressed faith in Christianity, but during the revolutionary period he was utterly indifferent to it. Ethan Allen derided Christian revelations as either deceptive or "spurious." Thomas Paine condemned the "monstrous belief" that God had ever spoken to man. George Washington, though he belonged to the Episcopal church, never mentioned Christ in any of his writings and he was a deist.[14]

Some, especially conservatives, claim that the founders uniformly believed in the necessity of religion and maintain, as a consequence, that we should too. U.S. Senator Orrin Hatch, in an essay published in commemoration of the bicentennial of the Constitution, insists the founders believed "self-government would work" only if the people "were moral," and that they could be moral only if "they were religious." Ronald Reagan, in a Thanksgiving Day proclamation in 1987, stated that the "acknowledgment of dependence on God's favor" was "our fledgling nation's very first order of business," a reference to the decision of the delegates to the first Continental Congress to overcome "discord by uniting in prayer." George Will, the conservative columnist, has made much of George Washington's farewell address, in which Washington said religion was indispensable for "all the dispositions and habits which lead to political prosperity."[15]

Certainly the founders weren't hostile either to religion or the clergy as, say, the French revolutionaries were soon to become. But neither did they insist, one and all, that religion was a pillar of liberty. Indeed, many of the most illustrious founders plainly rejected the idea. Historian John Diggins says those involved in writing and defending the Constitution, men like James Madison and Alexander Hamilton, "expressed profound ambivalence about religion, often seeing it as divisive rather than cohesive." And some of those who later came to believe in the necessity of religion, such as Adams, originally thought religiosity was of little matter. Adams said in 1787 that "Neither Philosophy, nor Religion, nor Morality" can govern people "against their Vanity, their Pride, their Resentment or Revenge"; "Nothing but Force and Power and Strength can restrain them."

Diggins is of the opinion that Abraham Lincoln was the first American president explicitly and meaningfully to affirm the usefulness of religion in politics. Others had used the rhetoric of religion, as modern presidents like Reagan have done in courting the religious vote. But Lincoln, Diggins says, was the first to ground his politics in Christian morals. With Lincoln, religion was essential to republican government. A good, old-fashioned Calvinist, even if he sometimes seemed to doubt God's existence, Lincoln believed that shame can save a people from self-righteousness.[16]

The founders have been pressed into the service of religion so long now and with such force that it is almost impossible to recover what they really thought. But we can certainly reconstruct their actions, and in their actions there are certain surprises. Consider the practice of public prayers, for example, opening meetings of Congress with a prayer. They are now so much a part of the fabric of American life that not even the atheists bother making an issue out of them. Maybe we are simply more in need of public praying than the founders were; but we do more of it than they ever did (not because they opposed praying but because they thought politics and praying didn't mix). The Constitutional Convention opened without a single public prayer and several of the first presidents, including both Jefferson and Madison, generally refused to issue prayers, despite importunings that they do so. Under pressure, Madison relented in the War of 1812, but held to his belief that chaplains shouldn't be appointed to the military or be allowed to open Congress.[17]

But if the conservatives err in overestimating the founders' willingness to mix religion with politics, the liberals err in overestimating the founders' willingness to keep them separate. Really all that the founders prohibited was the national support of religion. State support continued virtually unhindered. To be historically accurate, the founders didn't abolish state support of religion; the Fourteenth Amendment did (as subsequently interpreted by the Supreme Court), and the Fourteenth Amendment wasn't approved until after the Civil War.

Indeed, given the firm connection established between the founders and religious freedom, the extent of involvement of the states in religion after the Revolution is astonishing. One finds that Delaware required public officeholders to believe in Christ, that Maryland extended religious freedom only to Christians, that Pennsylvania insisted officeholders believe in God and the hereafter, and that New Jersey, Georgia, South Carolina, Massachusetts, and New Hampshire limited public offices to Protestants. Further, in defiance of everything we've been taught, three states—New Hampshire, Maryland, and Massachusetts—levied taxes to support state churches. Churches continued receiving state help in Connecticut until 1818, in New Hampshire until 1819, and in Massachusetts until 1833. Only Virginia, of all the states, firmly rejected the state support of religion, and Virginia only did so after a six-year campaign by Madison and Jefferson.[18]

Freedom of religion was spreading, of course, and the founders deserve to be associated with rationalism and the Enlightenment. But a distinction needs to be drawn between the founders and citizens in general, many of whom held less advanced views. The founding fathers may have been feasting on the rich diet of Rousseau and Locke and Montesquieu, but most people barely got a taste. The very month the Constitutional Convention convened in 1787, a mob in Philadelphia assaulted a helpless woman suspected of practicing sorcery. Two months later, while the constitution's framers were wrestling with questions of natural rights and democratic rule, a band of angry Philadelphians stoned her to death.

Though religion is thought of as being of great concern in the eighteenth century, it is barely mentioned in connection with the nineteenth. Probably most Americans could not name more than one or two developments of religious significance that took place then. Indeed, Americans probably know more about the Middle Ages than they do about the religious history of their own country a hundred years ago. From the movies, at least they know that people prayed a lot in the Middle Ages and that a lot of amazing cathedrals got built. And they know the period by a name: the Dark Ages, which is simplistic and misleading but is better than no name at all. The nineteenth century, in contrast, is a cipher. It shouldn't be.

The nineteenth century was a period of utmost religious importance. It was then that children began attending Sunday school, that the YMCA was established, and that Bible tracts began being published by the millions. And it was then that church membership first exploded nationwide: the Lutherans increasing from 225 churches in 1780 to 800 by 1820, to 2,100 by 1860; the Baptists from 400 to 2,700 to 12,150; the Presbyterians from 500 to 1,700 to 6,400; the Methodists from 50 to 2,700 to 20,000; the Roman Catholics from 50 to 120 to 2,500—in all, a rate of increase far faster than the growth in population. (The population increased from 4 million in 1780 to 10 million in 1820 to 31 million in 1860; church congregations increased from 2,500 to 11,000 to 52,000.) [19]

It was not only orthodox religions that suddenly attracted millions of new worshipers. If ever there was a great experimental age in American religion it was the 1800s, resulting in the creation of dozens of new and interesting churches. From upstate New York alone came the Shakers, founded by a woman who claimed to be Christ reincarnated; the Mormons, who sanctified polygamy*; the

* The practice of polygamy among the Mormons has, however, been exaggerated. Most Mormons did not approve of polygamy. Scholars estimate that at its height of popularity only about 10 percent of the Mormon population ever became involved with it. (Stanley S. Ivins, "Notes on Mormon Polygamy," in *American Experiences*, eds. Randy Roberts and James S. Olson [1986], I, 254.)

Millerites, who believed that the world would come to an end in 1843 *; and Oneida, the communist colony built around the idea of free love. [20]

As always, there was the fascination with the supernatural, which expanded in the nineteenth century far beyond the usual assortment of angels, devils, and witches common in previous times. To these were now added seer stones, spiritualism, mediums, seances, golden plates, and magical salamanders. Mrs. Lincoln held seances in the White House to talk to her dead children, and Lincoln himself reportedly attended at least a few of them.

And all this is largely forgotten—as if any other period has ever been richer in religious symbolism. It's as though the only thing that matters was the creation of religious freedom rather than how people subsequently used their freedom.

The sheer notoriety that attached to the Scopes Monkey Trial has contributed to the identification of Fundamentalism with the "ignorant rural South." But the fact is, Fundamentalism was conceived in upstate New York in the late nineteenth century and was led by intelligent and respected Protestant scholars. Indeed, it originally proved as popular among the northern urban middle classes as among the rural southern folk and initially was financially supported by two Los Angeles businessmen who had made a fortune in oil. It was they, in the early twentieth century, who dubbed the movement "Fundamentalism."

---

* And, when it didn't, they predicted it would end in 1844. But the Millerites are unfairly singled out. Many Americans throughout history have made similarly bold claims. Among these was the imperturbable Puritan divine, Cotton Mather, who made three different predictions about the end of the world based on "precise" calculations derived from biblical prophecies. Like the Millerites, Mather had the misfortune of living long enough to see his predictions not come true. His first prediction was that the world would end in 1697. His second was that the blessed event would happen in 1736. Subsequently, he settled on 1716. When 1716 came and went without incident, Mather stopped making predictions but remained persuaded that the world's end was calculable and that it was near. (James West Davidson, *The Logic of Millenial Thought* [1977], pp. 15–16.)

The sudden enthusiasm for Fundamentalism in the 1920s is usually attributed to the "frightening" and sudden popularity of evolutionism. However, evolutionism had by then been around for more
than half a century. Nothing more surprised mainstream America
in the twenties than the discovery that millions still found evolutionism controversial. By the 1920s, most Protestant theologians
had long ago made peace with the theory. What likely brought
about the growth of Fundamentalism in the 1920s was World War
I, which ended in broken dreams, widespread frustration, and social
turmoil. That more than anything else probably explains the Fundamentalist reaction against "modernism" and the desire to return
to traditional values. It doesn't, of course, explain why some Americans became Fundamentalists and others did not.

That the Fundamentalists' view of the Bible, the belief that it
should be read literally, is the traditional view is widely held, probably because Fundamentalists seem so identified with the "old values." But literalism is hardly traditional. Professor Ernest Sandeen,
in a book published by the University of Chicago, traced the origins
of literalism to the French Revolution, when Protestants concluded
that the French conquest of Rome and the banishment of the pope
fulfilled biblical prophecies in Daniel and the Revelations. Even
then the Bible was not widely taken literally, however. Sandeen
says no theology of literalism existed until after 1850. Until then
Christian faith was based on revelations and miracles; "the future
of Christianity did not hang on the infallibility of the Scriptures."

Indeed, not until the Fundamentalists came along did American
theologians believe the findings of science could undermine biblical
authority. Consider the Puritans, who are vulgarly regarded as Fundamentalists. According to Perry Miller, the single greatest authority on American religion, the Puritans never "dreamed that the
truth of scripture was to be maintained in spite of or against the
evidences of reason, science, and learning."[21]

3
Work and Play

Debauchee, n. *One who has so earnestly pursued pleasure that he has had the misfortune to overtake it.*
AMBROSE BIERCE

Reviewing the Victorian past,* it is astonishing that the average American is convinced that the work ethic has only recently slipped into decline. The evidence is overwhelming that it has been in decline for well over a hundred years.

Scorn for hard work, for instance, goes back at least to the middle of the nineteenth century. Henry Ward Beecher, the most popular preacher in the country after the Civil War, made a career out of celebrating leisure, advising people to take a "tranquil, dreaming, gazing" approach to life. Beecher himself took six-week vacations annually and observed that the "chief use of a farm" is "to lie down." He got into trouble in the 1870s when he was accused in a sensational sex scandal of committing adultery; critics charged he'd taken too seriously his own advice to enjoy life. But Beecher remained almost as popular as ever.

Beecher wasn't alone in advocating a leisure ethic instead of a work ethic. Henry David Thoreau did, too. "Work, work, work,"

* 1837–1901, the reign of Queen Victoria, a time of stuffy values in both England and the United States.

34

he cried in 1854. "It would be glorious to see mankind at leisure for once."[1]

Now, a healthy appreciation of leisure need not imply a repudiation of work. All know people who, during the week, feverishly work long days, and who on the weekend "party-hardy." And it is worth remembering the traditional farmer who spent the summer plowing his fields and spent the winter partly resting. But here was something new: leisure as an end in itself. It suggested a certain contempt for the Protestant work ethic that emphasizes work for the sake of work (or work to do glory unto God).[2]

It is true that the Victorians preferred working to loafing, but then most people do. Loafing is boring. What people want is time off to do something interesting, and the Victorians were experts in dreaming up interesting things to do. Think of all the ways Americans relax. Nearly every diversion was invented by Americans in the Victorian era. It was Victorians who introduced department store shopping, basketball, roller skating, bicycle riding, car racing, and modern baseball, the Victorians who pioneered trophy hunting, the Victorians who dreamed up popular dances like the two-step. Not for nothing were the 1890s known as the Gay Nineties.[3]

The Victorian was not so enamored of leisure as to hold work in contempt—that would seem to be our own generation's small contribution to American culture. We, not they, invented the "nerd," to express our hostility to those who work hard and succeed; we, not they, prefer winning money to earning it.[*]

We know that people in the nineteenth century worked longer hours than people do now, but that only seems to be because they had to. Nobody *wanted* to work long hours. Many of the most

---

[*] And we do enjoy winning it. Though some think the American is uncomfortable with lotteries, the source of the discomfort is misidentified. The secret joy we feel upon hearing that the lottery winner has, through some foolishness, lost his fortune stems not from the suspicion that it's wrong to win money but from the fact that it is someone else who has done the winning. To ourselves we think, "We would never be so stupid as they."

searing labor conflicts in the nineteenth century, including the famous Haymarket Riot in 1886, stemmed from labor's demand to work shorter hours.[4]

Indeed, almost everybody in Victorian America feared the danger of long hours, which was said to bring on neurasthenia, a newly discovered illness characterized by fatigue. For a time in the 1880s almost every illness was attributed to it, from headaches and dyspepsia to insomnia and spinal pain. In what must have been akin to the herpes scare of the 1980s, Americans in the 1880s suddenly became gripped by the terrible fear that they too might come down with this dread disorder. Adding to the tension was a warning by Herbert Spencer, the English philosopher of social Darwinism. On a three-month tour of the United States he told Americans they were dying early from an inadequate "adjustment of labor and enjoyment." A popular magazine captured in a headline the essence of the argument: "Fun Is a Necessity." Do without it, work too hard, and you just might find yourself in an early grave.[5]

The use of illness as an excuse for idleness, so common nowadays, was not unknown in Victorian days. Among the upper classes it was common. If historian Howard Feinstein is correct, several members of the famous James family, including William, the Harvard philosopher, and Henry, the novelist, arranged trips to Europe to recover from illnesses to which they actually hadn't succumbed. We cannot know for sure if they were faking. Feinstein suggests it's possible the illnesses were real, brought on by anxiety over the repressed desire to play. But more likely they were subterfuges. Certainly, Henry James seems to have developed a curious appreciation of the curative powers of the notoriously dull British sun. Sent on a tour of Europe to recover from a particularly bad case of "invalidism," he wrote home that the cure seemed to be working— but he needed more of it. "I have an impression amounting almost to a conviction," he wrote, "that if I were to travel steadily for a year I would be a good part of a well man." One supposes he was right.[6]

Nor was absenteeism unknown. Businessmen found they had to

keep the gates to their factories locked during working hours to prevent employees from leaving.

Nor did most workers show much perseverance. Turnover rates were shockingly high. At the Pullman plant, considered a model, a fifth of the work force left every year. At the mills in Lowell, Massachusetts, fully a quarter of the employees quit annually. (One reason Henry Ford, early in the twentieth century, instituted the $5 day was to make sure *his* workers stayed put.)

The belief that industrial workers worked hard is offset by the complaints of businessmen that they didn't. Perhaps the businessmen exaggerated. But it seems pretty clear that many of the complaints were well documented, especially those involving alcohol.[7]

Among immigrants, whose work habits are legendary, the work ethic was often palpably weak. Roy Rosenzweig, in a landmark book on the immigrants of Worcester, Massachusetts, says the immigrants there either questioned or explicitly rejected the Protestant work ethic, preferring instead to build a culture around the local saloon. This is an uncomfortable finding but apparently a true one. In Worcester the saloon was the focus of immigrant culture. There immigrants nursed suspicions about the work ethic, American materialism, homeownership, thriftiness, and punctuality. When temperance crusaders began in the 1880s to crack down on the saloons, the immigrants' resistance to middle-class morality stiffened, attacks on the saloon amounting to attacks on themselves. Of necessity, the immigrants eventually began to adopt more and more of the values with which they are popularly associated, saloon owners leading the way as saloons became increasingly prosperous. But the saloon culture endured for years. The only reason it is now forgotten is because it is at odds with the modern image of the ever-upwardly mobile, red-white-and-blue, Ellis Island immigrant stereotype.[8]

Of all immigrants, those from eastern and southern Europe seemed to have resisted the work ethic the most. Whatever they came to believe subsequently, early on they held to their European

values and these were inconsistent with the American work ethic.*
It wasn't that the immigrants were lazy. It's just that they thought
there were often better things to do with one's time than work. In
Europe, Polish weddings lasted days. The Greek church celebrated
eighty festivals annually. Immigrants saw no reason why they
shouldn't be allowed to celebrate here in America as often.[9]

The Irish resistance to the work ethic is well-known, though
misinterpreted. It is thought that they didn't work because they
liked to drink. But the truth is they drank because they weren't
allowed to work. ("Irish need not apply.") And when they were
allowed to work, they were often paid partly in booze—some contractors giving workers six shots of whiskey a day—apparently on
the theory that "the Irishman's shovel flew into the work after a
belt of whiskey and that without it he grew morose and idling."[10]

It is no small matter that many immigrants for a long time
remained indifferent to the work ethic. It was the immigrants, after
all, who worked most of America's factories. Roughly 75 percent of
all factory employees in the United States in the nineteenth century
were immigrants or the children of immigrants.[11]

If we have overestimated the work ethic of the Victorians, we have
in our ignorance underestimated our own. The amazing thing, says
Benjamin Hunnicutt, in his history of work, is not that we work so
little in comparison to Americans a hundred years ago but that we
work so much. Union workers then put in an average of fifty-four
hours a week. That's just ten hours more than typical factory workers do today.† And we are catching up fast. In 1980 government

---

* As history is written from the perspective of the present, of course, and in
the present the values of the industrial society are regarded as the "right
values," those who shared a different set of values have often been neglected.
Thus the widespread neglect of the immigrants' early indifference to work.

† American workers today of course receive better fringe benefits. But it is
worth noting that they receive fewer days off than Europeans. The "hardwork-
ing" Germans, for instance, get four to six weeks of vacation a year, even if
they have switched companies. The typical American, in contrast, gets one to

statistics show only 18 percent of full time workers spent more than forty-nine hours a week on the job. Ten years later nearly 25 percent did. And many people work even longer hours. Barely a week goes by that the newspapers don't include the obituary of yet another workaholic business executive. In Washington, D.C., government officials, contrary to popular opinion, ordinarily put in sixty-hour weeks. * On Wall Street, executives compete to see who can work the longest. Seventy-hour weeks are not uncommon. [12]

We are proud that people don't have to work quite as hard as they used to, and we take it as a measure of our nation's progress that they don't (even while we're concerned that people aren't working hard enough anymore!). But a hundred years ago many assumed that people by now would barely need to work at all. Our ancestors, no doubt, would be shocked to find out that though we had managed to make it to the moon we still have to work almost as many hours a week as they did.

Hunnicutt is of the opinion that by one standard we are rather more committed to work today than formerly, for today no one urges a reduction in the forty-hour work week. The last bold proposal to reduce the work week was made nearly sixty years ago, in the midst of the Great Depression. Most people today, one suspects,

---

two weeks of vacation a year the first five years on the job, and three weeks after ten years.

It's certainly possible that the average European works harder when he's on the job than the American, though that's unproven. But if he does, it may be due to the fact that he spends so much more time away from the job. Since the turn of the century studies have shown a connection between the dedication workers show to their jobs and the amount of leisure time they're allowed. Such studies in the 1920s helped persuade leading businessmen to join the movement for shorter hours.

* This is based on the author's own experience in 1989 during a stint in Washington, D.C., as a reporter on KUTV, a Salt Lake City television station. The experience convinced the author that politicians are not lazy. Literally from morning until night they are at work. Whether their work is useful or not is another matter.

would be shocked at the suggestion that the work week should be reduced from the current level, but for nearly a hundred years, from the 1830s to the 1930s, cutting the work week was one of the labor movement's prime objectives. Probably Americans would find it incredible that people once expected that by the year 2000 we would have a fourteen-hour work week. And yet that was precisely what the futurists in the thirties did expect. We wouldn't even take seriously a proposal to, say, mandate a thirty-hour work week, though during the depression the U.S. Senate actually passed a bill providing for a thirty-hour work week. [13]

There is no getting around the fact that the work ethic has declined; and no arguments or statistics could, in any case, convince people otherwise. Probably the greatest shock is the discovery that even before Victorianism belief in the work ethic wasn't universal. Herbert Gutman, after a lifetime of studying the subject, concluded that "at all times in American history . . . quite diverse Americans . . . made it clear in their thought and behavior that the Prostestant work ethic was not deeply ingrained in the nation's social fabric." [14]

Take urban workers in the colonial period. One doesn't read much about them in the history books, perhaps because they didn't work much. Alexander Hamilton, speaking for many, opined that the dedication of the workmen in America was suspect. How to industrialize, he wondered, "unless God should send us saints for workmen." Benjamin Franklin complained that "our working people" keep "Saint Monday" as much of a holiday as Sunday, the only difference being that on Monday they don't go to church; they go to "the ale house."

Between the Revolution and the 1830s, almost everybody in America thought everybody else had a drinking problem, and they almost were right. America was on a binge.* Work, in conse-

---

* See page 114 in chapter 7, "Alcohol and Drugs."

quence, suffered badly. While it is impossible to quantify the toll alcohol took on the working class, businessmen chronically complained that workers often showed up on Mondays with hangovers, and at other times they showed up plain drunk—if, that is, they showed up at all. One New Jersey manufacturer noted in his diary that one day "all" of his employees came to work drunk.

Next to drunkenness the most common complaint was absenteeism. Gutman found that the American workman frequently skipped work. He doesn't say how frequently, and really there's no way of knowing as most factories kept few records. But we do know from the factories about which information is available that absenteeism occurred on such a grand scale that it must not have been considered—by the employees—a major offense. At one factory all of the employees absented themselves from work one day to go play on the beach. Surely, unless they happened to be a uniquely delinquent bunch, they wouldn't have done so if the community treated absenteeism seriously.[15]

Between men and women, women often proved the more industrious. It was for this reason that women were employed by the mill operators in Massachusetts. But even the Lowell women, renowned for their attentiveness and punctuality, resisted (as one put it) the rhythms of the "Morning bells, I hate to hear./Ringing dolefully, loud and clear." One year a single Lowell mill discharged twenty-eight women for, among other things, "misconduct," "captiousness," "disobedience," "impudence," "levity," and, imaginatively, "mutiny." At another mill, in Nantucket, the women simply refused to work at all, preferring instead to spend their days at the beach. The mill, in consequence, had to close.[16]

That the industrial laborer had trouble meeting the expectations of business is interesting, because one frequently hears that the American was supposed to have been "made for industrialism." To the people who actually had to do the work, however, industrial work habits were difficult to master. Getting to work at a set hour, working for others rather than oneself, working away from one's home—in all these ways industrial life was strange, especially strange to those brought up on the farm. *

On the farm, for instance, one was allowed to relax while on the job. During house-raisings you could take a drink or have a smoke. In the autumn there were harvest festivals. On other occasions there were horse races and cock fights. At election time you could get drunk. But at the factory all one did was work.[17]

Worried as Americans are over the perceived waning of the work ethic, their real concern is with what may be behind it. Several explanations are possible, but by far the most popular is that the decline has been brought about by "moral weakness," which is variously attributed to the breakdown of the family, the disintegration of authority, or (the great bogeymen of the age) television, which is said to be largely responsible for the other two.

Upon analysis, the explanation that moral weakness is to blame is ridiculous. Nearly every generation feels that the one succeeding it has become morally weaker. Besides, if "moral weakness"—whatever that really means—is behind the decline of the work ethic, then we have been getting morally weaker for a long, long time. Presumably if "moral weakness" accounts for our own declining work ethic, it also accounts for the Victorians' and the immigrants'. And if that's true, then Americans have been on one long slide into the moral void since the nineteenth century. Even the most confirmed moralists might hesitate before accepting that idea.

Historians have another explanation for what has happened. They are of the opinion that the work ethic was largely done in by industrialism, which discredited the old idea of work as a moral obligation.

* Some corporations, out of sympathy for their workers, declined to enforce punctuality. Until the 1890s the Winchester Repeating Arms plant in Connecticut did not require employees to arrive on time. (Daniel T. Rogers, *The Work Ethic in Industrial America* [1978], p. 24.)

The main argument they make about industrialism, that it undermined the work ethic by forcing laborers to perform dull jobs, appears irrefutable. From the beginning of industrialism, social critics have observed the connection between dull factory work and spiritless workers. At congressional hearings convened to investigate the causes of labor unrest in the 1880s, clergyman R. Heber Newton noted that the industrial worker "*makes* nothing," and "sees no complete product of his skill growing into finished shape in his hands." Hence, concluded Newton, the worker feels dejected and lifeless. "What zest," he asked, "can there be in the toil of this bit of manhood?"

When Jewish glove makers in Chicago had to make their gloves on an assembly line, instead of the old-fashioned way, one glove at a time, one of them had the temerity to complain. The job, she said, is dull now. "You cling to the variety," she continued, "the mental luxury" of first making the "finger-sides, and then, five separate leather pieces, for relaxation, to play with!" Her complaint ended with a warning: "*Here,*" she said, "is a luxury worth fighting for!" [18]

Conceivably, those who felt disenchanted with work nonetheless persisted in believing in the work ethic. One suspects, however, that over time the fellow who's bored with his job begins to think the problem is not with him but the job. It is at this moment that the revolutionary thought occurs to the laborer that the work ethic may be bogus.

The other argument historians make about industrialism, that it sapped the work ethic by destroying the nobility of work, seems equally irrefutable. Anyone who has ever sat on an assembly line knows that factory work is humbling; the thought that a robot can do the same job you're doing—and that if you don't watch out a robot soon will be—is degrading. As a perceptive bishop in the nineteenth century put it, factory work turned the laborer "into a simple idiot." Growing complexity in the factory only worsened the situation; as work became more and more subdivided, the individual worker made less and less of a contribution to the finished

product. This further diminished his importance. With the introduction of Taylorism, the system of scientifically calculating the
precise way to do a job and the time in which it takes to do it,
work became hopelessly regimented. Workers, in turn, became
demoralized. Some complained that factory work had become
"un-American."

It will be claimed by some that work is work and by itself its
own reward, and that industrialism didn't change that. But industrialism transformed the independent yeoman into a dependent employee and in doing so robbed him of the hope that someday he
might become his own boss. This acted powerfully to undermine
the work ethic. For if one wasn't working for oneself—or for a
better future—why work hard? *

Industrialism need not always sabotage the work ethic. Presumably assembly-line jobs can be made more interesting and incentives
can be built into the system to give the worker the sense that in
helping his company he's helping himself. But as it existed in the
nineteenth century, industrialism was incompatible with the work
ethic. This was, after all, the era of worker exploitation. And no
worker was likely to give his all if he felt exploited. Indeed, by the
Civil War the conditions under which factory employees worked
had become so onerous that southerners argued that white factory
workers were less well off than slaves. This wasn't as preposterous

---

* The change in the work ethic was reflected in the advice proffered in "How
to Succeed" books. Whereas once they had recommended work and more
work as the key to success, by 1900 they were telling Americans it's best to
find a job where personality and drive count. Work and work alone, they
counseled, is insufficient; no matter how hard the factory worker worked, he'd
always remain "just a factory worker."

Daniel Rogers points out that none of Horatio Alger's heroes ever became
successful working at a factory. On the "rare occasions" when Alger started a
boy out at a factory, says Rogers, "he could only think to have the lad fired or
laid off at the outset, as if desperate for some contrivance to expel him as
quickly as possible into the world where a man can make his mark." (Rogers,
Work Ethic, pp. 38–39.)

as it sounds. While no sane white worker would have traded places with a slave, the North treated its workers so badly that when the Civil War broke out Europeans had trouble deciding which side was morally superior. Thomas Carlyle said, "There they are, cutting each other's throats, because one half of them prefer hiring their servants for life, and the other by the hour." [19]

The work ethic, to be sure, didn't simply vanish with the coming of the factory. There was a lot of life left in the old idea through the end of the nineteenth century. But by the 1920s, it had declined to about where it is now. The alarmists who think things have only recently reached the state they are in are mistaken. The damage was done long ago. Detailed studies by sociologists and historians show that by the twenties the work ethic had largely been replaced by the consumer ethic. The more things you buy, the better life gets. Want the good life? It's for sale! The goal in life is to live well, not to work hard. Don't have the money to get what you want? Remember you can always get it on credit. Loren Baritz reports that in the 1920s "$6 billion worth of consumer goods were bought on credit: 85 percent of furniture sales, 80 percent of phonographs, 75 percent of electric washing machines, and most of the vacuum cleaners, pianos, sewing machines, radios, and electric refrigerators." [20]

If any single cause is to blame, then, for the decline in this century of the much vaunted work ethic, it was the invention of the consumer culture. This, if true, is shocking. For it would seem to indicate that business has had a strong hand in undermining the very values it so often trumpets. For it is business that invented the gospel of consumption, and business that sold it through modern advertising.

The businessman indeed is misunderstood. While he extols the virtues of hard work so his employees will work hard, he is not really all that concerned with the survival of the work ethic. His greatest fear is not that people will stop working but that they will stop shopping. His secret nightmare is to wake up one morning and discover that Americans have become scrimpers and savers. What's needed are spenders! Scrimping and saving would spell ruin for the American economy.

Given the aggressive way in which businessmen have sold the message of consumption, it is remarkable that they have escaped the blame for the evisceration of the Old Protestant values. The whole thrust of modern advertising is to convince Americans you can spend your way to happiness.

To persuade Americans to become spenders, however, wasn't easy. Against the effort was the full weight of European history since the Protestant Reformation, which taught people the lessons of frugality and sacrifice, lessons that American experience reinforced. All remembered what had happened to the Jamestown settlers who came from England in search of gold and refused to work: They starved to death.

The amazing fact, then, is not that so many Americans continued believing in the work ethic as long as they did but that so many stopped believing as quickly as they did. Given the force with which religious and historical tradition must have pulled at their conscience, their willingness to adopt the gospel of consumption is astonishing.

Whether people should return to the work ethic is a moot question. The issue has already been decided. Much as they may regret the decline of the work ethic, people have clearly and definitely demonstrated a preference for leisure. What they want is for other people to work harder. It is always others who seem to be loafing.

But if Americans no longer seem as committed to the work ethic as formerly, they still demonstrate a genuine appetite for work, absent, we are told, in places like the Soviet Union. Indeed, there seems little reason to worry that Americans will ever become truly "lazy." For while people no longer think work is important in itself, it has proved important indeed in making money to purchase all those things business offers for sale and people seem so desperate to buy. As long as people want things—and no one shows more dedication in this than Americans—they can be expected to work hard. The great danger, then, is not laziness but empty store shelves. * [21]

While Americans' work habits are often debated and discussed, playing as a subject receives little serious attention, and what attention it gets often involves erroneous assumptions. Consider city parks. These are places to visit, not to think about. If they are thought about at all it's imagined they were established to provide pleasure. But any pleasure they supplied was purely incidental. Historians tell us the true purpose of city parks was to make people behave better.

This may seem a strange notion to us, knowing as we do all the things that go on in parks. But we know these things only in hindsight. When they were first proposed in the mid-1800s, parks were regarded as oases of pastoral morality. The hope was that parks would restore to the city the lost innocence of the rural village, which as cities grew and grew, seemed lost for good. [22]

An idea of the extravagant expectations parks aroused can be gotten from the statements reformers made in support of them. Andrew Jackson Downing, a leading American landscape architect, predicted in 1848 that parks would "be better preachers of temperance than temperance societies," "better refiners of national manners than dancing schools," and "better promoters of general good-feeling than any lectures on the philosophy of happiness." Frederick Law Olmsted, the creator of New York's Central Park, prophesied that parks would divert the "rough element of the city" from "unwholesome, vicious, destructive methods and habits" of recreation (that is, sex, drinking, etc.). Henry Ward Beecher predicted that their "divine" beauty would inspire the poor to "gentle thoughts and grateful silence." One official claimed that with sufficient funding, parks could reduce prostitution; apparently in com-

---

* Americans deprived of the right to "shop till they drop"? This may be what some social critics desire, but they should be careful. They could get what they want. One shudders at the consequences.

plete earnestness, he suggested that parks could cut prostitution by 98 percent.[23]

Historians caution that the reformers weren't only interested in social control. Roy Rosenzweig says they also seemed to have been motivated by "naturalistic visions of society, fears about urban disease, and infatuations with European public gardens." But it is hard to escape the conclusion that what really excited the reformers was the chance to do some reforming. Most reformers, it should be pointed out, only took up the cause after the immigrants had come to dominate the cities. This was not by coincidence. There was a strong feeling among the park-reform crowd against the southern Europeans who came to the United States in the late nineteenth century. If the great cities had remained in the hands of the old native stock, one imagines there would have been a great deal less emphasis on reform. We probably still would have had parks (if not so many of them), but other reasons would have been invented for having them.

Certainly the park creators were men of vision, but theirs was an unsuspectingly narrow vision and reeked of class consciousness. Thus one reads in George Burnap's seminal book, *Parks: Their Design, Equipment, and Use* (1916), that parks in poor neighborhoods should not be as elaborate as parks in wealthier ones as this could "cause resentment," and that parks in middle-class areas should be built with restraint, to counteract "the present tendency of our middle classes to ape . . . those of larger means and to covet their extravagancies and indulgences."[24]

Reformers did not believe that the poor should be prevented from visiting parks in better areas, which would have been impossible, of course. But some reformers slyly found ways to discourage the poor from making the effort.

The sliest was undoubtedly Robert Moses, a power-hungry civil servant, who in the 1920s, to accommodate his own narrow vision and completely on his own authority, restricted the access of the poor to Long Island's Jones Beach State Park, the biggest and best beach near Manhattan. To make sure that the poor couldn't come by rail, he denied the railroad the authority to build a station near the beach. To prevent their coming by bus, he successfully lobbied for legislation to prohibit buses from using the parkways that led to and from the beach. To make sure buses would *never* provide the poor with the means to reach the park, he deliberately built the bridges over the parkways so low that no bus could pass underneath them. The bridge clearances in most places measure 11 or 12 feet; buses need 13 or 14 feet. * [25]

The achievement of the park reformers, in the end, was large. America by the turn of the century was spending millions to build parks. From New York to Seattle, Olmsted left parks of magnificent scope and design. All who live in cities today must rejoice in their accomplishment. But in what they wanted to do they failed. People, it turned out, didn't choose to be reformed. And parks could not make them reform. People who drank too much before there were parks, drank too much afterward. People who loafed before, still loafed. And prostitution remained an awful moral blight. The only difference was that now people could do their drinking, loafing, and fornicating in the parks. Within ten years of the creation of Elm Park in Worcester, Massachusetts, the newspaper reported that a young Irish immigrant woman had become pregnant there. Rosenzweig reports that parks in immigrant neighborhoods quickly became places where people drank and caroused. From the outset,

* Moses's story is told by Robert Caro in a biography that contains an interesting quotation from Sid Shapiro, one of Moses's closest aides, leaving no doubt that in building those bridges as low as he did Moses knew what he was doing: "Mr. Moses had an instinctive feeling that someday politicians would try to put buses on the parkways, and that would break down the whole parkway concept—and he used to say to us fellows, 'Let's design the bridges so the clearance is all right for passenger cars but not for anything else.' . . . Mr. Moses did this because he knew that something might happen after he was dead and gone. He wrote legislation [to prohibit the buses] but he knew you could change the legislation. You can't change a bridge after it's up. And the result of this is that a bus from New York couldn't use the parkways if we wanted it to." (Caro, *The Power Broker: Robert Moses and the Fall of New York* [1974], p. 952.)

it would seem, people had more of an effect on parks than parks had on people.[26]

The biggest disappointment, however, was that nature seemed to have less of an improving effect on people's behavior than had been hoped. This was truly shocking. Since Jefferson, Americans had placed their faith in nature. Nature, in turn, had betrayed them. *

Like parks, playgrounds were also created to improve human behavior. Only the sentimental think that they were put here originally out of concern for children's pleasure. Established first around the turn of the century, they were designed to give the urban ragamuffin, as one reformer put it, "new social notions, and a better standard of what is acceptable to those 'higher up.' "

Indeed, the reformers expressly rejected the idea that the playground was for pleasure. To say it was for pleasure sounded frivolous. And playgrounds were serious. Some predicted playgrounds could virtually eliminate juvenile delinquency. Others said they would have as great an effect on childrens' morals as Sunday school classes and would help city children "keep their souls pure though they soil their hands." Jacob Riis, the New York muckraker, said the playground ranks high among the "wholesome counterinfluences to the saloon, street gang, and similar evils." The head of the American Civic Association counted the playground as a powerful weapon in the continuing duel with "the forces of evil."

It is certainly true that the reformers expected children to have fun at the playground, but their idea of fun was somewhat peculiar —at least from our perspective. To them fun meant performing exercises in unison under the guidance of a supervisor. The most

---

* We may look with wonder at their naivete. But are we any less naive? Summer advertisements for the Fresh Air Fund in New York suggest Americans today may be just as susceptible to the mythical appeals of nature as Americans a hundred years ago. Give kids a chance to fish in a pond, swim in a lake, and romp among the trees, go the promotions, and maybe the kids will turn out better. Maybe they will, but if they do, it's probably because they're finally receiving some personal attention and not because of the scenery.

interesting thing about playgrounds, though, is probably not that they were designed to improve children's character but that we have forgotten that they were supposed to. Here is a suspicious case of societal amnesia on a grand scale. One can only guess at the reasons. But it may have something to do with the fact that in the end the playgrounds—like the parks—didn't have much of an improving effect on anybody. We prefer to remember our successes.[27]

4
Business

Though the businessman did not live by his theory of laissez faire, it was all the theory he had.
GARRY WILLS

When it is *their* business that is failing, businessmen do whatever they can to obtain government help; anybody who reads the papers knows that. So it was with the railroads in the seventies, Chrysler in the eighties, the savings and loans in the nineties. But it was different in the past, we are told. Then businessmen were on their own!

Actually, American business has a long history of asking for help from the government and getting it. It is nonsense to say "in the old days" it was different. The nineteenth century is rich in examples of government aid to business. State governments helped by awarding businesses special franchises, bounties, grants, and immunities. The federal government gave business high protective tariffs and huge land grants. (In all, it's estimated that the federal government donated more than 130 million acres to the railroads, the states contributing an additional 48 million.) [1]

The history of American business, indeed, is sorely misunderstood. Business did not in its infancy start out strong and independent, only to succumb later to the temptation of government aid. It was suckled on government aid. In the early years, short on capital, businessmen depended on government to provide the money they couldn't raise elsewhere. Virginia invested in the railroads, and by the Civil War held a controlling interest in every line operating within its borders and named officers to the companies' boards of directors. Sixty percent of the money invested in southern railroads in the antebellum period came from public agencies. Pennsylvania invested heavily in banks, canal companies, and turnpikes, in all helping out more than 150 corporations.

Early businessmen, indeed, conceived of the corporation in starkly different terms from their current-day successors. Then as now, the corporations had stockholders and the stockholders liked to make money. But the corporation wasn't established primarily to earn profits, but to perform a public service. When someone wanted to set up a corporation, they couldn't just go out and do it. They had to ask the permission of the state legislature. Only if the legislature approved of the purpose of the corporation was it granted a charter and allowed to operate. Not until the nineteenth century did the states establish general incorporation laws.

Despite the Americans' legendary obsession with profits, the early businessman hardly knew what it meant to turn a profit. Most corporations fared poorly. By one estimate, fully one-third of all turnpike companies established before the Civil War never even broke ground. Another third found it impossible to sell their stock or to raise enough through stock sales to finance their ventures.[2]

Conservatives are under the impression that even though it may sometimes be necessary for the government to bail out a business, government should never own a business. All know where *that* can lead! * But if it's impolitic today to support government ownership, that has not always been the case. In the early nineteenth century, governments north and south owned and operated myriad businesses. New York had the Erie Canal. Georgia got into railroading. The federal government ran arms factories. We have all heard of

---

* Actually, of course, it need not lead anywhere. Since the 1930s the federal government has owned the Tennessee Valley Authority without seemingly sliding down the slippery slope to socialism.

Harper's Ferry. It was a gun factory, owned and operated by the U.S. government.

So much for laissez-faire.

It may be argued that if America's early leaders did not practice laissez-faire, they preached it. But even that's not true. While a few voices here and there echoed the view that is now ascribed to them, a clear majority believed in vigorous government action. E. A. J. Johnson, the foremost historian in the subject, says flatly that few eighteenth-century Americans believed in laissez-faire even in the abstract. "It is difficult," he insists, "to find any thoroughgoing, eighteenth-century proponents of laissez-faire, and even harder to find much explicit evidence of legislative acceptance of a theory of economic freedom." Professor Arthur Schlesinger, Jr., reviewing the vast literature on the subject, concluded that the founding fathers "were not proponents of laissez-faire." Their legacy, he reported, "was rather that blend of public and private initiative known in our own day as the mixed economy."[3]

What should be remembered, and rarely is, is that America in the age of Washington was an undeveloped country: few cities, few factories, few industries. And like third-world countries today, the question America faced then was how to get the economy to "take off." The easy part was knowing what not to do. Americans knew not to rely on the free enterprise system; the free enterprise system depends on the existence of private capital and at that time there was none. That left two options: having the government either directly taking over essential businesses, or lending them the money they needed. In typical American fashion, the founders, chose to do both.[4]

A third option—to wait until the day when capital had accumulated sufficiently in the private markets to meet business's needs without government help—was considered and rejected. None saw any need for waiting, and besides, waiting was dangerous. To men like Hamilton, waiting meant delaying the transformation of America from an agrarian weakling into an industrial giant, and that meant delaying the day when America could finally declare its economic independence from Europe. To the founders—ardent nationalists—that was intolerable.[5]

All knew of Adam Smith, whose book had been published in 1776. But Smith's "infallibility" had yet to be established. Hamilton, the chief advocate of the business class, had little faith in the invisible hand of Smith's free market and expressed the opinion that business should never be left "entirely to itself." When business is left "unbridled," he declared, the "spirit of enterprise" is apt to lead to "outrages, and these to reprisals and wars." Or, as he put it on another occasion, "speculation and enterprise" can be "made subservient to useful purposes" only if they are "properly directed."[6]

Thomas Jeffersons's idea that "that government is best which governs least" is sometimes used as evidence that he believed in laissez-faire, but the quotation barely hints at Jefferson's complex view of the matter. First, it wasn't Jefferson who said it; it was Henry David Thoreau, though Jefferson in his first inaugural address made similar-sounding statements. Second, Jefferson showed signs, at first tentative, but as time went on, more and more certain, that his deep-seated objection was not in the end to government per se but to governmnents headed by people other than himself. Once he had beaten John Adams and ousted Adams's Federalist apparatchiks from the bureaucracy, he seems to have become increasingly enthusiastic about government action.[7]

When Jefferson announced in his first inaugural that "a wise and frugal government" shall leave men "free to regulate their own pursuits of industry and improvement," he did not mean government had to adopt a hands-off policy toward business or society—or if he did, he subsequently changed his mind. For as Frank Bourgin observed in his history of laissez-faire, Jefferson actively involved the government in the promotion of science, education, and transportation. To promote science, he turned West Point largely into an engineering school (the only one in the country), and appointed the Lewis and Clark expedition. To advance education, he suggested the United States should establish a national university system like France's. To improve transportation, he proposed spending $20 million over a ten-year period to build new roads and canals.

One may have thought Jefferson would have harbored constitutional scruples about his plans, and to an extent he did. But he never let a cramped view of government authority prevent him from proposing needed social improvements. Thus, despite the fact that the Constitution nowhere mentions the promotion of education as a proper object of government, Jefferson proposed donating federal lands to the states so they could build schools. In 1806 he went so far as to propose a constitutional amendment to give the federal government vast new powers to solve the problems of "public education, roads, rivers, canals, and such other objects of public improvement as it may be thought proper." We may very well have had such an amendment but for the looming war with Great Britain. [8]

The American farmer did not resolutely embrace laissez-faire. The early farmer not only welcomed government aid but demanded it. Some wanted the government to establish model farms to test new agricultural methods. Others called for the building of better roads and canals so they could move their goods to market faster. (The roads were so bad in some areas that tobacco farmers often had to *roll* their product to market, sometimes over stretches of up to 40 miles.) Still others, including George Washington, wanted Congress to subsidize the establishment of a proposed national agricultural society.

It is true that farmers were self-reliant and often suspicious of federal power. But even the most suspicious farmers came to recognize the importance of the government to successful agriculture. Consider John Taylor of Caroline. A prolific writer, Taylor first earned a name for himself as a brilliant opponent of the Constitution and centralized power. But once the governmment was established, Taylor became a vigorous proponent of federal aid to agriculture. Far ahead of his time, he even suggested the employment of a permanent farm lobbyist to explain "respectfully to Congress" the types of assistance that farmers would find useful. [9]

It will be claimed, of course, that eventually Americans did embrace laissez-faire, whether the founders ever did so or not. Taken literally, however, this is nonsense. True laissex-faire has never existed in this country—much to the businessman's immense relief, no doubt. More often than is realized, the government has proved a willing friend to business. When railroads needed land out west to furnish a national transportation system, the government gave them land. When big businesses needed protection from foreign competitors, government gave them high tariffs. When businessmen needed help abroad in quelling rebellions that might result in the expropriation of their property, government stepped in to prevent it. When business was faced with strikes, government frequently sent in the troops to help end them. * [10]

The closest we ever got to laissez-faire in the United States was after the Civil War, a period of unfettered and robust industrialization. But the experiment was brief. In 1887 there was the Interstate Commerce Act. In 1890 there followed the Sherman Anti-Trust Act. And in 1907, amidst a financial panic, Theodore Roosevelt intervened directly in the economy to inflate the currency and force down interest rates. "Every man," announced Roosevelt, "holds his property subject to the general right of the community to regulate it to whatever degree the public welfare may require it." [11]

The whole idea, therefore, that it was Franklin Roosevelt who upset the laissez-faire apple cart is in error. Franklin Roosevelt is blamed only because his efforts overshadowed his predecessors', thereby turning business against him as it had never been against any other president. †

---

* The pattern of government favors to business established in this recital was not unanticipated. It had been predicted by the Jacksonians. They believed that government would always respond to those with money. For this reason, many opposed government interventions. (Arthur Schlesinger, Jr., *The Cycles of American History* [1986], p. 226.)

† A startling reminder of the intensity with which Franklin Roosevelt's name is still held in contempt in some quarters came in the course of an interview with Barbara Bush in 1989. When the interviewer compared the first lady to

It is hard to know why businessmen continue to insist that it's un-American for business to expect government aid. For the more they harp on the theme that it's wise not to help them, the harder it is for them to get help when they do need it. Politicians are so convinced of the general proposition that bailouts are un-American that a business needing a bailout has to beg for one. All know that from time to time business requires help—the bailouts of Lockheed, Chrysler, and the savings and loans attest to that. All seem willing in the end to see that help is provided (at least to the big corporations), but none seem willing to accept government assistance as a general principle.

The businessman, of course, cannot bring himself to admit the truth of his dependence on government aid. To do so would seriously undermine the cherished ideology upon which his whole outlook is based. The wonder is not that the businessman has kept his faith in laissez-faire but that he has been allowed to do so virtually unchallenged. Americans generally, it seems, cannot give up the romantic fiction that businessmen "stand alone."

Some will wonder why, if it was an early American tradition for the government to intervene in the economy, they haven't heard about it until now. Most of the story has been known since 1902, when G. S. Callender published an article on the history of banking and transportation in early America. Most of the rest was uncovered in the fifties. But teachers have chosen not teach it. Politicians have chosen not to explain it. And businessmen have taken the position that it simply can't be. Which all goes to demonstrate how sacrosanct the idea of laissez-faire has become. Powerful evidence is contained in a recent report on teenagers' knowledge of American history. The report showed that more teenagers can define the

---

Eleanor Roosevelt, in what was obviously intended as a compliment, Mrs. Bush was said to have been absolutely mortified. Mrs. Bush retorted that in her family's home when she was a young girl it was forbidden to mention Eleanor Roosevelt's name.

words *laissez-faire* than can say when the Civil War occurred or who Joseph McCarthy was.[12]

Laissez-faire gives the businessman the opportunity to succeed or fail, but it's the freedom to do as he pleases that is its chief attraction. To today's harassed businessman, fed up with the forms, rules, bureaucrats, and taxes that are the price of doing business in the modern world, it is especially appealing. But this preference is questionable. For while the lifting of controls would free him from regulation, it would also free his competitors, and if he wouldn't have to face the tediousness of complying with a surfeit of rules, he'd have to put up with the terror of ruthless competition, which might be worse. It's forgotten that America's period of greatest freedom for business—that so-called "golden age" between the Civil War and the 1880s—was also a time of great depravity. With unregulated competition came government bribery, unscrupulous deal making, child labor, violent strikes, and repeated, unprecedented business failure.[13]

The harassed businessman might think it best then to go back to an earlier period, when things weren't quite so out of control. But it may be doubted if he'd ever find what he so earnestly wants, since earlier in American history government exercised nearly as much control over business as it does today. In colonial times there were laws limiting what to make, how to make it, and what to charge. During the Revolution, tough price controls were put into effect, regulating the price of tea, salt, pepper, wood, hay, charcoal, leather, cotton, mutton, veal, and flour. At other times during the war, Congress limited the profits businessmen could make on goods sold to the military. After the Revolution, says E. A. J. Johnson, the "weird tangle" of state regulations circumscribing entrepreneurial freedom continued, creating a "maze of inspection laws" governing "the quality of goods offered for sale, and sometimes the prices at which they could be sold." In the 1790s, in Johnson's apt phrase, the "legislative harvest" of regulations increased. Under Andrew

Jackson businesses became less subject to national control, but re-cent studies show they continued to face stiff state restraints.

In probably only one area would the businessman of today be justified in looking back upon early economic history with fond nostalgia, and that would be with regard to wage controls. Wage controls were then adopted not for the benefit of labor but for the advantage of business. Controls were put in place to set a ceiling above which they could not go.[14]

That businesspeople oppose government regulation as a general rule is taken for granted by most Americans and with little wonder given the fiery denunciations that seem to greet the issuance of new regulations. But the businessman's animadversions, insistent as they are, must be placed against the evidence, and the evidence suggests that in times of trouble, when consumers are in revolt, merchants frequently welcome regulation in order to restore confidence in the fairness of their procedures or the quality of their products. Inevi-tably, business tries to get by with as few regulations as possible, thereby reinforcing the impression that it is hostile to all regulation. But it isn't. When it is convenient, business favors regulations.

The instances in which businesspeople have called for govern-ment regulation are numerous and easily documented. Consider, for example, the 1891 law passed to regulate the meat-packing industry that provided for the establishment of the first national food inspec-tion system. One might assume it came about as the result of con-sumer pressure, following, perhaps, some scandalous report on the noisome conditions of America's slaughterhouses. In fact, it was the direct result of the efforts of the meatpackers themselves.

The meatpackers acted after they had lost one of their key mar-kets: exports to Europe. Meat exported abroad had turned out to be so bad that European consumers had rebelled, forcing their govern-ments to impose a ban on American meat throughout much of the continent. To win back the market, the meatpackers had to reas-sure their European customers of the quality of their meats. Thus the meatpackers turned to regulation.

Under any rational system, all meats would have been affected by regulation and subject to inspection. But under the law of 1891 only meats exported from the United States were inspected. The domestic market had been unaffected by complaints of food quality. It remained unregulated. * [15]

If the idea of government interventionism was not born with Franklin Roosevelt, it's certainly true that he gave it a dramatic vitality it previously lacked. But it is often thought that he drew his inspiration from an Englishman, the so-called father of modern economics, John Maynard Keynes. This is a mistake. Keynes's major work came out in 1936. Roosevelt was elected in 1932. Thus the New Deal was well along its way before Keynes had a chance to affect it.

Who then helped provide the intellectual underpinning of the New Deal? Who provided the rationale for deficit spending? If any single person deserves the credit it is the improbable Marriner Eccles, a straitlaced Mormon banker from Utah, who in 1933 had the temerity to tell a senate hearing that the government should spend its way out of the depression. The problem, Eccles told the assembled senators, was that Americans were spending too little and saving too much to keep the economy going. The solution, therefore, was government spending. Roosevelt promptly seized on Eccles's suggestion and the next year rewarded the Utahan by appointing him chairman of the Federal Reserve Bank. †

---

* Eventually the American meat market was regulated, of course. That brings up another myth; see page 81.

† This is not to suggest that Roosevelt promptly became an enthusiastic proponent of deficit spending. Throughout the thirties he plainly stated his belief that deficits should be permitted only as a stop-gap measure at a time of economic crisis. We forget that Roosevelt's charges against Herbert Hoover included the criticism that Hoover ran a big budget deficit! Even after he himself became president, Roosevelt repeatedly tried to limit spending. In 1933 he cut veterans' benefits by $400 million. And in 1937 he vowed to deliver a balanced budget the following year: "I have said fifty times that the budget will be balanced for the fiscal year 1938. If you want me to say it again,

Eccles remains largely unknown, perhaps because businessmen find it inconceivable that one of their own—a banker!—was responsible for justifying Roosevelt's free-spending policies. Better that it should have been Keynes—at least he was a foreigner.[16]

The businessman's hostility to Keynesianism has always been difficult to explain, for it was Keynesian policies that ushered the country out of the depression and into prosperity, giving consumers the money to buy the things business sells. It is to be accounted for in two ways: either by sheer prejudice or by ignorance—or possibly by a mixture of both. The prejudice against a philosophy of state interventionism is deeply ingrained and can be expected to remain, but the ignorance is subject to remedy. It rests on the belief that Keynesianism did not end the depression—World War II did. But what brought about prosperity in World War II? It was government spending that did it, spending on such a scale that the New Deal looked like a children's experiment by comparison. If World War II proved anything in economics, it proved that Keynesianism (under certain circumstances) works.

It is perhaps unfortunate that the businessman prefers to attribute America's economic recovery to World War II rather than to Keynesianism. In doing so he reinforces the unpleasant association many make between war and business, reviving the old suspicion that businessmen welcome war as a generator of profits. One still hears, for instance, that America entered World War I at the behest of its bankers, who stood to lose millions if the Allies lost and defaulted on their loans. The charge carries with it the force of common sense, but it is based on the erroneous assumption that the bankers were seriously worried the Allies might lose. Actually, at the time America entered the war it was thought that the Allies were winning. Not until the veil of Allied propaganda was lifted after the conflict did it become clear how desperate the situation

---

I will say it either once or fifty times more. That is my intention." (James Savage, *Balanced Budgets and American Politics* [1988], pp. 166–73.)

really had been. (Some, no doubt, will cite the Nye committee hearings in the thirties as evidence in their indictment of bankers. Both the hearings and the bankers are misconstrued. It was outside the hearing room amidst a political campaign that the charges against the bankers were made. The hearings themselves proved nothing.) [17]

In fact, it is far from clear that business people as a group have been any more supportive of war than Americans generally. Indeed, the opposite case may plausibly be made. For war always leads to a certain amount of instability and businessmen hate instability. Thus, if anything, they maintain a deep prejudice against military action. By most accounts, they actively opposed the Spanish-American War. At the outset of World War II, many proved reluctant to abandon the lucrative civilian market to accommodate the needs of the government.

It will be observed that businesspeople were in the forefront of the Cold War effort to beef up the country's defense forces. By all accounts their contribution to the buildup—the largest military boom in the peacetime history of the United States—was large. One would be remiss not to give business the credit it so richly deserves for the buildup. In fact, business's contribution may have exceeded that of the Pentagon's. On more than a few occasions the defense industry persuaded Congress to approve weapons even the Pentagon opposed. But favoring the production of military hardware is not exactly the same as supporting its use. Indeed, given the numerous investigations that have shown how badly some key weapons perform, it may be presumed that the weapons' manufacturers would be the last people who would want to see them tried in combat.

Whether businesspeople have been specially predisposed to war or not, it's firmly believed that wars have proven to be a boon to business. The record would seem to suggest this is true. The Civil War is credited as a great force in strengthening industrialism. World Wars I and II are thought to have pulled the United States out of depression.

But when the details are considered, the economic utility of war is far less certain. Thomas Cochran, one of the country's finest economic historians, is of the opinion that both World Wars actually retarded economic growth in the United States. The only reason, he says, that they seem to have helped is because they occurred during periods of high unemployment. "The immediate effect of each, therefore, was to put men to work, to increase the national product, and to create an aura of prosperity." These effects, to be sure, were of great benefit, but it was not war per se that brought them about. It was concerted government action. War merely gave the politicians the excuse they needed to take radical measures.[18]

From the position of the losers, the Civil War must be judged as an unmitigated economic disaster. As losers, southerners enjoyed none of the advantages of war and suffered all of its liabilities: the destruction of property, the inflation of the currency, the collapse of their banking system, the loss of a generation of youth, and the impoverishment of a good part of their business class. The abolition of slavery, of course, must be construed as a positive economic development as well as a moral one. But it did nothing in the short run to mitigate the damage of a brutal and wasting, if necessary, war. One statistic is telling. Not until fifteen years after the war did the South produce as much cotton as it had before.* [19]

From the vantage of the victors, the Civil War is almost always considered an economic triumph. Arthur Schlesinger, Sr., said the war "had the effect of a hothouse" on the economy. Harold Faulk-

---

* Admittedly, it is possible to take the idea of the war's effects too far. The Mississippi professor who claimed in 1990 that his students needed to study the Civil War because "we never recovered" from it was doubtlessly sincere, and provided the newspapers with a good headline, but he was exaggerating. His evidence was that Mississippi had been the fifth richest state in the union before the war, "and when it was over we were thirty-sixth, and now we're fiftieth." But surely Mississippi's problems, to the extent that they reflect its past, are more the result of slavery and racism than war. (*New York Times*, April 22, 1990, p. 14.)

ner, in an economics textbook used by generations of students, said "it speeded the Industrial Revolution and the development of capitalism." Another textbook, coauthored by the esteemed Richard Hofstadter, said flatly that the war "led to American industrial expansion."[20]

None of this, however, is supported in the least by the available statistical evidence. As Cochran shows, in every category worth noting—from railroads to pig iron—the war's clear and unmistakable effect was to drive production down, or at the least, to hold it at the prewar level. Take the railroads, which are considered such a vital part of America's industrial development. If the war had been as powerful an engine of growth as it is usually portrayed, one would expect to find that more new tracks would have been laid during and after the war than before, but the finding is just the reverse. Before the war, railroad track increased at a rate of about 200 percent a decade. In the decade afterward, the rate barely reached 75 percent. During the war itself, railroad construction plummeted; only 4,000 miles of new tracks were built, a paltry 15 percent increase. Pig iron production fared even worse, increasing during the war by just 1 percent. Bank loans actually declined during the war, as did the total value of farm machinery and (no surprise) cotton textile production.[21]

That certain businesses have profited handsomely from war is beyond question. In the Revolution a few businessmen made so much money there was talk of enacting an excess profits tax. During the Civil War, financiers like Jay Cooke made huge fortunes through the sale of government bonds. In the thirties, the Nye Committee proved that in the First World War arms makers had profited fabulously. But it is one thing to suggest that war made people rich and quite another to say they dragged the country into war so they could become rich.[22] Of course, the very idea of someone profiting from war is repugnant, but there is not very much that can be done about it under a capitalist system.

That businessmen have sometimes made money from war in crooked ways is all too true, but many stories of corruption have become better in the telling than they really were. J. Pierpont Morgan, Sr., for instance, owes much of his considerable reputation as a Robber Baron to an incident from the Civil War that has come to be known as the Hall Carbine Affair (so-called because the man who originally designed the carbines in question was named Hall). However, Morgan's involvement has been exaggerated and the significance of the incident has been overplayed.

At the outset of the Civil War, the army, in a state of confusion, sold five thousand surplus rifles to a speculator for $3.50 apiece. Within literally weeks, it bought them back at $22 apiece. The resulting profits were shared by several men, Morgan among them. Obviously the main error was the army's for selling the rifles in the first place. It was utter folly to sell weapons at the beginning of a war even if at the moment the weapons seemed not to be of much use. But of course it is the men who made money off the deal who have borne the brunt of the scandal, since they are presumed to have taken advantage of the army at a time of confusion and national emergency. They are also thought to have made an obscene profit on the deal. On both of these counts they are guilty as charged.

The other charges usually made against them are bogus. It is inaccurate to say that they did nothing for their money. After buying the weapons, they had the barrels rifled by a machinist to improve their accuracy and range. This wasn't an expensive job, but it indicates they had something more in mind than sheer exploitation. It is also said that the rifles were dangerous and obsolete and therefore not worth $22, but they were worth the money. Though thirteen years old, the rifles had never been used. And despite stories that they had blown the thumbs off soldiers who fired them, they weren't dangerous. The thumb stories were fabricated. Union General John C. Frémont, who was the one who bought the rifles, averred that they were reliable and safe.

The misinformation is worth tracing. It comes mainly out of a book published in 1910 on the *History of Great American Fortunes,* written by a socialist named Gustavus Myers. The book didn't sell well, but it seemed so well-grounded in documents that in time it came to be regarded as a minor classic. Myers himself contributed to the impression that the work was beyond dispute, claiming he had sometimes spent months tracking down a single fact. Once he even wrote to the *New York Times* to complain that he wasn't getting the credit he deserved for the facts he'd singlehandedly dug up. The self-pitying attitude seemed ungracious. Rarely in the history of American letters had an author's work been cited as often as Myers's.

Myers remained undisputed for some thirty years. Then, in 1941, the Morgan men struck back. The counterattack was led by R. Gordon Wasson, a vice-president of J. P. Morgan and Company. In a book as thick with footnotes and documents as Myers's own, Wasson demonstrated that Myers had managed to neglect some of the key sources relevant to the scandal and had distorted others. Historian Allan Nevins promptly declared that Morgan had been cleared.

Whether Morgan was altogether clean is still a matter of dispute. What is clear, however, is that the scandal endured because of its association with Morgan. Had it not been for the Morgan connection, the affair would now be remembered only by those aficionados who have made Civil War trivia their personal hobby.

But what was the Morgan connection? What did he have to do with the army buying back weapons that it had just sold? It was Arthur Eastman, a little-known New Hampshire gun dealer, who arranged to buy the rifles from the army. It was Simon Stevens, a New York clubhouse politician, playing on his friendship with fellow Republican John C. Frémont, who sold them back to the army and who set the price at $22. Morgan's sole role in the affair was to loan Stevens some of the money needed initially to finance the deal. When the matter became public during the war, an investigating committee chastised the army officer who originally sold the weapons, condemned Frémont for buying them, and accused Eastman and Stevens of putting greed above country. Morgan, however, was never named.

One is rather tempted to believe the worst of a character like Morgan. Against him is the fact that he profited at the Union's expense (garnering between $6,000 and $10,000 in interest, commissions, and expenses*), that he delayed the shipment of the rifles to Frémont until his loan had been repaid, despite Frémont's plea that "good men are losing their lives while the men whom they defend are debating terms," and that he almost certainly knew from the beginning (despite the claims of his apologists) that the ultimate purpose in buying the rifles was to sell them back at an inflated profit. Add to it that Morgan hired a substitute in the war to do his fighting for him and you have more than enough reason to think him a coward and a knave. But he was not exactly the ringleader in the scandal that he's been made out to be, and he did not earn enough from the transaction—this transaction at least—to merit the notoriety attached to him.[23]

Far more difficult to determine is whether the businessmen of the late nineteenth century, men like Morgan, John D. Rockefeller, and Andrew Carnegie, deserve to be called Robber Barons. Some who think the term is inappropriate insist it reveals a naive contempt for materialism, reflecting, as one writer put it, a kind of "feminine idealism." They concede that bribery was rampant in the period, that children worked too hard at jobs that paid too little, and that men at the top often trampled those on the bottom to get ahead. But in the meantime, they say, a new age of manufacturing was arising. Markets were being "rationalized," inefficiencies were

---

* It is hard to know how much Morgan actually made from the deal. The records show he loaned Stevens $20,000, and that within two months he was paid back $26,343, earning 7 percent interest on the deal and a commission of a dollar a carbine. But he may have made an additional $3,797 for helping Stevens obtain additional loans from a man named Morris Ketchum, increasing his take to about $10,000. (Andrew Sinclair, *Corsair: The Life of J. Pierpont Morgan* [1981], pp. 18–21.)

being rooted out, and life was being made better.* In their telling it was a creative period, and businessmen were the leading creators, producing refrigerated meats, cheap steel, and abundant supplies of oil.[24]

In improving the life of the average person, however, their record was one of almost unrelieved failure. During the years they were in the saddle, between 1865 and 1900, Americans suffered through more depressions and panics than at any other time in history, enduring sixteen years of economic decline out of the total thirty-five. In employee relations their record was even more dismal. Between 1881 and 1885 there were nearly 500 work stoppages a year involving a total of 200,000 persons. Between 1896 and 1900 there were nearly 1,400 work stoppages annually involving more than 350,000 persons. Some idea of the cause of labor discontent may be found in the railroad safety statistics. In 1900 there were more than 2,500 railroad workers killed on the job; another 39,000 were injured.

The Robber Barons' most memorable contribution to human happiness is said to have been their phenomenal ability to increase the output of goods. But in the areas of agriculture, mining, construction, and manufacturing the output of commodities actually increased at a slower rate after the Civil War than it had before. Economist Allen Solganick, in an article summarizing the available research on the subject, concluded that "the United States developed more slowly during the era of the Robber Barons than it had before these 'creators' arrived on the scene."[25]

As risk-takers they are vastly overrated. Professor W. Paul Strassmann, after a careful review of manufacturing methods in the nineteenth century, concluded that they almost never took risks to try new technology. As a rule they waited for others to take the risks. Those like Carnegie, who indeed tried new technologies,

---

* Between 1850 and 1900 the United States went from being one of the least industrialized countries in the Western world to being the most industrialized. (Daniel Rogers, *The Work Ethic in Industrial America* [1978], p. 27.)

creating in the process the biggest and the best steel mills in the world, were the exception. "In short," says Strassmann of the iron and steel business, "the progressiveness of the innovating firms should not be taken as that of the industry as a whole."

That they did not reveal themselves to be great risk-takers is disappointing. It is thought that businessmen, when given the chance to operate without government interference, will naturally show the spunk of the stereotypical entrepreneur. The Robber Barons, however, showed the stereotype is apparently in need of revision. They proved that businessmen unburdened by red tape can be just as reluctant to innovate as businessmen living under close government scrutiny. Coke smelting, for instance, a major advance in steel production, was introduced in 1839; it did not become widely used until the 1880s. A fully automated loom was invented in 1888; it did not become widely adopted until the twentieth century. A cost-saving method of spinning yarn known as ring spinning was invented in 1828; as late as 1900 the old technology, which went by the name of mule spinning, was still being sold. When the Westinghouse air brake that is considered essential to modern railroading made its first appearance, railroad magnate Commodore Vanderbilt derided it as useless. The telephone was regarded at first as a toy. The typewriter was considered so unpromising that the inventor could barely pay off his personal debts with the money he got for the patent ($12,000).

The chief obstacle to innovation seems to have been the businessman's stubborn reluctance to scrap old equipment. All he cared was if the thing worked. If it did he kept it, even if it had clearly become obsolete, and even if it could be replaced with a new machine that would pay for itself quickly. The only time he seemed to welcome an innovation was if it could be adapted to existing machinery without too much trouble and at little expense.*

---

* George Draper, the man who developed the improved loom that nobody seemed to want, observed in 1878: "I find in all cases, almost without exception, that all of the principal machine shops are opposed to the introduction

It is not, it would seem, the better mouse trap that the world awaits. It is the better businessman. New and better mouse traps are being invented all the time. What there is a lack of is businessmen willing to take a chance on the newfangled things.

Big businesses seem to have been more willing to take risks than smaller ones, thus confirming the widespread belief in the superiority of the Robber Barons' large enterprises. But the correlation between big enterprises and risk-taking was weak. For one thing, then as now, increasing size meant increasing bureaucratization, and as the world needs no reminding, bureaucracies are often the greatest enemies of change. For another, increasing size meant greater business complexity, which bode badly for innovativeness as well. Take the case of Bethlehem Steel. As a simple matter of arithmetic, Bethlehem Steel would seem to have been better off modernizing its plants. The savings in labor costs alone would have justified the expense. With new equipment the plants could operate with a fourth as many workers. But nothing was simple where a behemoth like Bethlehem Steel was concerned. It turned out that the company had spent a lot of money building homes for its employees. If they were to be let go in substantial numbers, Bethlehem Steel would be stuck with a town full of homes and nobody to live in them. The prospect was frightening. Modernization, in consequence, was postponed.[26]

Contempt for the Robber Barons, great as it is for the rascally things they did, is greatest probably for the arrogance with which they defended their rascality. Most people probably can't remember a single concrete "crime" the Robber Barons committed, but every-

---

of improvements for the reason that it is costly for them to make the necessary changes, and it takes the personal attention of the leading men to the details that are required, and every point has to be considered, while in order to duplicate machines they have only to give the order; the patterns and the drawings and everything being ready for it and their hands being accustomed to do it." (Quoted by W. Paul Strassmann, *Risk and Technological Innovation* [1959], p. 99.)

body knows they made no apologies for their actions—that's what galls!

The trouble is that in maximizing their badness we have reduced them to caricatures of themselves. No more are they mere corporate criminals. They are sinister, scheming, blood-sucking villains. There is the tight-fisted John D. Rockefeller, the villainous J. P. Morgan, the scheming Cornelius Vanderbilt. Among their most villainous crimes was their espousal of social Darwinism. They didn't just say they believed in social Darwinism; it's held that they really did.

In fact, they didn't; they really had no philosophy at all. The business about natural laws and social evolution was taken to heart by only a couple of professors, namely William Graham Sumner and Herbert Spencer. It was they who strove for consistency in the application of the principles of evolution to society, they who advanced as scientific facts the idea that the social classes owe each other nothing and that "a drunkard in the gutter is just where he ought to be." The Robber Barons worried about money.[27]

Certainly, however much they talked about it, they didn't care much for the "natural law of competition." Let the birds and the rattlesnakes compete. Man was meant to get ahead by eliminating competition. Thus were the trusts born. As economist Dudley Dillard puts it, "Competition is profit-destroying. Consequently profit-motivated economic units attempted to establish monopolies whenever possible."[28]

A few, bothered by the inconsistency, tried to reconcile their avowals of competition with their practice of consolidation. When the Sugar Trust was formed, apologists said it wasn't to eliminate competition per se but to get rid of "excessive competition." When the railroad barons adopted monopolistic practices, they said it was because competition was a "fallacious idea" in their specific industry. While "the principle" applied to almost every other kind of business, it did "not apply to railroads."

That, at least, is what they said in public. In their private correspondence they were more candid. As one railroad magnate admitted, "the struggle for existence and the survival of the fittest" is "a pretty theory" but not much more.[29]

They were not wholly inconsistent. They firmly believed some economic "laws" were indeed inviolate. But these were the ones that—conveniently—applied to others, such as their employees. Thus they were convinced that though *they* weren't bound by the "law of competition," their employees were. Wages *must* be set at the very minimum. If more was paid, profits would go down. The company could go broke.[30]

Just what else they believed in besides money is unclear. Thomas Cochran, after an exhaustive review of the private business correspondence of sixty-one railroad executives, could find no rational basis for their beliefs aside from "pragmatism," in other words, what was good for them.

William Graham Sumner, in comparison, was sincere. When he enunciated a principle he stuck with it, carrying it through to its logical conclusion no matter where it led him. Thus, at considerable risk to his public position, he even came out against the protective tariff, calling it the worst form of "quackery." But then he was a professor, and as a professor he was expected to take principled positions. The Robber Barons, being businessmen, were just expected to make money. It is this they should be remembered for and not their social philosophy.[31]

The contempt in which businessmen and the rich were often held in the late nineteenth century is thought to have marked something of a turning point in American history. And indeed it did. There is nothing in the earlier history of the republic to compare with the invectives hurled at business in the Age of the Great Barbecue. * Previously, only politicians, Indians, slaves, and George III got as good a verbal drubbing.

The facts, however, show the businessman is only kidding him-

---

* The name given to the Gilded Age by literary critic Vernon Louis Parrington in his *Main Currents in American Thought* [rpt. 1958], III, 23.

self if he thinks the objections started with the Robber Barons and are due only to their obvious excesses. Businessmen in America have had to contend with public suspiciousness on many occasions. In the Revolution, war profiteers and monopolists came under scrutiny. In the War of 1812, New England smugglers were scorned. In Andrew Jackson's day, bankers felt the public's wrath.

Businessmen, it is true, were more secure in their wealth when the republic was young. All then agreed that the money a man made was largely his to do with as he wished. Not until 1913 did the United States adopt a permanent income tax. But it is a mistake to think that it took the fleecing of the common man in the late nineteenth century to produce the idea that the rich should be made to pay a greater share of their income into the government's coffers than the poor and the middling. As early as 1806, Jefferson argued that the rich should pay more. The first income tax was passed during the Civil War and was kept in place for ten years.[32]

Nor did the labor movement suddenly spring into existence in response to the Robber Barons. The seeds of the movement were planted long before the Civil War. The defect in understanding the situation is the consequence of oversimplified textbooks, which have, for convenience's sake, lumped in all of labor history with the Robber Barons.

A consequence of treating the labor movement strictly as a response to the Robber Barons is that it is made to seem minor in comparison. Indeed, in nearly every one of the labor battles that textbooks recount, labor is portrayed decidedly as the inferior group.

Upon investigation, however, it has turned out that this wasn't always so. Herbert Gutman, one of the country's leading labor historians, determined that the Robber Barons held overwhelming power only in the major metropolises, where it was often easy to get the police, say, to break up a strike since the strikers often seemed separate from the community-at-large. In the smaller cities, in contrast, strikers often were a vital part of the community and were less easily defeated. Thus, when a big Chicago coal operator tried to replace the local workers at his Braidwood, Illinois, mine with outsiders who would mine for less, he found he couldn't. Though he had the help of the state militia and the Pinkerton Detective Agency (which was often used to break up strikes), the locals had the support of the mayor and the sheriff. When the Pinkerton men asked the town for permission to carry weapons, the sheriff turned them down. When the miners asked if *they* could carry guns the sheriff said they could. Whether the miners threatened strike breakers with the guns is unknown. But when the out-of-town workers were told it was unfair for them to take the jobs of the local townsfolk, they quietly went home. Fourteen weeks later the mine operator surrendered.

Sometimes local laborers not only had the support of the local government but they were the government. In 1874 the congressman from Virginia City was the president of the local miners union. The postmaster in West Belleville, Illinois, was a leading trade unionist. The town of Evansville, Indiana, was run by the local labor party. And three labor leaders served on the city council in Joliet, Illinois.

The Robber Barons, to be sure, weren't on the run. But neither, apparently, was labor.[33]

5
Literature

If Alger ever kept a diary, I knew nothing about it. In any case, it was more fun to invent one. I had no letters ever written by Alger, which was fortunate. Again, it was more fun to make them up, as it was with letters persumably sent to Alger, none of which I had ever seen.

HERBERT R. MAYES, FIRST BIOGRAPHER OF HORATIO ALGER, JR. *

The most "shocking" and "interesting" event of 1926, the victory of boxer Gene Tunney over Jack Dempsey in the fight for the heavyweight championship of the world, would hardly have seemed either as shocking or interesting as it did had it not been for one simple, sorely misunderstood, but widely publicized fact published shortly before the bout. The fact? In his spare time, Gene Tunney liked to read Shakespeare. To true aficionados of the sport, the disclosure had decisively ended all hope that Tunney would beat Dempsey. For everybody "knew" Shakespeare is for snobs and snobs are weaklings.[1]

The logic exhibited in such thinking is plainly mistaken, though few at the time seemed to realize it, including Dempsey himself, who went into the match thinking Tunney was a pushover. The real error was not one of logic but of history.

What Dempsey didn't realize, and what nobody pointed out, was that there was ample reason for believing that Shakespeare could appeal to the brawny as well as the brainy. Historically, he

---

* On the controversy over Mayes's biography, see page 192.

had. Shocking as it may seem to us in the twentieth century, Shake-speare once was hugely popular with the masses. Lawrence Levine, a professor at the University of California at Berkeley who has written a book on the subject published by Harvard University, says that from 1750 until nearly the end of the nineteenth century, Shakespeare was "the most popular playwright" in America among all classes.

Evidence of Shakespeare's wide acceptance abounds. Mark Twain recalled that the pilot who taught him how to steer a steam-ship would read Shakespeare to him "by the hour," and "knew his Shakespeare as well as Euclid ever knew his multiplication table." As a young soldier, Ulysses S. Grant performed in an amateur production of *Othello* put on by his army regiment during the dull weeks preceding the outbreak of the Mexican War. As a boy, Lin-coln read Shakespeare for pleasure.

Shakespeare, then as now, bemused the uninitiated, but was popular with theater audiences. Historians who have examined the schedules of theater productions in detail report that in many cities in the antebellum period a quarter of the plays performed in any one season were Shakespeare's. Indeed, the British playwright was more in demand in America than in Britain.

His popularity was not confined to the cities. John Bernard, in the early 1800s a famous English performer, reported that anytime an actor found himself unemployed in America he "had merely to visit some town in the interior" and read Shakespeare to replenish his supply of money. Alexis de Tocqueville wrote that Shakespeare could be found in "the recesses of the forests," and said he could find "hardly a pioneer's hut that does not contain a few odd volumes of Shakespeare."

Shakespeare, in fact, in the nineteenth century provoked a far more passionate response among the masses than any pop poet or playwright ever has in the twentieth century. Consider the event that's come to be known as the Astor Place Riot, which occurred in New York City on the evening of May 10, 1849. The riot began with an attack on the Astor Place theater involving 10,000 people. By the time it was over at least 22 were killed, more than 150 were injured, and 86 were arrested. And the cause of all the commotion? A preposterous dispute between two Shakespearean actors, one American, one British, who were then performing in rival productions of Macbeth. The city had become caught up in the dispute, dividing along class lines, the rich favoring the British actor's production, the laborers favoring the American's. To followers of the American, it seemed that nothing less than democracy itself was at stake. Thus the deluge.

Some have suggested in the face of the evidence that people cared about Shakespeare, that they didn't really understand him, and they point out that the most popular of the Elizabethan's productions featured gore and action, the Shakespearean equivalent of the modern-day car chase. But that doesn't change the fact that people cared. And it certainly doesn't diminish in the least the Americans' commitment to Shakespeare, a commitment that is certainly all the more remarkable given the kinds of literature that subsequently became popular.

It's true that Americans in the nineteenth century did not approach Shakespeare the way we do today, on bended knee. Their Shakespeare lived: Actors freely tampered with the material, parodying Shakespeare's most famous lines, amending his language, eliminating scenes, and consolidating characters. But in tampering with Shakespeare the way they did—all to the horror of present-day purists—they were merely making him more appealing to American audiences. In the end what audiences got was still fundamentally Shakespeare.

At any rate, there is plenty of reason to doubt the premise that the level of the people's understanding was jejune or primitive. The fact that actors frequently parodied the plays, for example, is evidence that, at a minimum, audiences were familiar with the way they were originally written. As Levine observes "one cannot parody that which is not well known." Thus, only someone familiar with the original would find it funny to hear one character implore another to "Get thee to a brewery." *

Why Shakespeare suddenly declined in popularity is anybody's guess, but it undoubtedly had something to do with the emergence of cultural snobbery. We take cultural snobbery for granted, but historians say it didn't surface until around the 1880s. * It was then that Americans first began drawing the distinction between high and low culture, a distinction that owes its nomenclature to the old belief that persons with high brows were more intelligent than those with low ones, a belief borrowed from phrenology, the pseudoscientific study of the skull, which ridiculously associated certain skull bumps with braininess.[2]

Most of the mistakes made about writers stem from the attempt to

* But if Shakespeare enriched the popular culture of the nineteenth century, and if there were myriad theaters in which his plays were performed, one might wish, before growing nostalgic, to keep in mind the conditions under which the performances took place. For if there were more Shakespearean productions from which to choose in the nineteenth century than today, watching them in peace was considerably more difficult. Washington Irving recalled that when the common folk in the galleries were roused by something they saw on stage, they "commenced a discharge of apples, nuts & ginger-bread" on the heads of those below them. To this was added their cheers and jeers, which made the theaters, one imagines, about as serene as a stadium during a baseball game. Irving complained that the noise in the theater "is somewhat similar to that which prevailed in Noah's Ark; for we have an imitation of the whistles and yells of every kind of animal." And as if all this weren't enough, it seems that in some cases the galleries were opened to prostitutes to help sell tickets, making the off-stage performances almost as interesting—if not as enlightening—as the ones on-stage. (Lawrence Levine, *Highbrow/Lowbrow* [1989], p. 25; Claudia Johnson, "That Guilty Third Tier: Prostitution in Nineteenth-Century American Theaters," *American Quarterly*, XXVII [Dec. 1975], 581.)

* Until then Italian operas were attended by common folk and museums were designed for mass appeal. It wasn't just P. T. Barnum's museum that included "curiosities." Even Boston's Gallery of Fine Arts featured dwarfs along with Hogarths. (Levine, *Highbrow/Lowbrow*, pp. 86, 149.)

pigeonhole them, as Shakespeare is now pigeonholed as "high-brow." Thus, Noah Webster is remembered as the man who wrote the "nationalistic" American dictionary. Upton Sinclair is identified with the exposé that led to the reform of the jungle conditions inside the Chicago meat plants. Henry David Thoreau is lionized as a solitary, rugged woodsman. And Ernest Hemingway is celebrated for his love of war.

The main thing Webster is credited with doing—helping Americanize the American language—he didn't do and didn't hope to do. By H. L. Mencken's count, Webster's famous dictionary contained just fifty Americanisms, so few that when the dictionary was published in England it immediately became as popular over there as here. Professor Richard Rollins says Webster actually "was received more warmly across the Atlantic than in the United States." We will never know if the British reaction gave Webster as much satisfaction as the American reaction, but it did not dissatisfy him. Upon the publication of the second edition he sent a copy to Queen Victoria.

Once he had been an Anglophobe, but by the nineteenth century Webster had become an Anglophile. While other Americans were trying to establish an American culture independent of Great Britain's, he was hard at work trying to strengthen their mutual cultural ties. He told Queen Victoria he hoped his dictionary demonstrated that the "genuine descendants of English ancestors have not forgotten either the land or the language of their fathers."

If Webster seemed fascinated with Great Britain, he felt little but contempt for his own country. Anybody who thinks of him as a nationalist is mistaken; his nationalistic feelings ended with the revolutionary period. A reactionary at heart, he despised the Declaration of Independence, for "no person is born free," and he considered the Constitution dangerously democratic. In 1798, with Shays's Rebellion evidently still fresh in his mind, he warned Americans never to forget "that the cornerstone of all republican government is that the will of every citizen is controlled by the laws of supreme will of the state." Subsequently, he came out against the separation of church and state on the grounds that "all laws must have *religion for their basis.*" During the War of 1812, at the occasion of the Hartford Convention,* he ridiculed the notion of universal white male suffrage. Earlier he had suggested depriving Americans of the right to vote until they were forty-five, and believed no one should hold elective office until they reached fifty. All power, he wrote, should be vested in "our old men."

It is for his dictionary, of course, that Webster is remembered, and not for his views on politics. But Webster believed he could use his dictionary to affect politics and tried to by inserting his Christian morals and authoritarian views into his definitions and quotes. Professor Rollins says that "hundreds and perhaps thousands" of the entries in the dictionary plainly reflect Webster's attempt to use the work to promote his reactionary political agenda. In his definition of the word *love*, Webster wrote "The Christian *loves* his Bible. . . . we *love* God above all things. . . . In other words, the Christian *loves* God." The entry on *duty* is particularly preachy: "That which a person owes to another. . . . fidelity to friends is a *duty*; reverence, obedience, and prayer to God are indisputable *duties*; the government and religious instruction of children are *duties* of parents which they cannot neglect without guilt."

Just how much of an effect Webster had on mores no one may know. But he cannot have had anywhere near the effect that he hoped in his own lifetime—and none in our own day as far as can be discerned.[3]

Upton Sinclair is properly identified with *The Jungle* (1906), his exposé of the conditions inside the Chicago meat plants. However, the effect of the book on reform of the plants is overestimated. To be sure, *The Jungle* created a sensation. Regular eaters of processed meats gagged at the description of rats mixed with pork: "A man

---

* The convention of New England Federalists was called to protest the war, and was believed to have been inspired by radicals in the South and the West. Dominated by conservatives, the convention considered proposals to take New England out of the war and out of the union.

could run his hands over the piles of meat [at the plants] and swap off handfulls of dry dung of rats." The situation was so God-awful most Americans must have been thankful Sinclair had focused public attention on the problem—even if he was a Red! For the moment that seemed beside the point.

But his wasn't the first exposé of the meat plants, nor was it the first to produce a crisis. Processed American meat had been suspect for decades. During the previous century Europeans had banned it from the continent and in the Spanish-American War soldiers had died from eating it. All these events were widely publicized and condemned.

True, within four months of the publication of the book, which sold 25,000 copies the first week it appeared, Congress approved a tough new meat inspection law and Teddy Roosevelt signed it. But it wasn't *The Jungle* that proved decisive. Public interest in the issue had waned within weeks of the book's release and by that time the meat packers had organized sufficiently to sabotage the movement in Congress for a bill with teeth. Books by themselves are fine things, but a single lobbyist armed with threats and backed by a behemoth is often more powerful. The tough bill was defeated! In the end, the only thing that saved it was raw power. Roosevelt, believing he had an issue with which he could beat the meat trust (which he'd been unsuccessfully trying to break in the courts), used behind-the-scenes pressure to force the legislature to pass the law subsequently credited to Upton Sinclair.

Sinclair, incidentally, felt disappointment. While the book had sufficiently aroused the public to unsanitary conditions inside the meat plants, what he really wanted to change was the working conditions in the plants. He didn't.[4]

The belief that Henry David Thoreau (né David Henry Thoreau; he adopted the new name as a young man because he liked the sound of it better) was a hermit and a rugged individualistic woodsman is false but not wholly false. He did spend two years living in a cabin on Walden Pond. But we now know, as a result of research by Walter Harding in the 1960s, that a lot of things left out of *Walden* would have altered considerably the impression made by the statements left in. It is thought, for instance, that Thoreau lived the life of a recluse. But Harding proved that Thoreau either visited Concord or was visited by someone from Concord almost every single day of his stint by the pond. William Ellery Channing, the antislavery clergyman, stayed with him for two weeks. Every Saturday his mother and sisters visited. On Sundays Bronson Alcott came. One month a hundred Irish laborers arrived to cut up the ice in Walden Pond for shipment to Calcutta; when laborers fell in the water, which was often, they went to the cabin for help. Sometimes as many as thirty people visited Thoreau at the cabin in a single day. One year the antislavery women of Concord held an annual meeting at the cabin, which was used, occasionally, as a station for the underground railroad.

Nor was the cabin located in as remote an area as is usually imagined. "The well-traveled Concord-Lincoln road," says Harding, "was within sight across the field. The Fitchburg Railroad steamed regularly past the opposite end of the pond. Concord village was less than two miles away." Thoreau's parents lived even closer.

The cabin itself was sparse but hardly uncomfortable. If it seems primitive by our standards, it was more luxurious than the huts the Pilgrims inhabited and less austere than the shanty in which Lincoln grew up. It included a fireplace, plastered walls, and two windows. Outside there was an outhouse and a woodshed.

That Thoreau was a loner is laughable. Except for the two years he spent at Walden Pond, he lived nearly his entire life with his mother. When family members suggested he leave home to get a job, he broke down and sobbed. Touched, they told him to stay. (Not that Thoreau claimed to have been a loner. He merely left that impression because of his celebration of solitude.)

That he was a woodsman is true in the sense that he lived for a time in the woods. But he wasn't very rugged and he may have been indifferent to the forest. As a young man he and a friend set fire to the woods near Concord; a biographer has suggested he did so deliberately, perhaps in anger at the villagers for the contempt with which he was often treated. After alerting the village to the existence of the fire, Thoreau retreated to a nearby mountain to watch its progress, leaving the work of fighting the blaze to others. Some never forgave him. Little more than a year later, Thoreau— "America's nature lover"—moved to Walden Pond.[5]

The lament that "the mass of men lead lives of quiet desperation" is regarded as one of Thoreau's keenest insights, and it was. But few realize it was Thoreau who was desperate. That's why he went into the woods. A Harvard graduate, he never adopted a regular profession, was a disappointment to his mother, felt inferior to his gregarious brother, and long regarded his life as something of a failure. The one woman he loved he lost. He never married. When his brother died from lockjaw, Thoreau immediately came down with the same symptoms and was bedridden for months though doctors found nothing wrong with him. A psychobiographer has suggested Thoreau secretly felt he must—somehow!—have been to blame for his brother's death.

Despite the impression that he was lazy, an impression he himself liked to foster, Thoreau loved to work. It's forgotten that most of the time he spent at the cabin he spent writing, not playing with insects or watching birds. He wrote two books there: one on the trip he'd taken with his brother on the Merrimac and Concord rivers, and the other on Walden. The book on Walden, contrary to popular belief, wasn't a journal, dashed off at a leisurely moment between fishing and camping. Professor Leo Marx is of the opinion that it was "meticulously edited," but says it was written and rewritten to *appear* as if it had not been. It is true that Thoreau never wrote another book after *Walden*. But he constantly attended to his journals, writing some two million words in them in all before he died from tuberculosis at age forty-four. The journals alone, when finally published, are expected to take up twenty-five closely printed volumes.[6]

If Thoreau was really a writer who is thought of as a woodsman, he was also something of an engineer. Historians remind us it was Thoreau who helped perfect the development of the lead-lined wood pencil in America. His father ran a small pencil company; Thoreau's contribution was critical in making it a success. His achievement in the great scheme of things, though, was minor. It consisted mainly of borrowing a good concept already developed and demonstrated by the Germans.[7]

What is most interesting is not that Thoreau was engaged in pencil-making but that people seem so fascinated that he was. When news of his pencil-making activities first became widely known, upon the publication of a history of the pencil in 1989, it was treated as a major revelation. The *New York Times* named Thoreau in the headline accompanying its review of the book as if his contribution had previously been kept a secret. In fact, Thoreau's contribution had been well established for many years.[8]

We cannot know precisely why people were so taken with the news of Thoreau's pencil-making. But almost certainly the fascinating thing wasn't that Thoreau had been a pencil-maker—in itself that's hardly interesting—but that people hadn't been aware that he had been one. If Thoreau is currently remembered as a woodsman *and* a pencil-maker, almost certainly he will not be for long. Over time his pencil-making will be forgotten. What sticks in the mind are the myths: the figure of the lone woodsman retreating to the forest in search of truth.

A second Thoreau is often recognized in addition to the familiar woodsman. It is the Thoreau who refused to pay his taxes as a protest against the Mexican War and slavery and was thrown in jail. But rather too much is made of the event. It so happens Thoreau's night in jail was something of a staged event. He did not have to go as the jailer himself had offered to pay Thoreau's taxes for him. Thoreau was released the next morning after a relative— probably his aunt—paid the taxes. Nor was the idea of refusing to pay his taxes original. Bronson Alcott had refused three years earlier and was also jailed.

There is nothing to the charming story told about Emerson's visit to the jail. Emerson is supposed to have asked, "Henry, what are you doing in *there?*" Thoreau is supposed to have replied, "Waldo, what are *you* doing *out there?*" But it never happened. Emerson never even visited the jail. The jailer didn't allow visitors and Emerson didn't approve of Thoreau's action. He told friends it was "mean and skulking, and in bad taste."[9]

Thoreau's eloquent defense of his tax fight, contained in the essay "Civil Disobedience," influenced both Mahatma Gandhi and Martin Luther King, Jr., and is often quoted. But it is a mistake to think of the essay as a protest against slavery or the Mexican War. Scholars have indicated that the point of civil disobedience, in Thoreau's view, was not to protest a wrong but to save oneself from complicity in it: "It is not a man's duty [wrote Thoreau], as a matter of course, to devote himself to the eradication of any, even the most enormous wrong; he may still properly have other concerns to engage him; but it is his duty, at least, to wash his hands of it, and, if he gives it no thought longer, not to give it practically his support."[10]

Hemingway always pretended to have fought in World War I, and no doubt wished he really had, but he never fought in any war. In World War I, he served as a volunteer with the American Red Cross. In the Spanish Civil War and World War II, he was a reporter. If in the war novels he sounds like he was writing from experience, it was the experience of someone who knew war as an observer, not a participant (though he was certainly a close observer).

Hemingway was injured in World War I. Eager to see action, he signed up with the Red Cross and went to the front in Italy at age nineteen. There he was struck by mortar fire while serving chocolates to the soldiers. The Italian government even gave him a medal. But he wasn't nearly as brave as he or many of his biographers led people to believe. Professor Kenneth Lynn, after reviewing the usual claims made about Hemingway's service in the war, concluded they were all bogus. He was not the first American wounded in Italy. After he was wounded he did not carry an Italian soldier on his back to safety. He was not wounded by machine-gun fire. And after recovering he didn't join the Sixty-ninth Infantry and fight in three major Italian battles. All this he made up.

Hemingway's reputation as a macho American was undermined by the publication in 1986 of an unfinished manuscript* in which he entertained transsexual fantasies. To give him his due, it seems he may always have been far more ambivalent about sex than he seemed. Lynn is of the opinion that Hemingway's "best work was suffused by more sensitive and complicated feelings about himself and the world than the stereotypes of Hemingway criticism have ever allowed." As an example, Lynn cites *The Sun Also Rises.* Though Hemingway was criticized for avoiding in the book the subject of lesbianism on the Left Bank, which was extensive, he actually had "imported it, albeit obliquely, into the very center of his novel by encapsulating it within the story of its two principals." Somehow, suggests Lynn, the critics had missed the fact that the novel was about "a man who is passionately in love with a sexually aggressive woman with an androgenous first name and a mannish haircut, a man whose dilemma is that, like a lesbian, he cannot penetrate his loved one's body with his own."[11]

Say what you will about the misimpressions of Webster, Sinclair, Thoreau, and Hemingway, one can always come back to the pleasant fact that they are largely the work of the writers themselves. In America writers frequently find it necessary to adopt a pose in order to sell their books, and they do it with relish.

A great many errors are of our own making, however. A common mistake, for instance, is to naively define an author by the handful of celebrated written works or popular sayings for which he is famous. Take Ben Franklin. Because he wrote about saving money, he is thought of as a saver. But whether a penny saved is a penny earned, Franklin himself believed in spending money, not saving it, and often shocked his friends by his profligacy. In private he confessed that frugality was "a virtue I never could acquire my-

---

* *The Garden of Eden.*

self," a failing he tried to turn into an advantage in another proverb: "An egg today is better than a hen tomorrow."

Nor, past middle age, did he believe that "time is money." He retired at age forty-two from his printing shop (to get away from the "fatigues of business"), and he became so fond of leisure that he scandalized friends with his "natural inactivity." As an old man he confessed that while "now and then" he worried about spending time "so idly," he whispered to himself that the soul is immortal, and he wondered "Why then should you be such a niggard of a little time, when you have a whole eternity before you?" (Of course, by our standards, he probably would be considered a hard worker. Even when he was relaxing he was probably thinking, and thinking is work.)

Whether at the signing of the Declaration of Independence he actually said "We shall all hang together or surely we will all hang separately" is unknown, though it certainly sounds like him. But he wasn't nearly as committed to the cause of independence as leaders like Washington, and in his private correspondence he conveyed his doubts. On the eve of the Revolution he still believed the English had the "best constitution and the best King . . . any nation was ever blessed with." When Parliament passed the Stamp Act he supported it—until a mob threatened to burn down his house. Dixon Wecter says of Franklin: "He kept his foot in the door of conciliation so long that it nearly got pinched."

If Franklin's commitment to independence is exaggerated, it is partly because he wanted it exaggerated. The belief, for example, that he broke off his friendship with the king's printer after the war began is due to his famous letter to the printer in which he indicated he had: "You and I were long friends, but you are now my enemy, and I am—Yours, B. Franklin." In fact, the two printers remained friends throughout the war. Two years after the Declaration of Independence was signed the printer was still sending Franklin gifts.

The belief that Franklin was of a straitlaced character is due to the obscurity of his more racy works, especially his "Advice to a

Young Man on the Choice of a Mistress." Among Franklin's suggestions was that a young man should select an older woman over a young one because the older woman will be more appreciative and "below the girdle, it is impossible" to tell the difference between them. But we don't hear much about this Franklin and in the absence of information assume he must have been as prudish in morals as he seemed to be industrious in work. Who remembers that Franklin had his son out of wedlock or that he earned a reputation as a bon vivant in Paris?

Franklin is fortunate in that having mastered so many fields he is not confined, in the public imagination, to merely one or two of them. There are many Franklins and people are well aware of them: as inventor, scientist, philosopher, diplomat, statesman, and so on. But he remains hardly more than a caricature, and a nineteenth-century caricature at that. If we do not know much about the cosmopolitan Franklin it is because our image of Franklin was shaped by the Victorians, and Victorians did not cotton to the idea of the rakish founding father.[12]

Two writers are misremembered not so much for what they wrote as for the way they appeared.

Mark Twain, in almost everybody's mind, went around in a striking white suit—the Tom Wolfe of his day. It is as much a part of the Twain legend as his head of white hair and his Western-style mustache. But according to English professor Tom Burnam, not until Twain was in his seventies did he dress in the familiar white suit that actor Hal Holbrook made famous. Before then he wore black serge.[13]

Robert Frost, from appearances, both wise and avuncular, was neither. His official biographer, Lawrence Thompson, created a harrowing portrait of the artist as a monster, blaming Frost for the suicide of his son, Carol, and the commitment of his daughter, Irma. To be fair, friends subsequently challenged Thompson's account and defended Frost's behavior as a family man; Irma, whom

Frost had supposedly abused emotionally, publicly protested
Thompson's portrait. But even his warmest supporters agree he
could be ruthlessly ambitious and "disconcertingly feckless." [14]

Sex and sin are commonly associated with writers, but several who
deserve to be remembered for their debauchery are not. Prominent
among these is Horatio Alger, Jr., the celebrated author of the rags-
to-riches books.

Among the sophisticated, the Alger of popular imagination is
somewhat disreputable anyway, but not immoral. In their view, his
chief sin was that he was too romantic; to think that all it takes to
get ahead in the world are hard work and a little luck—what nonsense! To his loyal readers, of course, it didn't matter if his novels
were overly romantic. It was because of the books' romanticism that
Horatio Alger was one of the best selling authors of all time.

Alas, bad writing was Alger's least serious offense. His real
crime, as first detailed in a biography published in 1985, was pedo-
philia: having sex with young boys. It is not known with how many
boys he had sex or for how long he engaged in the practice, though
recent research indicates that once a pedophile always a pedophile.
We do know, however, that he had sex with at least several boys.
Unitarian church records confirm that in 1866, when Alger was a
young pastor in Brewster, Massachusetts, he was accused by boys in
his congregation of using his position of authority to lure them into
sexual relations. Confronted with the accusations, he fled town to
avoid a possible lynching and ended up in New York City, where
he befriended male bootblacks and street urchins. The church,
faced with the choice of keeping the matter secret or creating a
public scandal, chose secrecy. Alger, in consequence, was able to
begin life anew, as the writer of children's fiction. [15]

Often, the danger is not that a writer's faults will be overlooked
but that they will be exaggerated. Like everybody else, writers have
enemies, and enemies of writers often seem especially intent on
getting their prey. Of enemies there are two kinds: those who write

and those who don't, and of the two the worst kind to have by far are those who write. Beware the village gossip, but the writer with an ax to grind is certainly the more dangerous. His accounts are for the ages.

Ever since his death the reputation of Edgar Allan Poe has been besmirched by the lies of Rufus Griswold, a quarrelsome minor writer from the nineteenth century who published an anthology Poe had criticized. Poe, in Griswold's account, was capable of every imaginable kind of evil and excess. In his biography of Poe, Griswold reported that the writer had had "criminal relations with his Mother in Law," that he had been expelled from the University of Virginia for drinking and gambling, that he had been an army deserter, that he had been kicked out of West Point, and that as an adult he had been a drunk. All lies.

Of all the allegations Griswold leveled at Poe, only one—that Poe was always broke—had any basis in fact. (He was so broke that when his wife came down with a fatal illness, Poe was unable to buy food for her.) This, however, was less of a commentary on Poe than on society. In antebellum America anybody who wasn't independently wealthy and who chose to work as a writer full-time almost always lived in poverty, no matter how hard they worked and regardless of their financial acumen.[16]

The celebration of writers in the modern world is welcomed but suspect. Like others, literary folks are inconsistent, and the same writer who on one occasion seems a genius may another time seem a crackpot. In this century, writers have repeatedly demonstrated a remarkable gift for error. In 1937, Gertrude Stein proposed that Adolf Hitler receive the Nobel Peace Prize. After World War II, Charles Beard concluded that Franklin Roosevelt was to blame for the attack on Pearl Harbor. In the fifties, dozens of writers refused to back away from their support of Stalin despite conclusive evidence of his crimes. And so on and so on.

As for the way writers conduct their private lives, there is little need to go into detail here. Their dalliances and drunken orgies are covered amply in the newspapers. The wretched end to which they often come is the gossip of the common man. All are familiar with the accounts of writers who have blown huge fortunes.

Valuable for its sweet irony and worth mentioning in passing, however, is the story of Edmund Wilson, his generation's most highly esteemed "man of letters." Much of Wilson's reputation was built on the book he wrote about the Russian Revolution, *To the Finland Station*, for which he learned to read and speak Russian, and it is considered one of the most brilliant analyses of Marxism ever written. But this man who knew Marx inside out, and who presumed himself sufficiently expert in economics to put himself forward as an authority on capitalism, had difficulty mastering the one most basic fact of the American tax code—that you have to pay. Between 1946 and 1955 he failed to file any income-tax returns. His explanation, detailed at length in a book he later wrote to protest his tax bill, was that he hadn't realized he needed to. Because he was a little short of cash at the moment (rather a long moment—nine years), he thought he could delay paying his taxes until his situation had improved somewhat. Or so he claimed.

It is rather too simple to suggest, as Paul Johnson does in his book *Intellectuals*, that because a writer has trouble conducting his own affairs he can't be trusted to help others with theirs. Edmund Wilson's critique of capitalism was brilliant whether he knew how to balance his checkbook or not. * [17]

If many writers are taken too seriously as social critics, there are always those who struggle without success to be taken seriously at all. Among these was L. Frank Baum, the author of *The Wizard of Oz*, almost universally considered "merely" a children's fantasy, albeit a delightful one. In fact, it is much more.

---

* Economist John Maynard Keynes's ability to play the stock market successfully was no reflection on his abilities as an economist. But it sure made life sweeter for him.

Upon close inspection, the book (published in 1900) really appears to be, as Henry Littlefield points out, a "parable on Populism." Dorothy isn't just any little girl; she is a girl from Kansas. Her family isn't just any old family; it is a poor farm family, as Baum painstakingly makes clear. The prairie, he says, is "gray"; the grass around the farm is a "gray mass"; the house, once painted a bright color, is "gray as everything else"; Aunt Em is "gray"; Uncle Henry is "gray." Here, if ever there was one, is the portrait of a farm family down on its luck.

Consider the two evil witches. It's no accident one is from the East; the Populists felt tormented by the bankers back East. Nor is it an accident the other is from the West; drought conditions in the West were helping drive the Populists to bankruptcy. Dorothy and her gang, interestingly, are saved when the wicked witch of the West is drowned with water.

The color of Dorothy's shoes in the movie version of the story is misleading. In the movie they're red. In the book, however, they are silver, a not-too-subtle analogue to the Populists' belief that the free coinage of silver would help alleviate the farmer's problems,* returning him to a time when he took pride in farming, as Dorothy would again take pride in living in Kansas. "Your Silver Shoes will carry you over the desert," Glinda tells Dorothy. "If you had known their power you could have gone back to your Aunt Em the very first day you came to this country. . . . All you have to do is to knock your heels together three times and command the shoes to carry you wherever you wish to go." Whether Baum believed the free coinage of silver would actually have helped end the farmers'

---

* The movement of the free coinage of silver was supported by both farmers and Western silver mine owners: the farmers, for the reason that it would help spur inflation, making it easier to pay off their old debts; the mine owners, for the obvious reason that it would put silver in greater demand, especially if the politicians approved the plan to establish a value of 16 ounces of silver for 1 ounce of gold, a considerably higher value than silver was then fetching on the open market.

suffering is unknown. But in saying Dorothy always had the power within herself to save herself, he seems to be saying so did the farmer.

There is no mystery about Baum's opinion of politicians. He thinks they're phonies. They can no sooner make people smarter, braver, or more compassionate than the Wizard of Oz can give the scarecrow a brain, the Cowardly Lion courage, or the Tin Woodman a heart. The Wizard's not a great man; he's "a humbug." "It was a great mistake my ever letting you into the Throne Room," the Wizard confesses. "Usually I will not see even my subjects." Who is the man behind the curtain, then? He's the one-time circus balloonist, whose job was "going up in a balloon on circus day, so as to draw a crowd of people together and get them to pay to see the circus [read: Washington politics]." [18]

Speakers on the lecture circuit may be more disappointed than most to find out that many of the sayings attributed to writers are fiction. It could mean having to give up some of their most cherished quotations.

Emerson seems to have believed (without foundation*) that if you build a better mousetrap, "the world will beat a path to your door." The saying captures precisely the thought expressed in a journal entry written in 1855: "I trust a good deal to common fame, as we all must. If a man has good corn, or wood, or boards, or pigs, to sell, or can make better chairs or knives, crucibles or church organs, than anybody else, you will find a broad hard-beaten road to his house, though it be in the woods." But the scholars who have examined his writings in detail report he never mentioned mousetraps in connection with the things that can earn a man public attention. It seems to have been Sarah Yule and Mary Keene, in a book published in 1889, seven years after Emerson's death, who thought to add mousetraps to the list. Not even they, however, render the quotation as it's usually given; theirs is considerably less

* See page 70.

pithy: "If a man can write a better book, preach a better sermon, or make a better mouse-trap than his neighbor, though he builds his house in the woods the world will make a beaten path to his door." [19]

What Emerson said about consistency and what others say he said reminds one of Mark Twain's remark that the difference between the right word and the wrong one is the difference between the lightning bug and lightning. What Emerson wrote was that "a *foolish* consistency is the hobgoblin of little minds."

Speaking of Twain, it wasn't he who complained that "everybody talks about the weather, but nobody does anything about it." It was Charles Dudley Warner, with whom he collaborated on the novel, *The Gilded Age.* That, at any rate is what quote-master Bergen Evans wrote in *The Spoor of Spooks* in 1954. Later, however, he seemed a little less sure. In the *Dictionary of Quotations* (1968), he merely said that "some" attribute the quotation to Warner.

The words attributed to Barbara Frietchie, "Shoot if you must this old gray head, but spare your country's flag," are plainly John Greenleaf Whittier's. But she wasn't a creature of his imagination and he didn't invent out of whole cloth the scene that made her famous. He had been told that she really protested the Confederate conquest of Frederick, Maryland, by waving the Stars and Stripes in the face of General Stonewall Jackson's troops. At the moment of confrontation she reportedly remarked, after the troops had already fired at the flag's staff, "Fire at this old head, then, boys; it is not more venerable than your flag." But the story was based on what the friend of a friend (who was one of Frietchie's neighbors) claimed had happened. And after Whittier's piece on Frietchie appeared in 1863 in the *Atlantic,* several people wrote in to question the accuracy of the account. Some said Frietchie was too old and ill at the time even to have climbed out of bed. (She was ninety-seven.) One woman wrote to say that *she* was the one who waved the flag and challenged the troops. Whittier, in his defense, replied that since no one disputed "that there was a Dame Frietchie in Frederick who loved the flag," he didn't "feel responsible" if the rest of the story was wrong: "If there was no such occurrence, so much the worse for Frederick City."

Gertrude Stein's "A rose is a rose is a rose" is properly rendered, "Rose is a rose is a rose is a rose," which gives a better idea of her longwindedness, as is evident in her memoirs, where sentences (unpunctuated) run on for pages. Her famous lament that "there is no there there" is thought to have been a reference either to America in general or to Oakland, California, in particular, much to the regret of the residents of Oakland. In fact, what she was referring to was the disappearance of her childhood home in Oakland, not to Oakland itself.[20]

Everybody is familiar with the exchange "The rich are different from you and me"; "Yes, they have more money." It is supposed to have taken place during a conversation between Fitzgerald and Hemingway, Hemingway supplying the clever rejoinder. But no such conversation ever took place. Fitzgerald made the observation that the rich "are different from you and me" in a short story ("The Rich Boy"). Hemingway, ten years later, included the celebrated retort in a short story *he* wrote ("The Snows of Kilimanjaro"). The interesting thing is not that the exchange involved Fitzgerald and Hemingway but that it became a sore subject between them. In the original version of "The Snows of Kilimanjaro" a character plainly attributes the Fitzgerald line to Fitzgerald, which prompted Fitzgerald to complain. Hemingway, in response, kept the exchange but dropped the reference to Fitzgerald in future editions of the story.

It may be true that "there are no second acts in American lives," but in saying this Fitzgerald, according to professor Tom Burnam, didn't mean "there are no second *chances* in American lives." Burnam, sensibly, points out that most plays have three acts and what Fitzgerald must have meant was that Americans typically move from the first to the third act, skipping the second, "the one that builds or develops the plot and prepares the audience for the resolution or denouement" to come. "Like Jay Gatsby," concludes Burnam, Fitzgerald seems to be saying "Americans are fated to rush pell-mell from beginning to end, with no middle—a violation of Aristotelian principles in terms of the techniques of the drama; and only too often, in American life itself, a tragic rush toward a denouement which shocks or destroys because there has been no time to prepare against it."

6
Politics

They said he lived by symbols and mythic figures and that's why he was so drawn to those Reader's Digest *stories about the airman who went down with the wounded gunner, and why he was so moved by movies.*

But in turning to myth wasn't he being American?

PEGGY NOONAN ON RONALD REAGAN

Politicians peddle a lot of history, most of it nonsense, especially the wild claims made about the founding fathers. The patriotic insist the founders "never made a major mistake"—as if anybody's *that* good. The sentimental claim they loved mankind and adored "the people"—which makes the founders sound a bit like adolescent poets, though maybe that's a bit unfair—to the adolescents. Conservatives tell you the founders put a lot of stock in "virtue"—as if that is somehow going to make *us* more virtuous—and that they believed in balanced budgets. Of late, congressmen have begun insisting that in going home every week they are fulfilling the founders' commandment "to stay close to the people"—as if the real purpose in going home isn't to scrounge for votes.

That the founding fathers were nearly perfect is taken for granted by the politician. The lionization of the founders has been carried so far that nothing can be held against them. We all know that they really weren't saints: that Jefferson may have slept with one of his slaves, that Franklin was promiscuous, and that Adams could be a pompous ass. And we are aware that they had their limitations: Washington, though balanced, was not brilliant; Adams made a poor president, Madison an even poorer one. No politician dares to suggest that the founders possibly suffered from any serious flaws—or even minor ones. Warren Harding said, "I like accuracy in history; I love truthfulness in biography; I like the dependableness of tradition; but I do not like the iconoclast who would seek to destroy faith in those things which have inspired the most enthusiastic devotion to America."[1]

The celebration of the founders extends far beyond their military or political achievements. Everything they did is deemed worthy. Once it was considered enough that founders like George Washington were "first in war," and "first in peace." No more. Now Washington must be considered tops in everything.

Among those who labored hardest to give Washington his due —and then some—was the late Sol Bloom, the honorable representative from New York, who helped direct the celebration of the bicentennial of Washington's birth in 1932. In Mr. Bloom's opinion, Washington's reputation, great as it was, wasn't nearly as great as it might be. Few really seemed to understand "those sublime qualities of character" that made Washington "the outstanding American of his time, and perhaps of all time." To correct the situation, Mr. Bloom got Congress to publish a series of lavish, oversized books that would tell "the real story" about George Washington: how, in addition to his well-known strengths as a general and a statesman, he also possessed unappreciated talents as a businessman, surveyor, engineer, city builder, family man, religious leader, farmer, traveler, constitution-maker, landowner and inventor.* Upon reflection, Mr. Bloom confessed to finding only a single area in which Washington did not excel: colonizing! And it left him baffled. "Considering Washington's success as the manager of a great plantation and as an acquirer of western land," he wrote, "it is remarkable that he had no success as a colonizer."[2]

Such indeed is the reputation of the founders that those who criticize them are considered not merely contentious but misin-

---

* Mr. Bloom (falsely) credited Washington with inventing ice cream.

formed. But if misinformed is what they are, then a lot of well-known professors are misinformed, for many are of the opinion that the founders frequently erred. There is, for instance, as Garry Wills points out, the question of the founders' "expectations of the way our government would work." Madison's doozies included the expectation that the president would be weak, that the House of Representatives would be radical, that the House would be stronger than the Senate, that the Electoral College would usually deadlock (leaving the selection of presidents to the House) and, most astonishingly of all, that the creation of political parties would be disastrous. (It is now conceded that the weakness of the political parties is disastrous.) [3]

The belief that the founders shared a profound "faith in man" is tied to their reputation as "true children of the Enlightenment." In fact, the founders said a lot of nasty things about mankind. According to the professors, the one belief the founders shared was the belief that man is not trustworthy: "On this," says Harvard's Bernard Bailyn, "there was absolute agreement." Indeed, the Constitution was built on the premise that man is "ambitious, vindictive, and rapacious." [4]

It's a little dismaying to think that the founders didn't believe in the innate goodness of man, and a bit shocking as well. It is such a basic belief today that we can hardly bring ourselves to think the founders didn't share it. But the idea of our goodness is a product of modern politics. Prior to Jacksonianism, when politicians first began scurrying hat-in-hand for votes, they generally took a dark view of human nature. Hardly anybody indulged in the rhapsodies of airy optimism so common nowadays. Even radicals like Sam Adams conceded the "depravity of mankind" and the "ambition" and "lust of power" that are the "predominant passions in the breasts of most men." [5]

Neither, incidentally, did the founders express unalloyed faith in "the people." Mistrust of the people was the reason for, among other things, the system of checks and balances, the election of senators by the state legislatures, the election of presidents by the Electoral College, and the assignment of the conduct of foreign policy to the Senate and the presidency, the two institutions least subject to popular control.[6]

It may seem nitpicky to hold up the politician's well-labored odes to the people to scholarly standards. They are after all just odes, and sentimental and comforting odes at that. And if they are self-congratulatory and mythical, well, every people deserves the right to indulge themselves now and then in inspirational twiddle-twaddle. Who is hurt, after all, by the sentimental nonsense spread about the founders' faith in the people? No one really, but it is worth remembering that it is nonsense.

The survival of this bit of nonsense, in any case, is interesting. For it shows just how misunderstood the founders really are. Not only did they not believe "in the people" but they didn't believe in democracy either. America was founded as a republic, meaning it was based on a government of elected representatives drawn from "the best" classes. To say it was a democracy is anachronistic. Charles Beard, one of the great historians of the century, held the opinion that not until World War I did Americans generally begin thinking of their country as a democracy. In the eighteenth-century world of the founders, most people didn't even have the right to vote—not even most white adult males. Of the 4 million Americans alive in 1787, only 160,000 voted in the elections to select delegates to the state ratifying conventions—a measly 4 percent. Put another way, three-fourths of the white adult males did not vote, primarily because they could not meet the property qualifications then in existence.[7]

Conservatives are responsible for spreading the idea that the founders believed virtue is essential in a republic. Barry Goldwater has said the founders considered it indispensable. Utah Senator Orrin Hatch believes they considered virtue the "well-spring of liberty," one of the "mainsprings" of the republic, "the flower of freedom."[8]

Things weren't so simple, however. John Patrick Diggins has shown that many of the same founders often quoted in support of man's virtue frequently dismissed the idea. Jefferson rejected outright the belief that virtue alone is "sufficient security to the state against the commission of crimes," calling the idea "fantastical." Washington, though he "himself may have been praised by his contemporaries as a shining example of classical virtue and valor," believed that "people are moved by interest and expediency, which presuppose divisiveness, rather than by patriotism and virtue, which imply unanimity and duty." Noah Webster opined that virtue wasn't necessary at all.

Debate rages among historians as to exactly what the founders believed. But it is evident from the historical literature that one cannot easily generalize about the matter. And while there are historians who take the position espoused by the conservatives, it is asking too much to believe that the politicians arrived at their conclusions in as objective a way as the historians. Their conclusions are the product of their politics. It is evident that their purpose in advancing the argument about virtuousness is to help do in the welfare state, a system that they believe undermines virtuousness.[9]

Interestingly, the founders conceded they themselves were not driven by virtuousness. If they behaved exemplarily, they admitted, it was because they desired public fame. They had been taught, says Douglass Adair, that selfishness is inevitable, but that one can transform "egotism and self-aggrandizing impulses into public service."[10]

As for the argument that the founders believed in balanced budgets, there is the inconvenient fact that the patron saint of conservatism, Alexander Hamilton, did not. Even a passing review of his financial wizardry reveals that his entire program was based on the idea that a public debt is a public blessing. Hamilton reasoned that the more people owe the government, the more they want to see it survive. It was on this principle that he based his plan to require the federal government to assume the war debts of the individual states. If Hamilton had primarily been interested in balancing budgets, he never would have proposed a program antic- ipated to result in a dramatic increase in the government's debt load. *

That congressmen have a "sacred duty" to stay closely in touch with the people may be true, but the founders didn't think so. If anything, the founders believed legislators on the national level should make an effort to insulate themselves from public opinion. Indeed, they believed that only representatives who distanced themselves from their constituents could "discern the true interest of their country." One of the chief advantages of a republic over a democracy, it was thought, was the opportunity in a republic "to refine and enlarge the public views by passing them through the medium of a chosen body of citizens." [11]

Equally as misguided, if not as overwrought, as the generalizations about the nation's founding are those about other periods of Amer- ican history. Of these, three seem especially popular with presi- dents. From our early history, citizens are told, America—that "City on a Hill"—was established as a "beacon of liberty" by a "chosen people" committed to the creation of a "unique" society. In the modern period there's the idea that America is classless and that Americans don't fight among themselves about foreign policy —or didn't until Vietnam.

One hesitates to spoil the image of America as a City on a Hill, which is derived from a sermon delivered by the Puritan John Win- throp before an audience (as Ronald Reagan conjured up the movie-

* As a result of his plan the United States accumulated a mountain of debt, making our current debt almost puny in comparison. Then the government owed more than $50 million. Now, it owes $3 trillion. But in proportion to the government's revenues, Hamilton's debt today would total $10 trillion, more than three times as large as our own. (John Steele Gordon, "The Found- ing Wizard," American Heritage [July–August 1990], p. 42.)

set scene) of "a little group of Puritans huddled on the deck" of the tiny *Arabella* in 1630. Certainly, it is a pleasing image and presidents as diverse as Kennedy and Reagan have made the most of it. * By his own admission, it was one of Reagan's favorites. As he explained in his farewell address, he always thought of America as "the shining city," "a tall proud city built on rocks stronger than oceans, wind-swept, God-blessed, and teeming with people of all kinds living in harmony and peace, a city with free ports that hummed with commerce and creativity, and if there had to be city walls, the walls had doors and the doors were open to anyone with the will and the heart to get here."[12]

But for what purpose exactly was America founded? Why did the Puritans establish America as a City on a Hill—"the eyes of all people" upon us? It was not, as Reagan always insisted, to create a monument to liberty. Creating a free society was the last thing the Puritans wanted. What they really hoped to do was establish a model Christian community.†

Politicians, of course, do not content themselves with facts. The difference between a politician and a historian is that the politician is concerned with recalling an event for what it means to us. The historian's obligation is to try to tell us what an event meant to the people who participated in it.[13]

That Americans are a "chosen people" is, one supposes, a matter of personal opinion. Conceivably God has his favorites. But it is

---

* Kennedy used the image in a speech before the General Court of Massachusetts in 1961. It was a time when Massachusetts politics were notoriously corrupt. Instead of denouncing the corruption outright, which would have been risky—and for Kennedy, out of character—he slyly and cleverly confined his remarks to an ironic review of the state's glorious tradition of integrity. "We must always consider that we shall be as a city upon a hill—the eyes of all people are upon us," he told the legislators, using the quotation from John Winthrop. "For of those to whom much is given, much is required." (Theodore Sorensen, ed., *"Let the Word Go Forth"* [1988], pp. 56–58; Samuel Eliot Morison, *The Oxford History of the American People* [1965], p. 65n.)

† Others, of course, had different motives for coming here. Some came for freedom, some for riches, some just to be able to earn a living.

interesting that while it is still considered appropriate to claim God is on a country's side, individuals can't claim God is on their side anymore—*that's* egotistical. Perhaps countries are simply exempt from the normal rules that govern individual behavior.[14]

That America is different from other places in the world is indisputable. America is unique. For five thousand years it remained unknown to Europe and uncontaminated by the Old World's wars and corruption. After its discovery, it continued to exist in virtual isolation from the rest of the world for centuries, preserving its reputation as a pristine place. When Europeans were still fighting for basic freedoms, Americans (well, some of them, anyway) were enjoying theirs as a birthright. In no other country do so many people from so many different cultures live side-by-side in relative peace.

But unique as Americans are in so many ways, they are not quite as different as the politicians would have us believe. In killing Indians, enslaving blacks, and breaking labor unions, Americans proved themselves as able as any others in skullduggery and persecution. Among Western countries, only Cuba and Brazil continued slavery as long as the United States and not one fought as bloody a civil war. Recently, Americans have shown excellence in corruption. Other countries count their losses from bribes and defalcations in the millions. But it is America, which once looked down on countries known for "the greased palm," that has lost the most money in history in any one scandal: the billions absconded in the savings and loan mess.

It is interesting that American politicians take such pride in their country as a unique place. For it is just such pride—in others—that so often raises American hackles. What, indeed, is worse to an American than "conceited Frenchmen," "bragging Germans," or "supercilious Japanese"? Yet all claim nothing more than the American does. Indeed, they claim less. As historian Loren Baritz has pointed out, Americans think they're not only superior but that the rest of the world wants to become like them. "This," says Baritz, "is unique among the world's nationalisms."[15]

Class warfare is considered so un-American that many politicians are of the opinion it is un-American even to suggest that classes exist here. When in 1990 Daniel Patrick Moynihan, the New York senator, pointedly noted that the Reagan tax cuts benefited "the rich," George Bush chided him for talking that way, apparently in the belief that Americans never have. But this is just a case of historical amnesia, and a particularly good one at that. Even the founding fathers talked incessantly about classes. Like Karl Marx, they believed societies are divided into various groups and in public debates openly admitted that in this regard America is no different. They did not go so far as to believe in economic determinism, and they did not try to pit one class against another. But they did believe, as Madison put it, that "the unequal distribution of property" divides the members of society "into different classes," and that classes are "actuated by different sentiments and views."

If it is considered unseemly to admit the existence of different classes in America, it is considered absolutely repugnant to appeal to class pride. That's playing "the politics of envy." But the prejudice against class appeals, strong as it is, is of relatively recent origin. Through much of American history the rich routinely appealed to class pride in debates over taxes, labor strife, and reform. Alarm bells only began going off in the late nineteenth century when the poor began following their example.

Republicans employ the prejudice against class appeals more than Democrats, perhaps because they have more to fear from the appeal to classes. The Republicans remain stereotyped as the country club set. The Democratic Party is still widely identified as the party of the people.[16]

The nostalgic belief that Americans traditionally rallied round the president in matters involving foreign affairs is false but not wholly false. Sometimes they did, but more often they did not. In the 1790s, arguments over the Jay Treaty, which the Washington administration negotiated with Great Britain, became so acrimonious that anti-British patriots damned George Washington and deserted the Federalist party, leading to its irreversible demise. Anger over the treaty was so intense that when the House of Representatives, amidst the controversy, was asked to adjourn for half an hour in honor of Washington's sixty-fifth birthday, it refused.

The War of 1812 was so controversial that New Englanders seriously considered seceding from the union to avoid supporting it. The Mexican-American War aroused such passions that Abraham Lincoln gave a stirring speech in Congress against it. The Spanish-American War, despite its wide popularity, was sufficiently questionable to provoke a national debate about imperialism. World War I divided Americans so fiercely that when Woodrow Wilson blamed the Germans for blowing up the *Lusitania,* Secretary of State William Jennings Bryan resigned in protest, to the cheers of millions. Opponents to U.S. intervention in World War II disseminated the charge that FDR secretly maneuvered Japan into bombing Pearl Harbor to trick Americans into helping the Allies. The Korean War proved so unpopular that Americans wanted out of it almost as soon as they got in it.

But it is Vietnam, of course, and not these other wars, with which politicians are preoccupied, and Vietnam, all agree, was America's least favorite war, however much Americans may have expressed opposition to earlier ones. This view, firmly held as it is, seems to be held in defiance of the known facts. Public opinion polls show that Americans have expressed alarm over three of the four wars fought in this century. World War I seems to have been the least popular war, at least judging by a poll taken in 1937, the first to ask Americans about their feelings toward the conflict. To the question, "Do you think it was a mistake for the United States to enter the last war?" 64 percent of Americans said it was. Possibly, fewer may have thought so while the war was on, and fewer still when the war first began. Possibly, too, the high percentage reflected to a great extent feelings that surfaced in response to postwar international turmoil and to congressional hearings on war profiteering. Both contributed to fervent isolationism in the thirties. Still, conceding all that, the percentage was high enough to suggest deep dissatisfaction with one of the most important foreign policy decisions ever taken by the United States.

World War II is rightly remembered as a popular war, but even the so-called "Good War" provoked controversy. In 1944, a Gallup poll found nearly a third of all Americans believed that "in years to come people will say the United States should have avoided getting into this war." Fourteen percent said outright that "it was a mistake for us to have entered the war."

America's "forgotten war" in Korea confounds all expectations. The polls show that about as many Americans opposed the Korean War as opposed the war in Vietnam. Indeed, the statistics show that of the two wars the Korean was a bit more unpopular; 62 percent of Americans said the Korean War was a mistake. Only 60 percent said Vietnam was a mistake. And Korea was regarded as a mistake by a majority of Americans much earlier than was Vietnam. "The difference during the Vietnam War," says Loren Baritz, "was not the number of Americans who disagreed with government policy, but the number who took to the streets." [17]

In making their generalizations, politicians aren't merely betraying a weak grasp of the facts of history. Their real error is not understanding history at all. In this, of course, they have plenty of company.* But it can fairly be said that nobody mangles history quite as badly as politicians do.

Of the fallacies in historical reasoning frequently employed by politicians, half a dozen or so are worth mentioning. These include trying to transfer the prestige of famous historical figures to oneself, taking historical figures out of context (guessing what they would think if they were alive today), taking ideas out of context, misusing words, misusing quotes, and making false analogies.

Politicians no longer make the foolish mistake of insisting "God is on my side"—*that* is part of the long ago past. In our more enlightened times, they merely claim that the founding fathers are

* See page 183.

on their side and they artfully sprinkle their star-spangled orations with quotes from the demigods to prove it. But the new claim is nearly as presumptuous as the old one, and rests on the same dubious logic: That the sacred appeal to higher authority is as credible in politics as it is in religion. *

It may be useful or even fun to turn a hero from history into a supporter of one's own cause, but it's not very sporting. Heroes have enough trouble fighting their own battles without being dragged into somebody else's.

The politician cannot resist temptation, however. And neither can the public. All insist on playing the game, If "So-and-So" Were Alive Today. Never mind that "So-and-So" is so long dead that he never had the chance to ride in an airplane, listen to the radio, or take a drive in an automobile. Historical context counts for nothing. Our hero would think the same today as he did a hundred years ago.

The politician, of course, is indifferent to historical context. He "knows" how our hero would think today. Never mind the difficulty scholars have in deciphering our hero's thoughts about the issues of his own time and place. The politician is blessed. It is his special ability to be able to say what our hero would think about issues he never even heard of. A striking demonstration of this ability was provided some years ago by Arthur Vandenberg, in a book published before he was appointed to the U.S. Senate. In the book, *If Hamilton Were Alive Today*, Vandenberg reported that Hamilton would oppose the League of Nations, join the hunt for reds, condemn open immigration, and favor the strict enforcement of Prohibition. It was only coincidence, one supposes, that these happened, as well, to be the positions taken by Vandenberg himself.

---

* It is somewhat misleading to refer to these as new and old claims. Woodrow Wilson advanced both. In the presidential campaign of 1912, he said the founders were on his side. In World War I, he claimed God was on his side. Wilson being Wilson, he never seems to have asked himself if *he* was on either the founders' or God's side.

The usual practice in citing a hero, it should be noted, is for a politician to cite a hero with whom he agrees. All will concede there is a certain logic to this. But some reverse the practice, deliberately invoking heroes who are known to have entertained an opinion contrary to their own. This would appear to be less logical. But politicians have found that there are some causes that cannot go forward in the absence of support from particularly popular historical figures. In these cases the heroes' known views are simply wished away.

Thus was Thomas Jefferson, the purported champion of laissez-faire, enlisted in the cause of progressivism in the early 1900s. All knew that Jefferson opposed the kind of activist program reformers heralded.* But the reformers also knew it was essential in winning public support to show that the founders—Jefferson especially—would have approved of their somewhat radical proposals. The solution was to say Jefferson would have changed his mind. Woodrow Wilson said in 1913 that "I feel confident that if Jefferson were living in our day he would see what we see." The matter cannot be proven, of course. But that is the chief advantage in employing history in this way. For if Wilson cannot be proved right, neither can he be proved wrong.[18]

Another fallacy is taking ideas out of context. Consider the idea of virtuousness, which the conservatives like so well. Even if the founders had all uniformly believed virtue is a necessity in a republic, should we? Or do different circumstances call for different ideas? It so happens the founders' idea of virtuousness is now actually as out-of-date as their powdered wigs. It is totally inappropriate to a capitalist society based on self-interest. Here people do what's best for themselves. Out of the jumble of private interests emerges a public good. The public good is not (usually) the product of concerted civic-mindedness.

The concept of virtuousness derives from Montesquieu, who

---

* Or thought they knew. Actually Jefferson was far more willing to use government to meet social needs than people realized. See page 55.

believed that republics depend on private sacrifices for public gain. But Montesquieu was plainly wrong. As Alexis de Tocqueville noted, "Americans are not a virtuous people and yet they are free." To say this is not to say Americans always act out of self-interest only. Clearly they do not. Arthur Schlesinger, Jr., for one, has presented strong evidence that Americans have a history of public-mindedness. Periods of selfishness and greed have regularly been followed in America by periods of public spiritedness. Following the Gilded Age there was Progressivism, and following the Roaring Twenties there came the New Deal. But one would be pushing it to say that Americans are an especially virtuous people.[19]

Misusing words is, in politics, an art form. The politician who uses plain English is not likely to be a politician for long. Often it is better to be obscure. In using words from history, however, the politician is apt to be as unaware as the average voter of their true meanings. Take virtuousness again. What exactly does it mean? In practice it means whatever one wants it to. To John Kennedy it meant civic-mindedness: "Ask not what your country can do for you, ask what you can do for your country." To Ronald Reagan it seemed to mean entrepreneurship; in his speeches it was always the entrepreneur, pursuing his own interests, who seemed to rank among the most virtuous. To Andrew Jackson the virtuous were those who made a living working with their hands. Jefferson, more narrowly, indicated only farmers were virtuous. Thus it is hard to know what any given politician has in mind when he uses the term. It has come to mean so many things as to mean almost nothing.

Politicians love a good quote, or even a banal one, if it suits the purpose. From the *Congressional Record,* on any good day, one can cull several hundred quotes. But a politician's use of a quote in proper context is a much rarer find. One can quickly find, for instance, a hundred political citations of Jefferson's famous words about budget deficits: "The public debt is the greatest of dangers to be feared by a republican government." The quote is genuine, but it doesn't reflect the subtle range of Jefferson's true attitudes toward the subject. To the budget-balancers, of course, it's all very plain:

Jefferson opposed deficits. But Jefferson opposed deficits the way congressmen today do: when it's convenient. When it proved inconvenient—as when he wanted to make the Louisiana Purchase —he put away his scruples and ran up the debt. *

The phony analogy must be one of the politician's most common pitfalls in history. Certainly it's provided some of the best laughs. Lyndon Johnson's are nonpareil. They remind one of the old maxim that people who make history need not know much about it. No one in Johnson's book could assume a leadership role in the world without being compared with someone else. It was almost a rite of honor. Nguyen Cao Ky was said to be Vietnam's Rex Tugwell, the New Deal braintruster of whom Ky almost certainly was unaware. Ngo Dinh Diem was said to be Vietnam's Winston Churchill, when, that is, he wasn't being Franklin Roosevelt. Johnson, of course, was hardly singular in this respect among American presidents. Who can forget Ronald Reagan equating the contras with the founding fathers? [20]

History is always being used—or rather misused and abused—by average citizens and politicians alike. The great danger, however, is not that people will be lulled into accepting blatant propaganda as history. Nearly everybody now knows an average piece of propaganda when they hear it and can guard against it. The thing that gets by is the interpretation of history that passes itself off as a mere

---

* Taken at his word, Jefferson not only opposed running annual budget deficits but any deficits. More precisely, he was against any national debt that could not be paid off during the lifetime of the generation that incurred it. Fundamental to his vision of a "just society" was the belief that no generation should bind any that follows: "The earth belongs to the living generation." Thus if politicians today really meant to take Jefferson seriously, they would not only insist on yearly balanced budgets but on the elimination, over say the next twenty years, of the billions upon billions of dollars of debt accumulated in the lifetime of their generation. (See Dumas Malone, *Jefferson the President: First Term, 1801–1805* [1970], pp. 100–06.)

recital of "the facts." It is this interpretation that poses the genuine threat to truth and it is this interpretation at which politicians have become most expert. The leader to be feared is the leader who uses history in such a way as to appear he is only saying the obvious. Against the obvious we have few defenses.

7
Alcohol and Drugs

Nothing so needs reforming as other people's habits.
MARK TWAIN

The babbling nonsense spouted by drinkers "in their cups" is often matched in inanity by what's said about them. Consider the stories about the "hard-drinking" Irish. One frequently hears that they, of all peoples, drank the most. But Americans once were greater drinkers still. In his history of "the alcoholic republic," W. J. Rorabaugh reports that in the first third of the nineteenth century, Americans not only drank twice as much as the Irish but consumed more hard liquor * than anybody else in the Western world save the Swedes. In 1820, for instance, Americans drank enough distilled spirits to supply every man, woman, and child in the country with 5 gallons of booze; that particular year the Irish imbibed a third less. Rorabaugh, in his extensive study of the history of alcohol, concludes that between 1790 and 1830 the United States "had been one of the world's great drinking countries."

It was also then one of the great alcohol-abusing countries. In the early 1800s drunks became common in America and drunkenness came to be seen as the country's leading social problem. Between slavery and drunkenness, drunkenness was often regarded—

---

* Rum, whiskey, gin, and brandy.

even by many abolitionists—as the greater evil. Many reformers fought both.

Of drunks around the world, the American was, in many ways, the worst off. At least Irishmen typically drank in groups. Americans—virtually alone among the world's drinkers—imbibed in solitude. Worse, they also were about the only drinkers to go "on binges." And only in America did drinkers in any substantial numbers end up with delirium tremens (DT's).

No one can say for sure why Americans drank so much, but it probably had to do with the fact that they worried so much—and that they had so much to worry about. It's forgotten that while the government was becoming more and more stable in the early 1800s, the economy was undergoing profound changes as it industrialized, leading in turn to unprecedented anxiety. This anxiety, historians say, probably contributed to excessive drinking.[1]

In reviewing the layman's knowledge of early American history, the striking thing is not how much he knows about our alcoholic past but how little. Much is made, for instance, of the Pilgrim's grim first winter, but few realize one of the chief reasons the Pilgrims considered it so grim was that there was a shortage of beer and beer was their main drink. (They drank more beer than water; water was considered generally unsafe.) Nor are people aware of the extent to which soldiers in the American Revolution were dependent on alcohol. When supplies were available, soldiers in the Continental Army were given a daily ration of 4 ounces of hard liquor; to boost their morale after losing the battle at Germantown, Congress gave the soldiers involved an extra bonus of "spirits."

If little is known about the colonists' drinking, almost nothing is known about their habit of drinking to excess. But drinking to intoxication, says historians, was an American tradition. William Byrd, a Virginia gentleman farmer in the eighteenth century, reported in his diary that Virginians regularly got drunk at militia musters, court sessions, and elections. Foreigners, in astonishment, observed that Americans, women and children alike, regularly took a drink with every meal, including breakfast. During the Revolution, soldiers frequently got drunk and several times became so inebriated they couldn't function on the field. In their history, *Drinking in America,* Mark Lender and James Martin relate the story of a patrol that came across a barrel of whiskey during Washington's retreat across New Jersey in 1776: "Concerned that the booty not fall into enemy hands (or so the men said), they drank up the liquor on the spot. The result, an officer recalled, was a bad case of 'barrel fever,' with symptoms of black eyes and bloody noses."

In colonial times, as later, temperance leaders deplored drunkenness, but the amazing thing is the extent to which drunkenness was widely tolerated. At dinners where alcohol was served, for example, hosts often expected guests to drink to inebriation. Offense was given if a guest refused to do so. Indeed, only drunkenness that ended in public displays of rowdiness was scorned. According to Rorabaugh, hostility to drunkenness as a sign of moral depravity hadn't yet developed. As yet drunkenness was not generally associated with crime or violence. Not until the nineteenth century was mention made of "Demon Rum"; before then alcohol was considered aqua vitae, "the water of life."

Nor was drunkenness confined to the down and out. Byrd records numerous instances where public officials, including the governor, publicly became drunk. Others frequently reported seeing merchants drunk. When merchants closed a deal they would often celebrate by drinking until they could barely stand. Sometimes one wonders how people remained standing. At a dinner to honor the French ambassador to the United States, New York Governor George Clinton plied his 120 guests with over 200 bottles of spirits: 135 bottles of Madeira, 36 bottles of port, and 60 bottles of English beer. On top of this he served 30 cups of rum punch.

All of this doesn't make the United States a nation of drunkards. But it does suggest that drinking played a more important role in American history than the textbooks let on. Most history textbooks give the impression that alcohol only became a serious social issue in the 1920s, but that's hardly the case.

From the attention bestowed on the twenties, one would think that alcohol only then became an important economic commodity. But by then its economic significance was relatively minimal. In the past it had ranked much higher. In the early 1800s, for example, whiskey out West was the farmer's most profitable product. Until canals improved the transportation market for hogs and corn, whiskey earned men the most money. A thousand bushels of corn shipped to New Orleans in the 1820s fetched barely enough to cover the cost of getting it there. But turned into spirits, they could be sold for nearly $500. The farmers of western Pennsylvania had good reason to stage their unprecedented revolt against the federal government in the 1794 Whiskey Rebellion. When the government imposed an excise tax on their whiskey it put their very livelihoods in jeopardy. The idea that until Al Capone came along only "hillbillies" distilled moonshine and dodged liquor taxes is nonsense.

History books give rum some attention in connection with the burgeoning slave trade. Well known is the story of the Triangular Trade in which molasses, bought in the West Indies and distilled in America as rum, was sold in Africa to buy slaves. But that is about all the attention the subject receives. Less well known is the scholar's view that distilling was then the chief American industry, or that because of a dearth of specie, rum served as "the currency of the age."

It is hard to say why so little is made of our alcoholic past. It can't simply be that it's embarrassing; slavery is more embarrassing than alcohol and we've had no trouble admitting Americans owned slaves. And it can't be because we deplore the abuse of alcohol; alcohol abuse in the twenties is both conceded and romanticized. Most likely, our alcoholic past goes unacknowledged because it remains at variance with the image we have of ourselves in the Age of the Pioneer. We envision pioneers trapping animals, fishing, and farming, not distilling liquor. The national album must not include a picture of a pioneer tending a steam pot and condenser.

Nor, apparently, can it include a picture of Washington with a drink or workmen with a bottle. In a Currier and Ives print pub-

lished in 1848, Washington, upon bidding his fellow officers farewell, raises a toast to them; in his hand is a glass, on the table a
decanter of liquor. But in the reproduction of the print that appeared in 1876 the glass is gone and the decanter is hidden by a
hat. In the 1869 photograph of the Golden Spike ceremony held in
Utah to commemorate the joining of the Central Pacific and Union
Pacific railroads, workers are seen holding aloft several bottles of
booze. In the official painting of the event, the bottles are missing.[2]

The genteel way in which the drinking habits of "old-stock" Americans are treated stands in striking contrast to the stereotypes of the
alcoholic behavior of "wild" Indians and "dissolute" immigrants.
Everyone "knows" *they* had a drinking problem.

Concerning the Indians, it's almost universally believed that
they have had a racial proclivity to drunkenness. It is said they "just
couldn't hold their liquor." But that's pure moonshine. We know
from the people who knew the early Indians best—the explorers,
Jesuits priests, and fur traders who worked among them—that they
usually handled liquor well when first introduced to it. Jacques
Cartier, who was the first European to give alcohol to any Indians
(or at least the first to record having done so), noted in his journal
that the tribal members with whom he came in contact * drank in
moderation, neither getting drunk nor violent. Apparently, at this
early date it didn't even occur to Cartier that the Indians might "go
crazy" on alcohol; when he left he happily gave them liquor as a
gift. Lewis and Clark reported that the tribal members they met
either drank in moderation or not at all. Craig MacAndrew and
Robert Edgerton, in their pioneering study of Indians and alcoholism, cite dozens of tribes that behaved similarly. "Clearly," they
conclude, "the *initial* reaction of many Indians to liquor was anything but an epic of drunken mayhem, debauchery, and the like.
Instead, we find account after account of these earliest days in
which the Indians showed remarkable restraint while in their cups."

---

* The Micmac tribe of Gaspé Harbor, on the Gulf of St. Lawrence, in 1534.

Between whites and Indians, the whites often made the worse drunks. H. B. Cushman, who worked with tribal members along the Texas frontier in the middle of the nineteenth century, said that in his experience "A drunken white man is far worse than a drunken Indian, and more to be feared ten to one, than the Indian." Alexander Henry, earlier in the century, recalled that in his years as a hunter his white associates made "more d----d noise and trouble" when drunk than a "hundred Blackfeet." MacAndrew and Edgerton say it was common for drunk whites to terrify Indians.

Whether or not they behaved as badly as whites under the influence of alcohol, there is plenty of evidence, of course, that after their initial exposure to liquor Indians behaved badly enough. But if they did, it probably was because they'd seen how whites acted under the influence. Almost certainly, in the opinion of most experts, their behavior was derivative. Had whites acted passively when drunk, Indians probably would have done so as well; it is common for South American tribes to behave passively after drinking. It is now well established that drunks behave the way they think they ought to behave. From whites the lesson was learned all too well that drunks behave aggressively.[3]

As for the nineteenth-century immigrants, it's believed that they had a special affinity for booze. Although it's impossible to generalize, the widely held belief is that the Jews and Italians drank little, the Germans regularly drank light wines and beer, and the Irish regularly drank hard liquor. Irish drinking is especially notorious, not so much because they drank a lot but because the places in which they drank—the saloons—became the headquarters of the urban Irish Democratic machines that were challenging the political power of the Yankee elites. As Bernard Weisberger has pointed out, "*That* was the real sin."[4]

One cannot mention alcohol, of course, without touching upon Prohibition. It is one of the great romantic periods of American history. The thought of gun-toting gangsters running booze through dimly lighted streets puts movie audiences in rapture. Throw in a little blood and they swoon. They are especially fond of Al Capone.

Upon reflection, Capone is an unlikely hero. But to the common man it is not Capone's elevation that is considered bewildering. It is the enactment of Prohibition that befuddles. To think that Americans once thought they could legislate drinking out of existence. How ridiculous!

Yet how ridiculous was it? Unknown to the cavalier cynics who mock the effort is the confounding fact that to a great extent it succeeded. For drinking did dramatically decline during Prohibition. Its success is statistically demonstrable. In 1910, before the enactment of state and national prohibition laws, Americans consumed 2.60 gallons of pure alcohol per capita annually. In 1934, the year after Prohibition ended, consumption declined to 0.97 gallons. It rose a little thereafter, as people got used to drinking again. But as late as 1940, consumption remained lower than it had been before Prohibition, standing at 1.56 gallons. Joseph Gusfield, reviewing the available data, concluded that alcohol consumption declined during Prohibition anywhere from between a third to a half. (Correspondingly, the consumption of nonalcoholic beverages zoomed. Sales of Coca-Cola tripled. The Welch Grape Juice Company sold a million more gallons of juice. And per capita milk consumption in urban areas climbed from 34 gallons a year to 49.)

Deaths due to alcoholism also declined. Census figures show that at the beginning of the century there were 7.3 deaths from chronic or acute alcoholism for every 100,000 people; in 1932, the last full year of Prohibition, the figure was 2.5. In between the rate varied, increasing to 4.0 in 1927, but the experts say that was probably due to a temporary rise in the availability of illegal liquor, much of which contained alarming amounts of fatally poisonous concoctions.[5]

The famous writers from the twenties often left the impression that "everybody" drank more during Prohibition than they had before, but it turns out it was the writers who drank more. F. Scott Fitzgerald, Ernest Hemingway, Thomas Wolfe: All became drunks in the twenties, partly out of the inane belief that "true artists had to be alcoholic," and partly out of the belief (quoting one of their critics) that "once alcohol became forbidden . . . it was their moral duty to violate the law on every possible occasion." In their world, "It was a matter of principle to drink; people who had never cared much for alcohol now felt that drinking was the socially correct thing to do."[6]

There is, incidentally, nothing to the romantic impression, contributed by Fitzgerald himself, that in the 1920s he was a happy-go-lucky drinker. Far from it. When he did all those crazy things—skipping his way across the Plaza fountain, stripping naked at the Follies, boiling party guests' watches in tomato soup—he was frighteningly, uncontrollably, and undeniably drunk. We now know he drank so often that he suffered repeatedly from blackouts, often couldn't write, and once tried to kill his wife with a candelabra; only the intervention of the butler seems to have saved her.

Fitzgerald never accepted the fact that he was a drunk. Not even in the confessional piece he wrote about his "crack-up" was he able to bring himself to admit he cracked up because of alcohol. Indeed, he expressly insists he did not, claiming he hadn't taken a drink in the six months before the breakdown. But we now know he had; reliable reports indicate that just prior to his hospitalization he drank thirty-seven bottles of beer in a single day.

It may be thought that he dealt honestly with alcoholism in his books, for many of his characters are heavy drinkers. But he rarely admits in his fiction that the reason his characters behave badly is because they drink. Thomas Gilmore, in a celebrated book about writers who drink, concludes that Fitzgerald "clung to the denial" typical of alcoholics, and wrote "evasive and dishonest" stories about them. In Gilmore's opinion only one of Fitzgerald's novels successfully deals with alcoholism—The Beautiful and the Damned. Significantly, it was written before Fitzgerald's own alcoholism surfaced.[7]

If the famous writers of the 1920s drank more than they had in the past, one thing worth remembering is that it was because they could afford to. Most Americans couldn't—literally. Prohibition was so effective that the cost of drinking skyrocketed. Between 1916 and 1928 the cost of a glass of beer increased 600 percent, gin 520 percent, whiskey 310 percent. At a time when the average annual income barely topped $2,600, a mug of beer cost $.80.[8]

Critics relish the idea that Prohibition, which had been instituted to save the American family, in the end helped undermine it by corrupting youth. Samuel Eliot Morison, whose *Oxford History of the American People* contains the standard view on the matter, says "bravado" in the twenties "induced numerous young people to drink who otherwise would not have done so." But there is reason to believe that the standard view, Morison's endorsement notwithstanding, is flawed.

To begin with, we do not know for a fact whether youthful drinking increased in the twenties as there is an absence of hard statistical data on the subject. But even if, as likely, it did increase, Prohibition may not have been the reason it did. We now know that youthful rebellion seems to have occurred in all of the Western industrialized countries in the twenties, with a corresponding effect on the consumption of alcohol. That being the case, it would seem that World War I had a lot more to do with the "bravado" of youth than Prohibition.[9]

The introduction of Prohibition, without question, substantially increased the crime rate (though some historians even dispute that*) and bred disrespect for the law. But it is a mistake to think

---

* Norman Clark points out that organized crime didn't begin with Prohibition and insists that Al Capone would have surfaced as a major criminal whether liquor was legal or not. Capone got into organized crime before the start of Prohibition and earned most of his profits afterward in gambling and prostitution. "To see his career," says Clark, "as the consequence of a liquor law is to simplify a profoundly disturbing circumstance of American cultural pluralism. Capone and his lieutenants came out of subcultures which were indigenous to the massive urban growths such as New York or Chicago, and these men took brilliant advantage of an institutionalized commerce in illegal goods and services." (Clark, *Deliver Us from Evil* [1976], p. 150.)

that Prohibition proved "You can't force people to stop drinking!" The fact is hardly any effort was made to make people stop. Enforcement of the law was left almost entirely to the federal government, and the federal government spent little on the effort. In 1922, for instance, Congress appropriated less than $7 million for the Prohibition Bureau; police said $300 million was needed. With the little money it had, the bureau was able to hire just 3,000 employees, leaving huge stretches of the country barely covered. From Seattle to the Canadian border there were just 20 agents; in all of New England, 91; in New York City, just 129. (The U.S. attorney for New York City estimated it would take 1,500 agents to cover the city properly.)

The remarkable thing then is not that so many people got away with illegal drinking during Prohibition but that so many were caught. The effectiveness of the Prohibition Bureau was particularly remarkable given the extraordinarily high potential for bribery (the average agent earned just $150 a month), and the low ability, in the opinion of historians, of many of the recruits.[10]

Anybody with the cash who wanted a drink in the 1920s, of course, could get one. As the movies have shown, speakeasies were ubiquitous. But buying a drink wasn't quite as risk-free as is usually imagined. Agents regularly closed bars and arrested the patrons. A two-agent team in New York City in just five years confiscated 5 million bottles of booze worth more than $15 million and made nearly 4,500 arrests; 95 percent of those arrested were convicted. But then, they were the team of Izzie and Moe—Izzie Einstein and Moe Smith—and nobody else had the knack they had for collaring criminals. One of Izzie's favorite techniques was to be completely open about his intentions when he'd show up at a speakeasy to collect the evidence that people were drinking. "My boss sent me," the balding and overweight five-foot-five-inch Izzie would say. "I'm a prohibition agent. I just got appointed." And of course he'd be let in.[11]

All of this doesn't mean Prohibition was a great success and ought to have been continued. But neither can it be said that it was quite the failure it's been made out to be. A fair judgment would have to be that it (1) succeeded in reducing alcohol consumption, but (2) failed to do so at an acceptable social cost.

The belief that the Eighteenth Amendment forbid the sale of all liquor is widespread but erroneous. In actuality, the amendment only forbid the sale of "intoxicating liquors." That left open the possibility that weak beers and light wines could be sold. It was the Volstead Act, passed to implement the amendment, that blocked the sale of *all* alcoholic beverages.

That it was illegal to drink alcoholic beverages under Prohibition is plainly false. One could drink as much of the stuff as one wished—as long as it had been purchased prior to the enactment of Prohibition. The Yale Club throughout the twenties legally served alcoholic beverages bought before the deadline.[12]

Less common nowadays, but still sometimes heard, is the belief that Prohibition was instituted by women while the men were away during World War I. However, women still could not vote in most states at the time Prohibition was approved. Undoubtedly, women would have supported Prohibition enthusiastically, but then, so did the men. The belief that Prohibition slipped through by a slim majority is false. Only three states—New Jersey, Rhode Island, and Connecticut—rejected the Eighteenth Amendment. All the rest approved it with majorities of 80 percent or more. Only in hindsight did it seem such a stupid idea that people forgot how eagerly it had once been embraced.

Nor is it true that Prohibition was foisted on the American public by a conspiracy of reactionary hicks and hayseeds. Professor James Timberlake, who has made the most thorough and convincing study of the politics of Prohibition, says that it was actually promoted by progressives as a social reform. To them, the saloon was on a par with the corrupt urban machine, and the faster it could be eliminated the better the chance that city life could be cleansed and improved. Those who at one time or another supported some form of Prohibition included Wisconsin's Robert LaFollette, Idaho's William Borah, Theodore Roosevelt, Woodrow Wilson, and

Eleanor Roosevelt. Theodore Roosevelt charged that the "liquor forces" regularly torpedoed municipal reform. Wilson approved of local option laws that permitted the prohibition of alcohol on a county-by-county basis. Eleanor Roosevelt condemned her husband's fondness for highballs and firmly aligned herself (in the 1920s) with the "drys."

Popular belief of the conservative origins of Prohibition has its foundation in the fact that most support for Prohibition came from rural areas. But the conflict over Prohibition is best understood, says Timberlake, not as a "conflict between country and city" but as a struggle between classes: "For the movement cut across geographic lines: the old-stock, urban middle classes, which comprised about 40 percent of the urban population in 1910, tended to favor it, whereas the lower classes in the country were more often opposed." (It was those same old-stock middle classes, both urban and rural, that formed the backbone of the progressive movement.

Logic would seem to indicate, because Prohibition is so strongly identified with Herbert Hoover, that it was a conservative measure. However, through most of American history the campaign to outlaw alcoholic beverages was waged by reformers. Many of the most prominent abolitionists, for instance, considered drinking as great an evil as slavery and fought it just as hard. As for the impression created by H. L. Mencken that Prohibition was a triumph of Puritanism, there's nothing to it. In fact, the Puritans approved of drinking (in moderation).[13]

Hoover, incidentally, never called Prohibition a "noble experiment." His exact words were "Our nation has deliberately undertaken a great social and economic experiment, noble in motive and far-reaching in purpose." It was the Democrats who pinned on him the more pointed phrase. In substance it wasn't a whit different from Hoover's statement, but it was more memorable and for that reason more damaging.

The chief myth about drugs must be that Americans have only recently had much awareness of them. Underlying every discussion of drugs is the assumption that our concern with them is relatively new. It is the lament of the modern age that we alone have been afflicted with this dreadful scourge. Previous generations never even worried about drugs. Or so we, in our innocence, imagine.

Marijuana, for instance, is almost universally identified with the 1960s, but it was actually considered a problem in the 1930s and deemed a catastrophe in the 1940s. There is reason to believe the alarms were manufactured by the government and that marijuana use was actually quite limited. But there's no doubting that people worried about it. Social commentator Bergen Evans (in disgust) reported in 1946 that "the editors of half the popular magazines in the country" were then "addicted to marijuana—as a subject for copy—and sent their own and their magazines' circulations soaring with delicious dreams of high-school girls' abandoning themselves to orgies under the influence of this subtle drug."

Crack, of course, is of recent concern, but cocaine addiction was known in the latter nineteenth century. And opium and morphine addiction go back to the Civil War. Veterans of the war who were given morphine to relieve the pain of battlefield wounds found they couldn't get off the drug. Later in the century opium use became widespread among the educated, the wealthy, the elderly, and women. In 1889, it was estimated that there were 250,000 opium and morphine addicts in the United States, which, if true, was more addicts than in any other country in the Western world.

There is ample reason for thinking that the relationship between crime and drugs is far stronger now than ever before. But the belief that the two are linked goes back at least to the 1930s. Bergen Evans, by 1946, could write that crime and drugs "are [now] thought to be inseparable." In 1949, Kinzie Bluitt, a lieutenant with the Chicago Police Force, estimated that "80% of burglaries and 60% of robberies" in the city were committed by dope fiends. The good lieutenant may have been exaggerating; Evans believed he was. But that doesn't change the fact that the lieutenant *thought* that drugs were behind most of the city's burglaries and robberies, and in saying so, he led others to think so too.[14]

Most shocking of all, perhaps, is that some of the greatest American fortunes were made in drugs. Much of the money in the Roosevelt family fortune, for instance, was made in the drug trade in nineteenth-century China. We are accustomed, of course, to thinking it was the British who made money off the nefarious Chinese drug trade. It was they, after all, who started the infamous Opium Wars, using their superior military muscle to win the right to sell opium in China, "enslaving millions." What is forgotten, however, is that the Americans stood right by their side. Geoffrey Ward, in *American Heritage* in 1986, revealed that Franklin Roosevelt's grandfather, Warren Delano, was one of the most successful of the opium drug traders. During the Opium Wars, while the British were preoccupied with the fighting, Delano shrewdly used the time to expand his market in the drug: "While we hold the horns," an exasperated British trader complained, the Americans "milk the cow."

Christian missionaries complained that selling opium to the Chinese was immoral. But Delano seemed not to have been overly troubled by the practice. He wrote home: "I do not pretend to justify the prosecution of the opium trade in a moral and philanthropic point of view, but as a merchant I insist it has been a fair, honorable and legitimate trade; and to say the worst of it, liable to no further or weightier objections than is the importation of wines, Brandies & spirits into the U. States, England, &c."

Unquestionably, between the British and the Americans, the British shared greater responsibility for the disastrous trade in opium. But the Americans certainly made the most of the opportunity to make money from it. Not content with the lucre to be made from the shipment of the drug, they eventually joined the British in growing it. The British grew opium in India, the Americans in Turkey.[15]

None of this means that Americans were as familiar with drugs in the nineteenth and early twentieth centuries as they are today. But it does suggest that Americans have had more of a history with drugs than is generally admitted.

The great danger in neglecting our previous experience with drugs is that our attitudes about them will be strictly shaped by what we know of them from today's headlines. The debate over whether to legalize drugs, for instance, is conducted as if they have never been legal. Yet through most of American history, "hard" drugs *were* legal. Opium, which first came into use in America in the 1830s, was legal until 1914. Heroin was legally imported into the United States until 1924. Patent medicines in the nineteenth century frequently contained narcotics that are banned today. Bayer sold a heroin compound as a cure for the common cold. Others advertised that cocaine could help "cure sore throat, neuralgia, nervousness, headache, colds and sleeplessness." Laudanum, a liquid mixture of opium, was once as common as aspirin is today.

One of the main arguments against drug legalization is that it would encourage drug use. But just the opposite seems to have happened in history with opium. All the studies indicate that after it was restricted in 1914, it became more popular than ever. By World War I, it is estimated that there were a million opium addicts in the United States. * The more people violated the law, of course, the harder the police worked to apprehend them. But that only seems to have made matters worse, driving the poor addict further underground and giving the drug peddler greater profits.

Another argument against legalization is that drug use leads inevitably to the uncontrollable demand for drugs. Norman Clark, however, says that there is abundant evidence that this may not be so. In his history of alcohol and drugs he observes that when drugs were legal many prominent people proved that even if they couldn't end their addictions, they could control them. Dr. William Stewart Halsted (1852–1922), chief of surgery at Johns Hopkins School of Medicine, is said to have maintained a daily dose of three grains of morphine for decades. [16]

---

* Why the prohibition of alcohol seems to have reduced the demand for alcohol, whereas the prohibition of narcotics increased demand, is unknown. But it suggests we still don't know nearly as much about both as we should.

Two myths involving drugs have been advanced by those who want to justify their use. It is said that George Washington used marijuana and that Coca-Cola was originally made with cocaine. The association of Washington and marijuana is due to the fact that Washington grew hemp on his plantation. However, there's no evidence that he smoked it. He used it for its fibers.

Coca-Cola, because of the name and the secrecy surrounding its formula, was long suspected of containing cocaine. The Coca-Cola Company admitted as late as 1903 that its soda formula included cocaine, but the drug was used in exceedingly small amounts—so small that when federal inspectors conducted tests on the soda at the turn of the century they could not find even a trace of cocaine in the product.[17]

8
Women

"What's college?"
"That's where girls who are above cooking and sewing go to meet a man so they can spend their lives cooking and sewing."
GIMBEL'S DEPARTMENT STORE ADVERTISEMENT, 1952

Most American myths involve men—yet more proof of the neglect of women in American history. But the myths that do concern women we hold just as dearly.

We are virtually obsessed with the staid image of the nineteenth-century American Victorian lady. She is the great object of our pity. Weathered photographs have given us the impression she was the prisoner of the corset. Feminists insist men trapped her in a narrow role that deprived her of the freedom to express herself outside the home. Moralists say she was the hapless victim of the double-standard. Nobody doubts she was oppressed.

The favorite way of demonstrating the extent of her oppression is to show how much worse off she was than even her colonial forebears had been, which demonstration is thought to be definitive. To think that the condition of the American woman had declined! Harsh as life may have been in the colonial period, for example, women then were not "restricted to those jobs thought to be suitable for their sex." They could be almost anything they wanted to be: blacksmith, newspaper editor, lumberjack, or carpenter. Even under the Puritans the ladies supposedly had it better. For at least then, as one historian explained, men had not yet divided women into "sexual partners on the one hand and wives-mothers on the other." Only later, after "The Great Repression," was the artificial division made between good women and bad, a division that robbed "good women" of the opportunity to express themselves sexually.[1]

Our concern for the Victorian woman is misplaced. While she undoubtedly was repressed in her role as the heroine of the home,* she at least was in charge of the home. Earlier her husband had been. Only in the nineteenth century, for instance, did women begin taking the chief responsibility for child care. Earlier, child-care manuals had been written for men.[2]

And if the role of the Victorian woman as mistress of the home seems unduly narrow, by virtue of her identification with family and morality, she suddenly had the clout to do things outside the home she never had before. For if women were too pure for sex, the perception that they were pure gave them the chance to take leading roles in moral causes such as abolitionism and temperance. Say what you will about the female busybodies who joined league with the Comstocks and Sabbatarians in war on "immorality"; it was just such women who gave needed energy to the often moribund campaigns against slavery and drunkenness. Women, indeed, though regarded as apolitical, were given the political responsibility of maintaining American virtue, which was considered essential by many to the preservation of the republic.[3]

And if women felt less free than they once did to pursue traditional male jobs, they felt quite free to pursue jobs for which females were thought to be specially equipped. These included nursing and teaching. It was only because of the "cult of true womanhood" that women came to dominate these professions. If it sounds paradoxical that women would begin to work outside the home because they had become so identified with the home, it was. "The very perfec-

---

* Though sexually repressed, the extent of her repression is usually overstated. See the author's *Legend's, Lies & Cherished Myths of American History* (1988), chapter 5, "Sex."

tion of True Womanhood," according to historian Barbara Welter, "carried within itself the seeds of its own destruction. For if woman was so very little less than the angels, she should surely take a more active part in running the world, especially since men were making such a hash of things."[4]

The dominance of the "cult of true womanhood," in any case, is exaggerated. Many nineteenth-century women did not believe they ought to confine themselves to home and family issues, and by no means can it be maintained that women universally adopted the pose of the leisured, frail maiden, which was considered an essential part of the "cult of true womanhood." Frances B. Cogan, in her history of the "all-American girl," suggests that millions of women emulated a different ideal that "advocated intelligence, physical fitness and health, self-sufficiency, economic self-reliance, and careful marriage."

It is a little hard to prove conclusively what ideal people held, as any one individual usually held different ideals at once, even though the ideals may have contradicted one another. But it is hard to discount the evidence that many women seemed to scorn the image of the weak-kneed woman foisted upon them by men. Certainly the young ladies at Vassar College rejected the notion that they should be timid, as did the avid readers of the popular novelist Marion Harland. Harland's female characters, described as having "muscles like harp-strings," boasted of their physical prowess. Says one (sounding like a female Teddy Roosevelt): "I can row six miles without fatigue and walk ten. I can drive and swim, and ride twelve miles before breakfast on a trotting horse. I eat heartily three times a day, and sleep soundly for eight hours out of the twenty-four. . . . Do I ever have headaches? Once in a while, but not so often as do my collegian cousins. Hysterics? No; nor the blues!"[5]

And if many women wished to lead a life of leisure and frailty, it is a fact that many couldn't. They couldn't afford to. Nearly half of all adult black women had to work outside the home to make ends meet, as did millions of immigrant women. As early as 1816, when industrialism was still in an inchoate stage, 66,000 women (mostly single) worked in cotton textile factories. Thousands more worked as prostitutes (as many as 7,000 in New York City alone in the early 1800s). And thousands more worked as school teachers, though teaching, of course, was regarded as a "proper profession."[6]

If the Victorian woman represents in American consciousness the extreme example of weakness and dependency, Rosie the Riveter represents the opposite. We have never had a stronger female. But who was she?

It is popularly assumed that the women who flooded the factories during World War II were "young, white and middle class" and that they joined the labor force "out of patriotic motives." When war ended, it is thought, they eagerly left their jobs to go back to their families.

Actually, a clear majority seem to have gone to work in the factories because they needed the work. The statistics show most of the women came from working-class backgrounds and that by 1941 they already had chalked up years of experience in the labor force. Thirty percent had worked for at least ten years. Nearly 50 percent had worked five years. Only 25 percent had worked fewer than two years. World War II, to be sure, increased the ranks of working women. In 1940, 25 percent of women worked; in 1945, the number rose to 36 percent. But if more women worked, the significant thing that changed is the kind of jobs at which they worked. For the first time in American history women were given the high-paying jobs men formerly monopolized. Just as soon as the war was over, however, returning veterans were given back their old jobs. Female employment remained the same—at the new higher level established during the war—but women once again were forced to take the lower-paying jobs.

If we think of Rosie the Riveter as a middle-class housewife, it is because the government wanted us to. For one thing, the government believed that housewives would be perceived as temporary workers and that would help win public acceptance of women in men's roles. Who could object to a woman in a man's job if she took the job just to be patriotic (and if it were clearly understood she'd give up the job as soon as the man returned)? For another, by insisting it was housewives who took the jobs of men, the government could ease the fear that the women might want to keep their jobs at war's end. "Mere housewives" wouldn't want to. If it seems strange that World War II did not have a greater effect on women's liberation, it is because the campaign to enlist women in the war effort was expressly designed to minimize the idea that women should define themselves in terms of their work. Their "real" job was in the kitchen; war work was temporary.

Women hardly could have been pictured any other way than as temporaries. For if it was believed they had a right to their jobs it would have been unconscionable to ask them at war's end to give them up to the veterans.[7]

The stay-at-home housewife of the fifties is remembered for her traditionalism. In cooking and cleaning, in chauffeuring the kids and attending the PTA, she seems the epitome of conventionalism. We can hardly do without her. How else would we know how far we've come?

Hers is a false standard by which to judge our progress, however. The fifties' housewife was an anomaly. By many yardsticks women then were less liberated than those who came earlier. Proportionately more got married than in their mothers' generation. More got married younger. And more had bigger families. In 1941 the great majority of American women said they wanted two children; in the fifties most said they wanted three or four. The more children they had, of course, the less easy it was to have a career.[8]

To be sure, more women worked in the fifties than ever before: 38 percent by 1955. But fewer seemed to want to work in jobs traditionally held mainly by men. Relatively more women earned college degrees in the thirties than in the fifties and relatively more were awarded Ph.D.'s. Quoting Page Smith, "In 1930 two out of five B.A.'s and M.A.'s were awarded to women; and one out of seven Ph.D.'s. By 1962 the figures had dropped to one in three and one in ten." In 1879 thirty-eight percent of the teachers in the universities and colleges were women; by 1959 only twenty percent were.[9]

The new passivity of women was reflected in the new ways women were featured in the movies and in magazines. It has been noted that Doris Day and Debbie Reynolds replaced stars like Katherine Hepburn and Joan Crawford. And actresses who had once hidden the fact that they were pregnant now advertised it. In the magazines, as Betty Friedan reported, none of the heroines of fiction seemed to find success in a career of their own as they had in the thirties. "The image of woman that emerges . . . is young and frivolous, almost childlike; fluffy and feminine; passive; gaily content in a world of bedroom and kitchen, sex, babies, and home."[10]

If the fifties are misperceived as a typical period, our era is misunderstood as an atypical one. Thus, almost everybody makes the mistake of thinking that the woman who faces a choice between a career and a family is facing a choice few women ever had in the past. But college women have long confronted the same problem. Consider the lament of the *Smith College Weekly*, from 1910: "We cannot believe that it is fixed in the nature of things that a woman must choose between a home and her work, when a man may have both. There must be a way out and it is the problem of our generation to find the way."[11]

If much of what is taken for granted about women's history is suspect, all is not suspect. Women, for instance, really did win the constitutional right to vote in 1920, with the passage of the Nineteenth Amendment. But even that simple fact is less simple than it seems. In the colonial period some women with property were allowed to vote in local elections in Massachusetts, New York, New Jersey, Rhode Island and Pennsylvania. And between 1776 and 1807 they had the right to vote in New Jersey (if, that is, they were worth at least 50 pounds). Kentucky gave women the right to vote in school elections in 1838; Kansas did the same thing in 1861. In 1869 the Territory of Wyoming granted women the suffrage in all

elections and the following year the Territory of Utah followed. *
The Territory of Washington awarded women the vote in 1883. By
1920 women had the vote in fifteen of the forty-eight states.

Some women voted in elections where they legally weren't allowed to. Susan B. Anthony, joined by more than a dozen other
New York women, voted in the 1872 presidential election. A short
time later she was convicted in a court of law for doing so and was
fined. [12]

It is said, no doubt in all sincerity, that women finally got the
constitutional right to vote in 1920 because of a "long and hard
fought battle" for equality. But while the fight was long and it was
unquestionably hard, it wasn't waged so women could play an equal
role in politics. The expectation was that women would play a
superior role. Being purer, it was thought, they would contribute to
the moral improvement of politics. Then, as now, women leaders
alleged that a world run by females would be far less likely to be
plunged into war than one run by males. [13]

They made no such argument in favor of their right to sit on
juries. That was considered just a matter of simple justice. But few
realize quite how long it was before men came to agree. As late as
1942, only twenty-eight states gave women the right to sit on a
jury. Not until 1957 were they guaranteed the right to sit on federal
juries. And not until 1973 were they finally given the right to sit
on all juries in all fifty states.

Beyond the question of the woman's right to vote and her right
to sit on a jury, there's the question of her right to be her own
person. This took long to establish as well. In 1970 the Ohio Supreme Court, echoing the colonial view that a woman should be
accorded the same rights as lunatics and infants, ruled that a wife is

---

* Wyoming acted in the hope that extending the suffrage would make women
want to come live there (women were in short supply). Utah's reasons are
more obscure, but apparently the Mormons hoped that by giving women the
right to vote non-Mormons could be prevented from taking control in the
territory. But it also may be that they wanted women's help in defending
polygamy. (Eleanor Flexner, *Century of Struggle* [1975], pp. 164–66.)

a husband's servant with "no legally recognized feelings or rights." In 1974 the Georgia state legislature declared that husbands are the "head of the family" and insisted that the wife is subject to her husband's will.[14] Perhaps she was —on paper.

While women have been preoccupied with winning their political freedom, their husbands have been celebrating their wives' freedom from household drudgery. To the American male that's been the real advance of the century!

Thus, the husband who leaves his wife at home to cook and clean often thinks to himself that at least there are appliances to help her. But the truth is "modern conveniences" (as the advertisers call them) historically have helped him as well as her. In this century dishwashers reduced the work husbands formerly did in drying dishes, while garbage disposals decreased the amount of trash husbands needed to take out to the curb for pickup. In the last century the invention of the coal-burning stove saved the husband the chore of cutting and hauling wood for cooking.

Industrial progress, indeed, commonly had the ironic effect of increasing the work of the housewife while decreasing the labor of her husband. The switch, for example, from home-grown grains to store-bought flour, which was made possible by the development of the railroads, eliminated the husband's job, which consisted of growing and milling grain, but dramatically complicated the house-wife's. There are only a few simple ways to cook with the whole flour and meal made from home-grown grains. Store-bought fine flour, in contrast, can be used to bake cakes, cookies, and pastries. Similarly, on the old open-hearths housewives had been limited to the preparation of single-course meals. With the conversion to stoves, however, women could—and it was expected they would—cook complicated meals including soups, appetizers, main courses, and desserts.

Ruth Cowan, after surveying the various jobs men performed around the home in the nineteenth century, concluded that indus-trialism eliminated "virtually all" of them. After industrialism, she says, the average American male didn't cut wood, butcher animals, mill grain, or make shoes. *

There is no question industrialism eased the drudgery of house-work. Women after industrialism certainly worked less hard than they had before; and they did so while increasing the family's stan-dard of living. Those cakes and pastries tasted better than bran. But women still worked longer hours than their husbands. Housewives in 1900 typically put in a twelve-hour day seven days a week † (and that doesn't include time spent on child care).

That housewives today work less than they did, say, a hundred years ago, owing to improvements in technology, is undoubtedly true. But there's no justification at all for the snide remarks of husbands who wonder "what their wives do all day." For housewives still don't have as much free time as one might expect given the abundance of "time-saving" machinery. Studies show that in 1965 the average housewife worked about fifty hours a week (half on child care, half on housekeeping). At that rate of progress, she was just then approaching the workload of the typical affluent housewife (with an income of up to $3500) of 1912. And as if that weren't disconcerting enough, it turns out, that she was about even with the typical housewife of 1935. The historians don't yet have precise figures showing the impact of microwaves on the housewife's regi-men. But even in 1965, TV dinners were common, so there might not be much of a difference in statistics compiled today.

If there has been a dramatic change in the work of housewives in the last century, it is in who's doing the work. A hundred years ago the affluent middle-class housewife had at least one, often two, servants to help her get dinner on the table and do laundry. Today almost no one but the rich hire full-time servants. Thus, what

---

* Not that the husbands had it easy under industrialism. In the 1880s men who worked in factories typically worked twelve-hour days, six days a week. In 1900, they put in ten-hour days.

† Two hours on laundry, six on cooking, two on cleaning, and two on sewing. (Stanley Lebergott, *The American Economy* [1976], p. 92.)

technology has achieved is greater democracy. Today, the affluent housewife is as likely as her lower-middle-class counterpart to do her own housework and to do it in about the same amount of time.

Women who work outside the home do less work inside the home, and technology is surely one reason why they can. But even women who work for pay put in a lot of time cooking, cleaning, and taking care of the kids: on average about thirty-five hours a week. Their husbands contribute ten minutes more a day to housework than husbands whose wives stay at home.[15]

9
Freedom and Democracy

What caused the American Revolution? This is indeed a rhetorical question that for many years historians have begun chapters with. As well they should. For the American Revolution is without doubt the single most important historical event ever to occur in this nation except of course for Super Bowl III.

DAVE BARRY

These days no one talks about the "grand and impressive" saga of American freedom and democracy. *That* kind of rhetoric is out-of-date! But we still think of our "mighty national development in Political Liberty and Free Civilization" in the overly romantic way Americans always have.* The Mayflower Compact continues to be thought of as the "cornerstone of American democracy." The New England Town Meeting is "a peculiarly democratic institution." John Peter Zenger's acquittal is "a landmark in the history of freedom of the press." The Boston Massacre is the glorious spark of the Revolution. Valley Forge is the winter of "cruel hardships."

---

* "Grand and impressive, beyond all that is written in the Volume of Human History, will be that transcendent Chapter, which shall unfold, in philosophic narrative, the birth and onward march, in greatness and power, of the Republic of the United States,—the completion of its First Century of mighty national development in Political Liberty and Free Civilization, and the momentous relations of that development to the interest, progress, and destiny of mankind." (Quoting R. M. Devens, *Our First Century* [1976], p. 7.)

140

The advantage of associating the birth of democracy with the signing of the Mayflower Compact is that it is easy to do so. The public loves a simple explanation, and none is simpler than the belief that on November 11, 1620—the day the compact was approved—a cornerstone of American democracy was laid. Certainly it makes it easier on schoolchildren. Marking the start of democracy in 1620 relieves students of the responsibility of knowing what happened in the hundred some years before, from the arrival of the *Santa Maria* to the landing of the *Mayflower*.

The compact, to be sure, demonstrated the Englishman's striking capacity for self-government. And in affirming the principle of majority rule, the Pilgrims showed how far they had come from the days when the king's whim was law and nobody dared say otherwise.

But the emphasis on the compact is misplaced. Scholarly research in the last half century indicates that the compact had nothing to do with the development of self-government in America. In truth, the Mayflower Compact was no more a cornerstone of American democracy than the Pilgrim hut was the foundation of American architecture. As Samuel Eliot Morison so emphatically put it, American democracy "was not born in the cabin of the *Mayflower*."

The Pilgrims indeed are miscast as the heroes of American democracy. They spurned democracy and would have been shocked to see themselves held up as its defenders. George Willison, regarded as one of the most careful students of the Pilgrims, states that "the merest glance at the history of Plymouth" shows that they were not democrats.[1]

The mythmakers would have us believe that even if the Pilgrims themselves weren't democratic, the Mayflower Compact itself was. But in fact the compact was expressly designed to curb freedom, not promote it. The Pilgrim governor and historian, William Bradford, from whom we have gotten nearly all of the information there is about the Pilgrims, frankly conceded as much. Bradford wrote that the purpose of the compact was to control renegades aboard the *Mayflower* who were threatening to go their own way when the ship reached land. Because the Pilgrims had decided to settle in an area outside the jurisdiction of their royal patent, some aboard the *Mayflower* had hinted that upon landing they would "use their owne libertie; for none had power to command them." Under the terms of the compact, they couldn't; the compact required all who lived in the colony to "promise all due submission and obedience" to it. * [2]

Furthermore, despite the compact's mention of majority rule, the Pilgrim fathers had no intention of turning over the colony's government to the people. Plymouth was to be ruled by the elite. And the elite wasn't bashful in the least about advancing its claims to superiority. When the Mayflower Compact was signed, the elite signed first. The second group consisted of the "goodmen." At the bottom of the list came four servants' names. No women or children signed.

Whether the compact was or was not actually hostile to the democratic spirit, it was deemed sufficiently hostile that during the Revolution the Tories put it to use as "propaganda for the crown." The monarchists made much of the fact that the Pilgrims had chosen to establish an English-style government that placed power in the hands of a governor, not a cleric, and a governor who owed his allegiance not to the people or to a church but to "our dread Sovereign Lord King James." No one thought it significant that the Pilgrims had adopted the principle of majority rule. Tory historian George Chalmers, in a work published in 1780, claimed the central meaning of the compact was the Pilgrim's recognition of the necessity of royal authority. This may have been not only a convenient argument but a true one. It is at least as plausible as the belief that the compact stood for democracy. [3]

---

* The Pilgrims were supposed to plant their colony at the mouth of the Hudson River, in what was then considered "Northern Virginia." But when they came upon New England they decided at the last minute to stay there, perhaps because it would give them an opportunity to settle in a place not already under the authority of the Church of England. They landed first at Provincetown, then went on to Plymouth—a fact they remember in Provincetown.

In associating the Pilgrims with one type of freedom, that of religion, Americans at least do the Pilgrims the courtesy of remembering them as they would want to be remembered. Religious freedom—or at least the freedom to practice *their* religion—was a Pilgrim cause. Democracy, though, was not.

Pride in the venerable New England Town Meeting is entirely understandable. Nothing else so embodies the democratic ideal. Its usefulness as a symbol of democracy alone makes it powerfully important. Who can resist the thought that life would be better if we the people could just run our own affairs the way they used to in the old-fashioned New England Town Meetings?

A mainstay of the New England mythology is the presumption that at town meetings everybody was allowed to vote.* But the impression that the town meetings of old were free, democratic, and civilized is far too simplistic. In the seventeenth century it wasn't "the people" who ran the town meetings; it was the town selectmen. It was they who levied the taxes, passed the laws, punished the disorderly, and settled disputes between neighbors.†⁴

Historians who study the operation of the town meetings have revealed that the people in the colonial era exercised little control at all over their own affairs. For one thing, meetings were held so infrequently that townsfolk had little opportunity even to monitor their elected representatives. On average two meetings were held a year. When meetings were called, it was the selectmen who set the agenda and they who controlled the discussion. Only rarely did

---

* Everybody, except, of course, women, blacks, Indians, and white men without property, but in the national mythology they don't become worthy of notice until the nineteenth century.

† In early colonial Dedham, Massachusetts, there was a time when the townsfolk—and not the selectmen—actually made all the big decisions at town meetings. Here was the direct, participatory democracy in which Americans, New Englanders especially, take so much pride. A great and noble experiment, it lasted all of three years. By 1639, three years after the town was established, Dedham abandoned participatory democracy. (Kenneth Lockridge, *A New England Town* [1985], p. 80.)

townsfolk challenge the decisions the selectmen made. Historian Kenneth Lockridge found that in the first fifty years of Dedham, Massachusetts' history, the townsfolk never overturned even one of the board of selectmen's substantive decisions. Only once in all that time did they vote a board out of office.

Ultimately in New England power did rest with the townsfolk if they wanted it. But frequently, they didn't. The people were too busy plowing their fields and clearing the forests to bother with government. More importantly, many didn't think they were equipped for governing. In Dedham, people willingly left governing up to those who were well-off, old, and devout. "Year after year for half a century," says Lockridge, "the town selected a wealthy and experienced group of respected friends, took their suggestions, obeyed their bylaws, and left them to run the town without interference." Elections were held annually. But once elected, selectmen tended to be elected over and over again, remaining in office for ten, twenty, even thirty years. Not until a later day did voters begin the honorable practice of "throwing the bums out."

It can be argued that because the selectmen were elected by townspeople, the process was indirectly democratic. It was. The statistics show, for example, that in the 1640s up to 90 percent of the adult males could vote in Dedham in town elections. (Somewhat fewer—maybe 80 percent—could vote in colony-wide elections.) Some historians go so far as to say anybody could vote. All one had to do, says Clifford K. Shipton, was show up, even if one could not meet the legal property qualifications. "So far as one can determine from the colonial record," says Shipton, "the situation in town meeting was then precisely what it is today, when the chairman of the finance committee tries in vain to get the moderator to exclude unqualified persons from voting."[5]

Perhaps, but the suffrage laws must have meant something, and through the seventeenth century, contrary to the expectations of the Believers in the Law of Progress, the suffrage was increasingly restricted. America, along the March of Democracy, marched backward. While upward of 90 percent of adult white males could vote in Massachusetts in the 1630s, by the 1680s, says Lockridge, "a majority of men held no suffrage whatsoever." For by then property qualifications had been dramatically stiffened. Under one law new voters had to possess eighty pounds of taxable estate—four times the requirement in the 1660s. In Dedham only a quarter of the adult males could meet the new property standard.

Whether the seventeenth-century New England town meeting was or was not especially democratic, the impression remains that the towns themselves were incubators of democracy. Out of the towns grew the country that became a "beacon of freedom to all the world." But what did the founders of say, Massachusetts, or Connecticut, really desire? What were they trying to achieve? It wasn't democracy.* What the Puritans wanted was social order.

Like the peasants of old England, the citizens of New England feared social chaos above all else. They were, after all, not far removed, as Lockridge says, "from the baronial feuds which had kept England in turmoil for generations." Layered on top of their English fear of disorder was their Christian faith in love, which reinforced their belief in cohesion. While Puritans believed in the

---

* John Cotton, the Puritan's Puritan, said, "Democracy, I do not conceive that ever God did ordain as a fit government either for church or commonwealth. If the people be governors, who shall be governed? As for monarchy, and aristocracy, they are both of them clearly approved, and directed in scripture . . . as the best form of government in the commonwealth, as well as in the church." (Perry Miller and Thomas Johnson, eds., *The Puritans* [rev. ed., 1963], I: 209–10.)

That by democracy Cotton meant what people do today when they use the term is unlikely. To the Puritans of Cotton's generation there was nothing like representative government, universal suffrage, or tolerance. As the English historian J. R. Pole says, when they used the word democracy they meant the popularly elected element in a government of king, lords, and commons. "When they said that the government was becoming 'too democratical' or 'leaned towards democracy,'" Pole observes, "they meant that the popular element was too weighty for the proper balance of a mixed constitution." (J. R. Pole, "Historians and the Problem of Early American Democracy," *American Historical Review* LXVII [April 1962]: 634.)

individualism of self-reliance, they demanded, as Perry Miller says, "that in society all men, at least all regenerate men, be marshaled into one united array. The lone horseman, the single trapper, the solitary hunter was not a figure of the Puritan frontier; Puritans moved in groups and towns, settled in whole communites, and maintained firm government over all units." As John Cotton remarked, "Society in all sorts of humane affaires is better than Solitariness."

Nothing indeed would have shocked the Puritans more than the reputation their little towns have earned as democratic workshops. Take the question of tolerance, presumably a staple of democratic communities. The Puritans detested the whole notion. The charter drawn up by the founders of Dedham, for instance, explicitly rejected tolerance as an insidious belief. Not only did they limit the number of people who could settle in their area (less than fifty families for 200 square miles); they also expressly excluded anyone who was "contrary minded." Only good, Christian Puritans need apply. When one is building "the good society," as the Puritans were, one cannot afford to let outsiders in to despoil the beauty of oneness. (The original name of Dedham was Contentment.)[6]

If the Puritans weren't democrats, what were they? Historians disagree on this. Lockridge, ambiguously, says he can't think of anything to describe them. To him they were neither democrats nor oligarchs—perhaps something in between. Miller is clearer. The government of Massachusetts, he says, was a "dictatorship, and never pretended to be anything else." Not the dictatorship of a tyrant "but of the holy and regenerate," which could be just as suffocating, if not more so. Little wonder then that Anne Hutchinson and Roger Williams were banished from the colony when they started to take a dissenting line. New England leaders had no appreciation of dissent. When late in the seventeenth century Europeans began to grow more tolerant of others, New England Puritans could not fathom why they would want to. When some in Massachusetts claimed the colony's founders had approved of toleration, Boston clergymen disagreed. Oh no, said Samuel Willard, minister of Boston's Third Church, the Puritan founders were the "professed Enemies" of toleration.

Few actually get the Puritans' attitude toward democracy wrong. Debunkers like H. L. Mencken have seen to it that the Puritans are remembered as autocrats. But those towns of theirs retain their image of innocence, perfection, and democracy—as if, somehow, the towns could be democratic while the people in them were not. The error consists, fundamentally, in the common habit of layering new interpretations of the past on old ones when the old ones need to be jettisoned. Thus, the Mencken attack on the Puritans did not supplant the older, more favorable view; it was simply added to it. Hence, the jumble of contradictory myths held about the Puritans and the towns they created.

A further complicating factor is that the town meetings eventually did become more democratic. It happened in the eighteenth century when the descendants of the Puritans, beset by fights between established towns and breakaway precincts, and one religious faction and another no longer deferred to the power of a single group of wise and old leaders. Out of the conflict came tolerance for diversity and the wider distribution of power. By the early 1700s, townsmen had even taken control of the towns. They set the tax rates, hired the treasurer, and determined the business to be considered at town meetings.

When in Massachusetts the colony tried to frustrate the popular will by imposing convoluted procedures in town meetings, the townsfolk demonstrated a democratic genius for getting around them. To give themselves the right to bring up new business at meetings without having to undergo the laborious filing of appeals in advance to get a place on the agenda, they simply made the last item on every meeting's agenda "new business." Over time they began electing watchdog committees to monitor their selectmen. When they wanted something done, they appointed ad hoc committees to the job. The committees, in turn, were responsible to the town, not to the selectmen. Over time the suffrage was widened to include most everybody (most everybody, that is, who was white, male, and had a little money or property).

Town meetings, even then, did not measure up to romantic stereotype. The more open meetings became, the more they became riddled by faction and roiled in argument. As elections began to be contested, campaigns for office became downright ugly. Controversy replaced peace. And when one group did not get its way, it fought hard—and sometimes duplicitously—to outmaneuver the opposition. When the old guard in Dedham lost control of the selectmen's board in 1704, it declared the election illegal on trumped-up charges relating to the time the election was held. (Not enough notice had been given in advance, they claimed, though they themselves had been in charge of calling the election.) When another election was held and all the proper notices had been given, they lost again, and so arranged to nullify that one as well. A third election was held and (surprise) they lost it, too.

The very tumult of democratic politics was evidence of its vigorous health, but in the mythical New England town meeting everybody was polite. And everybody played fair. And while Americans today put up with extensive disorder in their own politics, they prefer to think colonial politics in New England somehow were "better." *

The misunderstanding may have to do less with history than with democracy. The very idea that democracy is "better" if practiced in an orderly fashion is a delusion. An orderly democracy is,

---

* That democracy was practiced so wildly in colonial days in an overwhelmingly English population is very interesting not only for what it tells about democracy but for what it says about ethnicity. Even the most enlightened Americans take for granted the assumption that democracy is messy in modern America partly because the country is made, like a puzzle, out of so many diverse groups. Perhaps it is so. But the history of New England demonstrates that when power is at stake the Anglo-Saxons in old New England could be just as "wily" and "expedient" as the Boston Irish, the New York Jews, the Chicago Italians, and the blacks in Reconstruction.

one suspects, almost certainly an apathetic one, with real power in the hands of an unchallenged elite. A study of history is the cure for this lame view of democracy, but few seem willing to undertake it. And so the myth proceeds unabated.

Since in the end the New England town meeting finally proved to be as democratic, if not as pacific, as legend would have it, some may conclude the legend remains substantially intact. The trouble is "in the end" the institution did not remain democratic, forever and always, right up until the present. According to one study, by the eve of the Revolution the once vibrant and busy meetinghouses in Massachusetts had become virtually moribund. At a Plymouth town meeting in 1776, only five people showed up. At another in Amesbury in 1783, only seventeen appeared. Brookline became so used to small turnouts that in 1781 the town adopted a rule regarding meetings when fewer than half a dozen voters attended.

That so few turned out may have been due to plain old apathy, which in itself is at odds with the image of a vibrant, boisterous democratic institution. But a more nefarious cause may have been to blame. Attendance at town meetings may have been deliberately kept small to give town elites extra leverage over their community's affairs. If larger meetings had been desired, for instance, meetings could have been held when the weather was warm. But often they were held when it was cold and muddy and snowy, making travel difficult and sometimes impossible. Of course, it may simply have been thought better to hold town meetings in the winter months when they wouldn't interfere with farm chores, but historians suspect the real reason was more insidious.

He who controlled the scheduling of a meeting often controlled the outcome. Some politicians, according to David Syrett, went so far as to hide the occasion of a town meeting to "exclude voters who did not intend to vote as the town officers desired." In 1780 in Sudbury, Massachusetts, for example, politicians in one part of town tried to keep the time of the next general meeting secret from voters in another part. Some politicians, craftier yet, deliberately convened meetings illegally if they knew they were going to lose;

that way they would later be in a position to challenge the vote and possibly win again on a second try. Syrett's conclusion was that the town meeting was "neither better nor worse than the men who controlled it. As such, it was a form of government that was frequently dominated by the minority, and almost always characterized by the willingness of its officials to break or ignore the rules by which they professed to live."[7]

As late as the nineteenth century—if Stamford, Connecticut, is representative—democracy in the town meeting did not flourish. We know about Stamford because Estelle Feinstein has studied it carefully. And she found that town meetings in the Gilded Age were run very much as they had been in the seventeenth century, with an old established elite in control. Between 1868 and 1893, she reported, virtually all of the major matters brought before the Stamford town meetings were initiated by leading businessmen in the community. Of the eleven major intitiatives considered by the town meeting in those years, a clique of industrialists, bankers, merchants, attorneys, and realtors proposed nine of them. When the measures were put to a vote, only a minority of the eligible voters participated. National and state elections drew far more interest. When in 1872 a critical vote was held on whether to consolidate the schools, a matter affecting virtually the entire town, only 455 turned out to vote. (The measure barely passed, 235 to 220.) That same year, by comparison, 1,300 cast ballots in the gubernatorial election.

On the surface, naturally, the Stamford town meeting appeared entirely democratic. Except for the unschooled Irish, who had trouble surviving the state-mandated literacy test imposed expressly to limit their power at the polls, virtually all adult white males could vote. And anybody who wanted to could, theoretically, stand up and speak his mind. But between the theory and the practice, as Estelle Feinstein pointed out, "lay the parliamentary rules of order." And they counted more than all the votes of all the farmers, Irishmen, and clerks put together. As anyone who has ever sat through a formal legislative debate can readily testify, meetings run by the rules can become tedious and complex. In Stamford the lawyers saw to it that the town meetings were both. Each side on an issue was represented by a lawyer, ensuring the ssemblance of a fair debate, but the prominent role played by attorneys at the meetings discouraged others from participating. Thus, what was supposed to be a popular forum became instead an adversarial proceeding between attorneys arguing fine points of law.[8]

The myth of John Peter Zenger is typical in its simplicity. A printer accused of seditious libel in 1735 is acquitted and freedom of the press is established. Snap, just like that! It makes one wonder why other countries seem to have so much trouble with the issue. Maybe we were just lucky.

Maybe. But even after the Revolution freedom of the press was largely a theory, not a right. Remember, it was under John Adams that the sedition act was passed and Americans were thrown in jail for insulting the president. Zenger himself was acquitted only because the jury agreed with his attack on New York's royal governor. His attorney, the flashy and articulate Philadephian Andrew Hamilton, never argued that citizens had the right to criticize the government. Both sides took it for granted that the government had the absolute right to punish citizens who dared to question its policies.

So did the Zenger case matter? Leonard Levy, regarded as one of the soundest authorities in the field of constitutional freedoms, has said it didn't, for in fact we never had a truly free press prior to the Revolution. "No cause," Levy wrote, "was more honored by rhetorical declamation and dishonored in practice than that of freedom of expression" in pre-Revolutionary America.

The startling thing, actually, is how little press freedom there was in colonial American, not how much. In the seventeenth century the New York press was not even permitted to report the votes of legislators without the express permission of the speaker of the house. When two printers published an anonymous article drawing attention to the dismal economic conditions in Orange and Ulster counties, the legislature jailed them for a week. Then they were made to reveal the author of the article. He subsequently was jailed as well. His crime: creating an "irritation."[9]

The Boston Massacre is steeped in myth. For one thing, it wasn't the first violent incident of the Revolution. In 1765 there were riots against the Stamp Act. In 1766 British troops clashed with a group of New York patriots, wounding one of them with a bayonet. In 1768 a Rhode Island man was killed in an argument with a British naval officer. In January 1770 there was a pitched battle between redcoats and patriots in New York. In February an eleven-year-old boy was killed during a patriot attack on the home of a Boston Tory. The Boston Massacre came the next month.[10]

Crispus Attucks, about whom so much was heard in the 1960s, is a far more shadowy figure than is now generally conceded. No one knows if he was a black, an Indian or a mulatto. Nor is it known why he joined in the fray. We don't even know if he was the first to be killed. The familiar Attucks story, in all its glorious details and fine ironies, was wholly the creation of the propagandists of the Revolution.

We do know who started the fight that ended in the deaths of five Americans and the wounding of six others: It was the Americans. Disturbed over a scuffle earlier that day between a British soldier and a ropemaker, the Americans roamed the city that night looking for trouble. At 9 P.M. they found it. Armed with clubs and rocks they laid seige to a British sentry. The idea that the British mowed down a peaceful group of civilians is nothing but propaganda —propaganda rich with purpose but propaganda nonetheless. The real lesson of the day wasn't that the redcoats were ruthless but that a group of soldiers, when pushed far enough by a club-wielding mob, will sometimes fight back. The British mistake, of course, wasn't in fighting back but in firing their weapons. This, however, was apparently done in confusion.

The remarkable thing about the Boston Massacre is that we continue to celebrate the event with pride. Some take comfort from the fact that the redcoats weren't really punished. * But the outcome of the trials in no way attests to the nobility of the jury, the sanctity of the American system of justice, or the highmindedness of John Adams, who defended the redcoats at trial. Hiller Zobel, co-editor of the Legal Papers of John Adams, is of the opinion the proceedings "marked the nadir of law, authority, and justice" in colonial Boston on the eve of the Revolution. Not only did the radicals in Boston scheme to bring on the trials of the soldiers immediately after the incident, the better to exploit the passions of the moment, but they also stooped to physically intimidating the judges in the case. Further, the happy outcome of the Preston trial apparently turned on Adams's successful strategy of packing the jury with British sympathizers. One juror was known to have repeatedly declared prior to the trial that Preston was "as innocent as the Child unborn." Two others subsequently became loyalists and left the country. Another had actually helped Preston with his defense by lining up the witnesses willing to support the officer's version of events. Yet another juror, a baker, was a supplier for a British regiment. As

---

* Captain Thomas Preston and six of his soldiers were acquitted outright. Two others were found guilty of manslaughter, branded on the thumbs, and freed. They escaped more severe punishment through an old English custom known as "benefit of clergy." For most crimes in colonial America one could avoid the death penalty simply by reading a verse of the Bible. Originally the concession was given only to clergymen, who were tried in special ecclesiastical courts, where the punishment was lighter than in secular courts. Later it was extended to lay people. By the time of the Revolution even illiterates were permitted to invoke it, apparently in an attempt to leaven justice with mercy. The custom applied in all but the most heinous of crimes and was frequently used. Arthur M. Schlesinger found that in New York alone it was "invoked no fewer than seventy-three times between 1750 and 1775." Most of the states dispensed with the custom after the Revolution, but South Carolina refused to give it up until 1869. The brand on the thumb was intended to prevent offenders from claiming the privilege twice. (Schlesinger, *The Birth of the Nation* [1981], pp. 109–10; Lawrence M. Friedman, *A History of American Law* [1973], pp. 61–62.)

Zobel observes, if justice was so prized in the community, why then was it apparently "necessary to go to such extraordinary non-legal lengths to ensure it"? [11]

More disturbing was the manner in which Adams succeeded in winning over the jurors. He did it not by appealing to their sense of fair play but by exploiting their prejudices against blacks, foreigners, and the poor. In giving his summation Adams told the jurors it was time to stop avoiding the ugly truth about the colonists who had provoked the soldiers. "Some have called them shavers," he remarked sarcastically; "some call them geniuses. The plain English is, gentlemen, [they are] a motley rabble of saucy boys. Negroes and mulattoes, Irish teagues and outlandish jack tars. And why should we scruple to call such a set of people a mob? I cannot conceive, unless the name is too respectable for them."

That Adams agreed to represent the redcoats is often used in his defense. Here, it is thought, is clearly the case of a man putting conscience above politics. But the claim that, in representing the British, Adams put his popularity in jeopardy is somewhat exaggerated. However unpopular the defendants may have been, Adams seems to have suffered little for his decision to take their case. Shortly after he agreed to do so he ran for the Boston General Court and won, handily. Certainly Adams was taking a risk, and all can feel for him given the immense pressure he must have faced. He himself greatly feared that his action would deprive him of a meaningful role in the resistance to Parliament. But even his loyal biographer Page Smith acknowleges that Adams's fears were largely unfounded. [12]

The Boston Tea Party is another widely misunderstood event in our early history. In the hallowed story told in grade school, average citizens, irritated at Parliament's latest scheme to levy an onerous tax without their approval, tossed some chests of British tea overboard from a ship anchored in Boston Harbor. It is all very stirring stuff. The colonists even dressed up as Indians and called themselves Mohawks. Adding to the romance is the mysterious code of silence taken by the participants. To this day no one knows how many people joined the conspiracy, or who actually showed up the night the tea was dumped.

In fact, much of the traditional account of the Boston Tea Party is wildly misleading. Consider the business about taxes. It is said the colonists feared the effect of British taxes on the economy. But in reality, the Tea Act *reduced* the duty on British tea imported to America. It was this reduction that caused the controversy. Historians say the cut in duty made British tea suddenly competitive with the tea smuggled into the colonies from Holland by American merchants like John Hancock. It was this—the prospect of cheap British tea, not higher taxes—that precipitated the Boston Tea Party. American smugglers wanted to save the lucrative American tea market for themselves. (Three-fourths of the tea sold in America was smuggled in.)

It may be thought that surely some principle was at stake here. And it was. It was the oldest principle in history: self-preservation. Parliament had passed the Tea Act in order to give an advantage in the American market to the British East India Company, which was going bankrupt. The smugglers thought it unfair that their economic fortunes should be determined by a government thousands of miles away whose chief interest was protecting somebody else's business.

None of this, of course, is ever explained to Americans. That the Boston Tea Party was organized to save America's smugglers from economic ruin is rather too dreary a truth to find general acceptance. Certainly no one ever mentions the role of the smugglers in organizing the Boston Tea Party. All we ever hear about are people like Sam Adams. But without the smugglers—and the businessmen allied to them—Sam Adams never would have had a revolution. Indeed, throughout the Revolutionary period it was the gentry that led the opposition to Parliament, for it was the gentry that stood to lose the most from Parliamentary interference in colonial affairs. The small tax increases Parliament passed had little impact on the average American. Average Americans paid fewer taxes than their British counterparts. But British regulation of colonial commerce could ruin the gentry. It was they who suffered from the "long train of abuses and usurpations" that ended in the call for independence. * [13]

Despite the success of the Boston Tea Party, it is worth noting that it wasn't universally sanctioned—even by patriots. George Washington worried it would lead to British retaliation. Benjamin Franklin suggested the colonists ought to reimburse the East India Company for the lost tea. Indeed, it is remarkable that the incident ever became an accepted part of American mythology. What other crime of property destruction in American lore—and it was a crime —has been celebrated like the Boston Tea Party? One would have thought there are enough patriotic events in the Revolution to pick from that this one could have been forgotten. It may be too easy to suggest that the celebration of the Boston Tea Party shows that Americans are less concerned with the rights of property than is usually imagined. Perhaps Americans just can't resist a good romantic drama. Here, after all, is history as myth in all its sentimental glory. The tale of the Greeks and the Trojan Horse is hardly any better.

Worth noting in passing is the slogan that surfaces in almost any discussion of the Revolution: "Taxation without representation is tyranny." This, it's believed, is what the Revolution was all about. Actually, the slogan rings hollow. The fact is most Americans went unrepresented in the legislatures at home, let alone in Parliament. In Virginia, only 6 percent of the adult whites owned enough land to be entitled to vote. In Massachusetts, only 16 percent did—and

---

* Knowing this, some assert that the people were duped into supporting the gentry's cause. Perhaps, it's suggested, the colonists would have been better off letting Parliament have its way. At the least they would have gotten cheaper tea! But the colonists sensed that the smugglers' struggle for independence was their own. This isn't really very mysterious. At bottom it was just plain old nationalism—the same nationalism that leads Americans today to resist foreign inroads on American industry. Besides, to enlist popular support the gentry had to frame their appeal in egalitarian terms. This inevitably had consequences of its own, enhancing the power of the people.

only a fourth of those actually exercised the right. In Philadelphia, 2 percent could vote. Not until the nineteenth century was the suffrage widened, and a majority of adult white males enfranchised.

Nor did the colonists really want representation in Parliament. Though they frequently complained that they did, it wouldn't have done them much good if they had gotten it, and they knew it. Outnumbered by the English, they almost certainly would have found themselves outvoted on almost any issue of vital importance. Surely the biggest mistake the British ever made was to deny the colonies a voice in Parliament. Giving in on this particular demand would have robbed the Americans of one of the key propaganda themes of the Revolution. But of course the British couldn't. Better to lose a substantial part of the empire than make room in Westminster for a few country cousins. [14]

Valley Forge is surrounded in myth. We are told that the soldiers there nearly froze and starved to death, that this was the hardest winter the army suffered in the Revolution, and that the men were so naked they left their bloody red footprints in the white snow. Washington, it is recalled, warned Congress that if help weren't provided to relieve the awful deprivation the army would "dissolve or disperse."

The seriousness of the soldiers' plight, however, is exaggerated. Studies by the National Park Service, performed by a team of archaeologists and historians in the 1970s, show that nobody starved or froze and that morale was high. Consider the availability of food. The researchers found that in December, January, and February, the 10,000-man army was supplied each month with a million pounds of flour and a million pounds of meat and fish. Broken down, that means each soldier was allotted more than three pounds of flour and more than three pounds of fish or meat per day. Of course, the availability of food didn't offset the fear of the soldiers that they might starve, a very real fear indeed given the army's inadequate lines of supply. But most of the time the soldiers seem to have kept their fears in check. And only once, during the last two weeks in February, was the supply of food seriously interrupted. The belief that they went "naked" stems from a misunderstanding of the eighteenth-century use of the term. "Naked" then meant going without *proper* clothing, not going without any clothing.

Barbara MacDonald Powell, considered one of the leading experts on Valley Forge, says the shortages of food and clothing at the camp "were not much worse than during other periods of the war, and none of the privations suffered were any more severe than those of preceding or succeeding winters." Indeed, Powell is of the opinion that the dread winter of all time for the army was the one spent at Morristown, New Jersey, from 1779 to 1780. Morristown guidebooks sardonically note today: "We suffered more."

The impression that things were worse at Valley Forge than they actually were was the responsibility of George Washington, who in his own crafty way overplayed the adversity at the camp to obtain more aid from Congress and to fend off criticism from officials who thought the army should spend the winter on the march. The mistake Americans have made is in taking Washington at his word —as if the general of the American army really couldn't tell a lie. It's forgotten that Washington was shrewd and not above orchestrating a little propaganda now and then. Not for nothing did Washington show up in a general's uniform when the continental congress was deciding who should lead the U.S. army. He knew it helped to look the part. Only the naive think of Washington as the simple soul who chopped down the cherry tree.[15]

Other myths about American freedom and democracy concern the abolitionists, Charles Sumner, the frontier, and the election process. The conventional image of the abolitionist, the sworn enemy of slavery who, driven by a stern conscience, eagerly sacrificed his own comfort to improve the fortunes of others, is consistent with the image the abolitionists had of themselves. Most textbooks continue to perpetuate it. But one wonders: Is motivation in such a great struggle so simply determined?

All the world loves a hero, and the abolitionists are surely worthy of emulation and commendation if anyone is. But it is naive to think that they were such simpletons as they have been made out to be. Sincere as they undoubtedly were, sincerity doesn't begin to explain why they, of all the Americans born up until then, alone devoted their lives to the extermination of slavery. Were they morally superior to the Americans who came earlier? Purer? More enlightened? More public-spirited?

Upon investigation, one discovers that the abolitionists may have joined the movement as much for their own good as for the good of the slaves. Professor David Donald of Harvard says the abolitionists appeared to have been on a "double crusade." In addition to seeking the freedom of blacks, they were also attempting to reclaim the dominant position of their social class. After examining the backgrounds of 250 of the country's leading abolitionists, Donald found that virtually all belonged to an old New England rural elite that stood in danger of being eclipsed by the rising generation of urban go-getters who suddenly appeared in the 1820s and 1830s. In abolitionism they would have the chance to reassert their role as social leaders, wresting from the new urban elites control of the nation's political agenda.[16]

Donald, of course, may be mistaken in his assessment, and plenty of historians think he is. Some think he places too much of an emphasis on the loss of the abolitionists' social status. But he surely is right in suggesting that something more than sincerity accounted for the abolitionists' involvement in the antislavery cause. Only an incurable romantic could think otherwise.

Whatever their motives, the abolitionists' success is overrated. The heyday of abolitionism was in the 1830s. By the 1850s, the movement was largely in hibernation. It had little to do with the secession of the South or the coming of the Civil War. What sparked southern rage was the movement to limit slavery to the places where it already existed. Almost no one in a prominent position seriously considered abolishing it outright. When Lincoln finally issued the Emancipation Proclamation, it wasn't in response to the demands of the abolitionists but in reaction to the war. To save the union, Lincoln realized, he had to kill slavery. Then and only then did Lincoln agree that slavery had to be abolished.

Those discouraged by Lincoln's refusal to adopt abolitionism may be comforted by the knowledge that many other Americans did. But not too comforted. Abolitionism only won support among Americans in the 1830s when they began to realize that slavery posed a threat to *their* own liberties. Few cared about the liberty of blacks. The single biggest factor in the growth of abolitionism was not the exposés of the dreadful conditions under which slaves lived, shocking as these were. It was the attempt by southerners in Congress in the 1830s to prevent the consideration of antislavery petitions on the floor of the House of Representatives. Now, white liberty was subject to the "gag rule" of slave masters. This was intolerable.[17]

The ordeal of the abolitionists cannot be recalled without thinking of Charles Sumner, the Massachusetts senator who was clubbed over the head with a cane by a slaveowner on the floor of the U.S. Senate in 1856. The incident has become one of the set pieces of Civil War mythology. Even the textbooks pause long enough in their hurried chronicle of events to mention it, if only to cherish the irony inherent in the situation: that the attack followed a speech by Sumner on the "barbarism of slavery." What could be more perfect?

It has been found, however, that the harm done to Sumner has been overestimated. Almost all accounts mention that the attack was so severe that Sumner was nearly incapacitated by it and that for the three years following he couldn't resume his senatorial duties. But the chief difficulty seems to have been psychological, not physical. David Donald, in the course of a Pulitzer prize–winning biography of Sumner, reports that modern neurologists can find nothing in the senator's medical record to justify his continuing absence from the Senate. Their conclusion is that though his symptoms were real they were, in effect, of his own making. This in no way diminishes the significance of the attack or his ordeal, but it robs the story of some of its heroic dimensions.[18]

Of all of the factors said to contribute to American democracy, none is considered more decisive than the frontier. The seed of democracy planted by the Pilgrims may flower in the New England Town Meeting. But it's on the frontier that the March of Democracy begins and individualism flourishes.

Alas, the frontier era of democracy is no longer idealized quite so much as it once was. Historians today are almost all agreed that democracy did not (as alleged) come "out of the forest." Thus, it is no longer considered significant that women won the right to vote in Wyoming two generations before they did nationally. The scholars now seem more impressed with the fact that New Jersey gave women the right to vote even earlier, in 1790. True, more people could legally vote out West than in the East through much of the nineteenth century, but that's only because it was easier out West to meet the property qualifications. Thomas A. Bailey, himself a westerner, states that "on balance" the West borrowed more democratic concepts from the East than the East did from the West.[19]

As for the belief that the frontier encouraged individualism, the less said the better. The truth may be too disconcerting. It seems that most people traveled west in groups. To survive, they perforce remained together. It was the rare soul who pulled up stakes back East to face the frontier alone.

More surprising to the average American may be the fact that the West did not act as a safety valve for eastern discontent. People might be willing to accept the notion that democracy did not develop exclusively on the frontier, but they'd be reluctant to give up the idea that people back East fled west to find greater opportunities.

The argument, however, is backward. The movement of discontented Americans was from the farm to the city, not the other way around. For every one urban dweller who packed up his belongings and moved west, twenty farmers moved east. Most of the huge increase in urban population between the Civil War and World War I was due to the migration of rural folk to the metropolis. Thus, it was the city that served as the safety valve for discontent.

The mistake is in thinking that it would have been an easy matter for the urban dweller to pick up and move west. Nothing could be more untrue. The American in the mid-nineteenth century who chose to abandon the East for a nice farm out west had to have money in the bank. Historians estimate it cost the typical family $1,000 to avail itself of the opportunity to buy a vacant spread and build a farm from scratch. The Homestead Act, much ballyhooed, barely changed the equation. Clarence Danhof reports that "the fact that the land was free did not change circumstances materially." An underpaid workman, of course, could have traveled west to find work if he so chose, but why he would want to do so is a mystery. Wages on the farm were lower than in the city and the problem of seasonal layoffs was worse. Nor would he be tempted to travel west in the event of bad times back east. When the East was depressed, so was the West. * Indeed, it's been determined that the migration west was greatest during times of prosperity.[20]

Those who fret that the loss of the old safety-valve theory seriously undermines the traditional explanation of American democracy may also want to remember that it also undermines the idea that our democracy is possibly headed for self-destruction. Some

---

* The successful migration of an eastern worker to the West was rare. Stephan Thernstrom, after reading through thirty years of newspapers covering Newburyport, Massachusetts, reports finding only a single instance (between 1850 and 1880) in which a local laborer moved west and made it. It was one Michael Welch, "who had been the treasurer of one of Newburyport's volunteer fire companies; when he left for the frontier he took the treasury with him!" Welch wrote home to his parents that he was doing so well he would soon be able to repay the money he'd stolen. (Thernstrom, "The Dimensions of Occupational Mobility," in An Interdisciplinary Approach to American History, eds. Ari Hoogenboom and Olive Hoogenboom [1973], p. 69.)

have feared, as Charles Beard commented half a century ago, "If the free land did it all, then we are busted when the free land goes." *

The election of 1876, all agree, was unfortunate. Republican Rutherford B. Hayes won office after a special commission with a Republican majority conveniently awarded him all of the disputed electoral votes cast by three states (though his opponent had won a quarter million more popular votes). But *that* was an isolated case! Through most of American history, it's believed, Americans have held honest elections.

Actually, though, the belief that American elections have been conducted fairly and honestly and with a minimum of manipulation is not entirely true. Upon reflection, it will be recalled that several of the most important elections in American history were tainted by fraud and won through artifice. In 1840, William Henry Harrison was elected by falsely passing himself off as a poor boy who had made good (though he actually had been born on a plantation). In 1960, John Kennedy won thousands of apparently stolen votes in Illinois (though historians say he probably would have been elected even without them).

But these elections are well-known and worth mentioning merely in passing. More interesting are the little-known contests in the eighteenth and nineteenth centuries involving lesser offices. These often were won by the candidate who dispensed the most alcohol. It was the custom then for local candidates to treat voters to free drinks. Those who didn't, didn't get elected.

---

* When did the frontier end? Frederick Jackson Turner, the great historian of the West, said it ended in 1890, and most historians have agreed with him. The source of Jackson's information, whether they know it or not, is the census of 1890, however. And that census is now under attack. Gerald Nash, an acknowledged statistician, is of the opinion that the 1890 census was so flawed as to be unreliable. It was compiled by amateurs, presided over by a Republican Party hack, and generated so much controversy as to provoke a government investigation. (Gerald Nash, "Where's the West?" *The Historian* [November 1986], pp. 5–7.)

Consider George Washington's run for a seat in the Virginia House of Burgesses in 1758. Already a famous soldier by then, he had plenty of friends and important connections. But historians say what determined the outcome of the race was alcohol: 144 gallons of rum, beer, wine, and punch. "My only fear," he confessed, was that his agent, in a desire to save Washingtoan some money, had spent "with too sparing a hand." Washington had reason to worry. Everyone agreed a lack of spirits had cost him victory in a previous election. This time around, however, he won easily, obtaining 307 votes: 2 gallons for every vote gotten.[21]

Taking pride in our elections is clearly justifiable—certainly in light of how other countries run theirs. But it is not now and never has been the pristine process commonly imagined. In numerous elections someone, either at the behest of the candidate himself or on his behalf, tries something underhanded. The interesting thing about the recent revelations involving the U.S. Senate election of 1948, for example, in which Lyndon Johnson won by 87 votes, was not that Johnson got stolen votes but that, in fact, both candidates had.

10
Saints and Scalawags

There were giants in the earth in those days.
GENESIS 6:4

If sometimes it seems that leaders today are less heroic than those in the past, it is because many *are* less heroic. We have never had fewer heroes. Even the giants of baseball have proved disappointing. One opens the paper each morning half in wonder and half in fright to see who will be exposed next as a gambler, a philanderer, or a cheat.

One notes, however, that one reason heroes may seem in such short supply nowadays is because we can read all about them in the paper. The more one knows about a person the less a hero that person seems. About the leaders of the past, in contrast, we often know next to nothing. To take just two examples, consider the cases of Ethan Allen and John Brown. If people knew as much about them as they do about Gary Hart or Pete Rose, they wouldn't be heroes either.

Allen is a national hero, exalted for his daring assault on Fort Ticonderoga and his bravery in battle. A furniture store chain is even named after him. But he may be the most improbable hero in American history. He was a crafty land speculator. He secretly negotiated with the British during the Revolution to take Vermont out of the war in exchange for a huge tract of virgin forest. And in the 1770s, with the help of roving bands of mounted Green Mountain Boys, he launched a campaign of terror to prevent New York from taking possession of land he claimed as his own in an area in dispute between New York and New Hampshire. Before he was through he burned down several homes, destroyed a few mills, and set up a kangaroo court in which he condemned colonial officials to punishment by whipping. Of all this, though, the average American knows nothing.[1]

John Brown is remembered, no doubt, the way he would liked to have been remembered. People recall that he sided with the slaves, was killed by southerners, and died a martyr. Louisa Alcott called him "Saint John the Just." Emerson opined that Brown's hanging would "make the gallows glorious like the cross." Few realize what he was really like. He was a complete failure in business. He welshed on his debts. He almost certainly was insane. And in 1856 he nearly plunged Kansas into civil war by ruthlessly murdering five helpless members of a mildly proslavery family, in the process "splitting open heads and chopping off arms and fingers," as Dixon Wecter reminds us. Yet people remain ignorant of these facts.[2]

If it is true that some heroes have been overrated, it is also true that some villains, in a nicely compensating way, have been underrated. Pirates weren't unmitigatingly evil. Chief Justice Roger Taney, author of the Dred Scott decision, wasn't a vicious racist. Tammany Hall's Boss Tweed didn't singlehandedly loot New York City of millions. General George Custer did not die for your sins. Lizzie Borden, the "ax murderer," did not commit murder. William Jennings Bryan, the "reactionary" laughingstock of the Scopes Monkey Trial, was not a reactionary.

Among the scalawags who least deserve consignment in the popular imagination to the nether world is the "fiendish" pirate. Recent research indicates that the pirate's reputation as a terrorist is largely unmerited. Usually pirates didn't terrorize innocents; they just robbed them. Most pirates became pirates to escape cruelty, not to inflict it. Thus, when a ship was captured its captain usually was executed only if he was known to have treated his men badly. "To pirates," as Marcus Rediker says in his study of eighteenth-century mariners, "revenge was justice; punishment was meted out to barbarous captains, as befitted the captains' crimes." Captain William Snelgrave recalled that when his ship was taken in an incident in 1719 the pirates told him he "was safe provided none of (his) People complained against [him]." None did and Snelgrave was spared.

Nor, incidentally, did they usually make their victims "walk the plank." That seems to be the melodramatic creation of their enemies. In fact, they commonly seem to have disposed of their victims simply by throwing them overboard.

Nor were they totally uncivilized. It may indeed be the case that pirates behaved in a more civilized fashion than many of their maritime counterparts. To provide help for the poor and the lame, they established a formal welfare system funded from the ship's booty. To aid fellow pirates injured in accidents they paid out benefits like an insurance company, compensating sailors who lost an eye in a storm or a leg in battle. To prevent the arbitrary rule common aboard regular ships, they limited the powers of the captain and chief officers, and required that all major decisions be approved by the crew in a majority vote. When a despotic captain tried to lord it over his crew as was the custom in the merchant marine, chances are he'd be deposed. According to Rediker, "even the boldest captain dared not challenge" the crew's will. The only time the captain aboard a pirate ship was given the power to make decisions unilaterally, in Daniel Defoe's pungent phrase, was "in fighting, chasing, or being chased."

The average pirate also lived better than other sailors. He had more to eat and more time to sleep. And everybody earned about the same pay as everybody else.[3]

Few Supreme Court justices have been misquoted as often—and with such devastating consequences to their reputation—as Roger B. Taney, who wrote the majority opinion in the infamous Dred

Scott case. His statement that the Negro had no rights that a "white man was bound to respect" is usually quoted as shocking evidence of Taney's depravity and of the insidious effect of slavery on the thinking of white southerners like Taney, who grew up on a Maryland plantation. In his own day as in ours it had been used to demonstrate the antebellum southerner's fundamentally uncaring attitude toward blacks. Ken Burns, in his 1990 PBS documentary on the Civil War, refers to the Taney quotation to show just how deeply slavery had corrupted the South and how important it was that slavery be abolished, even if abolition could only be achieved after a brutal and bloody civil war.

But to be fair, Taney never said he believed that the white man need not respect the rights of blacks. What he said was that's what the "public" believed at the time of the Declaration of Independence. In fact, he was mistaken, since many of the founders agreed blacks had rights. But his failure was in misunderstanding history. He was not, as often charged, a "malevolent old man who had prostituted himself before diabolical slavery interests." If anything, Taney deserves to be remembered as one of the South's most enlightened citizens. He considered slavery (in his words) "a blot on our national character," and thirty years before Dred Scott, freed his own slaves, whom he had inherited from his parents. His biographers tell us he generally held liberal views in politics and remind us he was appointed to the Supreme Court by Andrew Jackson. When the South seceded, Taney, unlike many fellow southerners, remained with the union.[4]

New York City corruption under Boss William Tweed reached such an astonishing level that he is always likely to be remembered as the most corrupt politician in American history. From his day to ours his Tammany Hall organization has epitomized Gilded Age greed and graft. Textbooks recount his many crimes: how he accumulated a fortune in the millions while working on the public payroll; how he "joyfully" bilked the taxpayers out of $11 million for a county courthouse that should have cost a third as much; how he approved the purchase of so many chairs for the courthouse that if they were placed side by side in a single line "they would have extended seventeen miles"; how he used taxpayer funds to pay a friend $3 million for plastering the building; and so on.

Certainly few politicians have ever looked the part of the criminal as well as Boss Tweed. With his "ugly features, small beady eyes, huge banana-like nose, vulturish expression and bloated body," he personified fraud and malfeasance. If he hadn't existed, as one historian put it, they would have had to invent him. Rome had its vandals; England its King John; New York its Boss Tweed.

Worse, his critics are thought to have been especially virtuous, which made Tweed's vices particularly obvious and irksome. Never was a criminal politician done in, in the popular view, by a more solid, well-meaning, and good-hearted bunch than Tweed's. Arrayed against him was the *New York Times, Harper's Weekly,* and *Harper's* famous cartoonist, Thomas Nast, whose drawings are said to have been so devastatingly accurate that when Tweed fled to Spain after a jail escape he was identified and captured on the basis of one of Nast's cartoons.

It is all so perfect—too perfect. To begin with, though he was repeatedly indicted for fraud, Tweed was never convicted of it. Leo Hershkowitz, professor of history at Queens College and the author of a book about Tweed, has concluded there was "no direct evidence of Tweed's thievery." This isn't the same as saying Tweed was innocent; for we know at one point his bank account contained nearly a million dollars in cash, and that city contractors admitted paying him off. But if he was so blatantly guilty of fraud, it's surprising he was never convicted of it. All he was ever convicted of was "failing to audit claims against the city"—a misdemeanor. He was never even tried on the charge of fraud, apparently because prosecutors feared they couldn't make fraud charges stick.

Guilty or innocent, his trial was a sham. Several jurors, before they were seated, admitted they thought Tweed was guilty but were picked anyway over the objections of the defense. Evidence was withheld from Tweed's lawyers, including the list of witnesses who appeared against him before the grand jury. The judge in the case was friends with the prosecutors and in an incredible midnight switch decided to treat each of the 220 counts of the single misdemeanor charge filed against Tweed as separate crimes, each punishable by up to a year in jail. (An appeals court later overturned the judge's decision, ruling Tweed could only be sentenced to a single year in jail.)

If Boss Tweed was unjustly treated by the courts—as is now the consensus—he has also been unjustly regarded as only a political boss. In fact, he was a man of substance and in his long career as a congressman, state senator, and commissioner of public works he initiated innumerable worthwhile reforms. Among other things he is credited with improving the welfare system, opening the schools to Catholics, establishing public baths, preserving a place in Central Park for the Metropolitan Museum of Art, and most important of all, securing home-rule for New York City, whose authority had been shackled by the barons of the state legislature.

It is painful in defending Tweed to have to attack the great Nast, but we must. For Nast, despite his greatness, was flawed. Like many Americans, he was a bigot. He detested Tweed because Tweed (though not Irish himself) headed the party of the "drunken-ignorant Irish" and Nast hated the Irish. Not by accident did the Irish always look like monkeys in Nast's drawings; he thought they were as stupid as monkeys and often said so. Like many reformers from the old elite, Nast felt threatened by the Irish and wanted to dethrone them. Getting Tweed was one way to do it.

The story of Tweed's capture on the basis of a Nast drawing is so delightful and so detailed that it seems it must be true. We are even told which drawing led to his identification: a cartoon in which Tweed is seen holding two young street urchins who are supposed to represent "Tweed-le-dee" and "Tilden-dum" *; behind them a sign reads "IT TAKES A THIEF OR ONE WHO HAS ASSOCIATED WITH THIEVES TO CATCH A THIEF." Be-

---

* "Tilden-dum" is a reference to Samuel Tilden who, like Tweed, was a Democrat.

cause of the drawing the Spanish are supposed to have believed Tweed was guilty of "kidnapping two American children." "To the Spanish officer, [who made the arrest and] who did not read English," one of Nast's friends later explained, the urchins looked like "two children being forcibly abducted by the big man of the stripes and club." (Nast had dressed Tweed in prison garb and given him a menacing club.) "The printing on the dead wall [behind Tweed] they judged to be the story of his crime." Absurd? Well, yes, it was. But "absurd as it all was, the identification was flawless."

Or so we were led to believe. Actually, Tweed had been identified by a low-level American counsel in Cuba a short time before he fled to Spain. His arrest in Spain was arranged by American authorities. "The outlandish legend of his being recognized from a Nast cartoon by some simple Spaniard," says Hershkowitz, "is a complete fiction." * 5

George Armstrong Custer, once the beneficiary of excessive praise, is now the target of excessive abuse. His very name has come to stand for all the awful crimes ever committed by whites against Indians. Best-sellers proclaim, "Custer Died for Your Sins." The movies charge, "Custer had it coming." Some hint he was mad; in the 1970 hit movie, *Little Big Man*, he insanely reels around the Little Bighorn battlefield shouting incoherent insults at the Indians closing in around him.

It is all rather a dismal end for the dashing blond-haired "Boy General" who became a hero in the Civil War at the tender age of twenty-three and who was revered in his own lifetime as a great frontiersman. Few heroes have sunk so low so fast. Even Richard Nixon gets better press now.

His true crime, however, apparently is not that he won so many Indian battles but that he lost one. A lot of other Americans won

---

* Many have been taken in by the Nast legend, including the author of this book. See my *One-Night Stands with American History* (1980), pp. 138–39. It is not as much fun refuting a myth I myself have had a hand in spreading, but far better for me to point out the mistake than someone else.

many more Indian battles and killed far more Indians than Custer ever did, but nobody remembers them. Who's ever heard of Nelson Miles? Of George Crook? Of Ranald S. Mackenzie? Between them they routed the Sioux, defeated the Apaches, and broke up several other tribes, breaking the Indians' hold on the plains and in the Southwest. But they are forgotten. It is poor, miserable George Custer, the one Indian fighter to go down to ignominious defeat at the hands of the Indians, and who in going down took with him more than 200 other white men, who is made to bear the guilt of genocide. If he'd won, almost certainly no one would pick on him.

If Custer's misfortune is to be remembered as a devilish killer, it is also his misfortune to be remembered as a bungler. Almost everybody thinks he acted foolishly, out of either egotism or self-glory, or both, in attacking a bigger Indian force than he could handle at the Little Bighorn. Certainly he was outnumbered. To his 600 men, there were 8,000 Indians, 2,000 of whom were fighters. With these kinds of odds, we are told, disaster was inevitable. If only Custer had waited a day for reinforcements, he would have had his attack and victory, too, even though he would have had to share the glory with another commander.

All this, however, may be as misguided as Custer's attack is said to have been. Robert Utley, considered the most knowledgeable expert on the battle, is of the opinion that "given what he knew at each decision point and what he had every reason to expect of his subordinates, one is hard pressed to say what he ought to have done differently. In truth, at the Little Bighorn 'Custer's Luck' simply ran out." Utley dismisses criticism that Custer was outnumbered; experience had taught Custer that he could beat any Indian force of any size. As for the complaint that Custer should have waited for reinforcements, Utley says, he couldn't afford to—or didn't think he could. Custer (mistakenly) thought he'd been spotted by the Indians and worried that if he waited they would disperse; in every other Indian battle Custer had ever been in the thing to be concerned with was the Indians dispersing. Like Washington in the

Revolution, the tribes survived by withdrawing. How was Custer to know that this time they would decide to take a stand and fight?

Interestingly, the assumption is that Custer should have won. But why? Were the Indians so inferior as fighters that any white man should always have been able to prevail against them? On the plains the Indian often was in a superior position to the white man and was certainly brave enough to beat him. It is ethnocentrism, plain and simple, to think the Indians couldn't.

Defeat, in any case, perhaps was avoidable. Utley says if Custer's two chief subordinates had behaved better—one dawdled, the other cut and ran—the attack might have worked. The Indian fighter who took Custer's place—Nelson Miles—succeeded eventually in routing the tribes using the same approach Custer had, staging surprise attacks on big tribal forces with light and mobile ones.[6]

Nothing said in her defense is ever likely to exonerate Lizzie Borden of the charge of murder leveled against her: "Lizzie Borden took an ax/And gave her mother forty whacks; /When she saw what she had done/She gave her father forty-one." But it may be worth pointing out that although she was arrested for murder, she was subsequently acquitted of the charge. Her only "crime" was refusing to talk to the press about the tragedy, which, of course, only increased the public's suspicion of her.

Two credible books have been written about the incident. One concludes she did it, the other she didn't. The chief evidence implicating her in the crime was that she was in the house at the time it took place. But then, so was the maid. Perhaps the maid did it. That may sound suspiciously like the tired murder-mystery writer's handiest refuge: "the butler did it." But she may have. That, at least, is the conclusion reached by the author of the book that clears Lizzie.[7]

William Jennings Bryan's vigorous defense of Fundmentalism in the Scopes Monkey Trial has left the impression that he had repudiated progressivism, betraying both his ideals and his supporters. Movies about the trial have made the one-time liberal hero look like a bigoted conservative villain, ill-informed and "hopelessly outdated." It's so astonishing a change as to almost seem surreal, rather as if Hubert Humphrey had become a Republican or Edward Kennedy a Reaganite. If it is excusable at all, one supposes, it was only because by the time of the trial he was old and ill.

It is true that at the trial Bryan was sick; he died within days. But there's no evidence he'd become senile and no reason to think he'd abandoned his progressive politics merely because he'd recently adopted biblical literalism. In Bryan's mind they were perfectly compatible, and if we think they weren't, that's our problem, not his. He remained politically liberal to his last days. In the 1920s he supported the League of Nations, a minimum wage law, the abolition of monopolies, aid to farmers, and federal insurance for bank depositors. To Calvin Coolidge's chagrin, Bryan continued to see himself as a watchdog for the common man. When Coolidge nominated a railroad executive to help run the Interstate Commerce Commission, Bryan publicly objected that the man could not possibly "sympathize with railroad patrons."

Certainly his adoption of the cause of Fundamentalism put Bryan in the company of some fairly conservative people, and between the liberals and the conservatives in the Fundamentalist movement, he gravitated to the conservatives. But to his way of thinking, promoting Fundamentalism was promoting reform. "There has not been a reform for twenty-five years that I did not support," he recalled in 1923, but "I am now engaged in the biggest reform of my life. I am trying to save the Christian Church from those who are trying to destroy her faith."[8]

Few villians from history are as well known and as passionately hated as Tokyo Rose. She is commonly ranked among the worst of World War II's criminals. Reporters, allowed in to visit Japan after the surrender, engaged in a competitive frenzy to see who was going to be the first to find and interview two people: General Hideki Tojo, who planned the attack on Pearl Harbor, and Tokyo Rose, the siren broadcaster with the velvet voice who demoralized the troops with suggestions that their girlfriends back home were cheating on them. Like Benedict Arnold, she's considered one of the most devious traitors of American history.

Millions swear they heard her voice. Soldiers returning home from the Pacific front told how they listened to her nightly broadcasts on Radio Tokyo. In the summer of 1949 the U.S. government tried and convicted her of treason. The night before she was scheduled to be released from prison in 1956 reporters hid in a nearby farmhouse all night so they could catch a glimpse of her as she emerged. In 1977, the day before his term expired, President Gerald Ford gave her a pardon.

Given all this, and given the fact that the government itself officially confirmed on numerous occasions that Tokyo Rose existed, it would seem almost impossible to deny she did. But deny it people have, including the late Edwin O. Reischauer, the famous Harvard scholar, considered one of the most well-informed experts on Japanese society. Even the federal government itself has held that she did not exist. In August 1945, in a report publicized in the *New York Times,* the U.S. Office of War Information announced "There is no Tokyo Rose; the name is strictly a G.I. invention. . . . Government monitors listening in twenty-four hours a day have never heard the word 'Tokyo Rose' over a Japanese-controlled Far Eastern Radio."

The woman accused of being Tokyo Rose was actually, say Reischauer, "a helpless and hapless young Japanese American girl, Iva Toguri, who had been stranded by the war in Japan." She indeed broadcast on Radio Tokyo during the war, but she was made to by the Japanese because she spoke good English. She never denounced her U.S. citizenship. She didn't have a sweet, seductive voice. (Her biographer says she actually sounded like Gracie Allen, of Burns and Allen.) And she never said anything to demoralize the troops. The broadcasts in which she was involved, in fact, were slyly orchestrated by an Australian POW to comfort the troops. The Japanese never caught on.

The key witnesses who testified against her during her trial for treason and who claimed that she had broadcast propaganda, subsequently admitted they had lied. "We had no choice," said one of the witnesses, a Japanese businessman. "U.S. Occupation police came and told me I had no choice but to testify against Iva, or else." When he and the other witnesses were flown from Japan to San Francisco for the trial, "We were told what to say and what not to say for two hours every morning for a month before the trial started." The judge in the trial privately indicated while the case was still being heard that he thought she was guilty and was shocked that his son—a veteran who had been stationed in the Pacific— felt no animosity toward her. They "just laughed" about her, he reportedly commented. "I can't understand it." In his instructions to the jury he excluded virtually all of the arguments Toguri's lawyers had raised in her defense. The jury foreman afterward said, "If it had been possible under the judge's instructions" to acquit her, the jury would have.

The question of whether there really was a Tokyo Rose was supposedly settled in 1945 by the reporters who were after an interview with her. They told the world that Iva Toguri had admitted she was Tokyo Rose. They had a contract with her to prove it. The contract says she is "the one and original 'Tokyo Rose.' " But she apparently signed the contract only because she'd been promised $2,000 to do so, which in war-ravaged Japan was quite a sum. In fact, when the reporters first asked if she was Tokyo Rose, she had told them she was merely one of a half-dozen or so English-speaking women who broadcast on Radio Tokyo. If the name applied to all of them, she said, it applied to her, too. But she had no idea that Tokyo Rose was considered a traitor and certainly would not have admitted to being one.

That she never should have signed that contract is obvious. But it was equally obvious to the officials who investigated her that she wasn't Tokyo Rose and that she hadn't committed treason. And they said so. * But by then the media had so sensationalized the

* "Considerable investigation [wrote Assistant Attorney General Theron L. Caudle, in 1948, in a letter to the attorney general] has been conducted in

story that reporters and broadcasters found it hard to back down from it. The leading sensationalist was Walter Winchell. When he began using his radio pulpit to proclaim her guilt, the Truman administration, worried about appearing soft on traitors, and worrying too about the 1948 election, decided to indict her. Thus began what Reischauer calls "a postwar disgrace to American justice."

Interestingly, while Tokyo Rose remains one of America's great villains, almost no one remembers Axis Sally (Mildred Gillars), the Maine native who broadcast for the Germans, though she really existed and she clearly did commit treason. "Damn Roosevelt! Damn Churchill! Damn all the Jews who have made this war possible!" she blared during one of her broadcasts. "I love America, but I do not love Roosevelt and all his kike boyfriends." Why Axis Sally should be forgotten and Tokyo Rose remembered is anybody's guess. Both were brought back to the United States to stand trial at the same time and both were convicted. But Axis Sally was white and Tokyo Rose was Asian. That surely had something to do with it.[9]

Of all the wicked groups that have robbed, cheated, and murdered their way through American history none is considered more wicked than the Mafia. The very name carries blood-curdling connotations. But how much of what's said about the Mafia is accurate?

---

this case and it appears that the identification of Toguri as 'Tokyo Rose' is erroneous, or, at least, that her activity consisted of nothing more than the announcing of music selections. . . . A few recording cylinders of her broadcasts and a large number of her scripts were located, and they, as well as the transcripts of the only two broadcasts of her program which were monitored by the Federal Communications Commission, do not disclose that she did anything more than introduce musical records. . . .

"It is my opinion that Toguri's activities, particularly in view of the innocuous nature of her broadcasts, are not sufficient to warrant her prosecution for treason." (Quoted in Masayo Duus, *Tokyo Rose: Orphan of the Pacific* [1979], p. 104.)

It is not now and never has been a single, monolithic organization. The links between the Mafia groups in different cities have always been weak. Even to speak of "the Mafia" is a mistake. There are many Mafias. Mafia chieftains in New York have little to do with Mafia chieftains in Chicago. They don't even use the same name to describe themselves. The New York Mafia refers to itself as "La Cosa Nostra"; the Chicago Mafia calls itself "The Outfit."

It is probably because of the Kefauver hearings in the early 1950s that most people think of the Mafia as a single, threatening entity. But the experts are of the opinion that Senator Kefauver "merely assumed its existence. He did not prove it." Just because mobsters from different cities occasionally get together, says Professor Joseph Albini, doesn't mean they necessarily belong to the same organization. "When several executives from different corporations meet to discuss mutual problems or mutual concerns [he asks] does this mean that they constitute an organization? Why is it, then, that when syndicated criminals from various syndicates in the country hold a meeting that almost without question, they are viewed as belonging to some form of secret national crime organization?"

Innocent citizens are no better off because "the Mafia" is in actuality a collection of criminal groups rather than a single one, of course, and in fact they may be worse off. One suspects mobsters are more effective because their organizations are run locally. Fearsome as a centrally driven syndicate of crime might be—one imagines scenes like the one in Goldfinger where a board of seedy characters meets around a big table to consider knocking off Fort Knox—it almost certainly would be more inefficient than the present system and easier to undermine. Part of the difficulty the police have had in infiltrating "the Mafia" is that they have had to infiltrate it in every city in which it operates. Because different cities' Mafias act independently, convictions won against any one group seem to have little effect on the others.

Fearful as the image of "the mob" is as a kind of criminal octopus, as one writer imaginatively put it, it is a secondary fear. "The mob" really inspires fear because mobsters are violent. They are always killing people. Think of "the Mafia" and you think of dead bodies found in the trunks of cars, "cement boots," "rub-outs," tommy-guns, restaurant assassinations, and all the other lurid images that make up the popular stereotype. But the fact is that the innocent citizen has almost never had to fear mob violence. The chief victims of mob violence are other mobsters. As Benjamin "Bugsey" Siegel observed, only somewhat inaccurately, "We only kill each other."

Fear and hatred of mobsters is certainly justifiable; though "the Mafia" is now said to be in decline (*New York Times* front-page headline, October 22, 1990: "A Battered and Ailing Mafia Is Losing Its Grip on America"), in the past Mafia mobsters have been responsible for a major proportion of the crimes committed in at least a dozen cities, from New York to New Orleans. And in certain places, such as New York, "the Mafia" remains powerful. But much of the furor over "the Mafia" stems from the belief that it is an Italian import. Probably a majority of Americans believe that if it weren't for the Italians—particularly the Sicilians—we wouldn't have organized crime in this country.

It's true the Italians dominate "the Mafia," but the fact is there was organized crime in America before "the Mafia" appeared and it's likely organized crime will continue to exist in this country if "the Mafia" disappears. In San Francisco in the 1840s there was the Hounds gang. In New York in the 1860s there was the Hell's Kitchen Gang. Cincinnati in the 1870s had syndicates of gamblers. Chicago, from 1872 to 1907, had Mike McDonald, a gambling kingpin known as the "Boss of Chicago."

A further objection to the argument that the Italians are to blame for organized crime in America is that it emphasizes the behavior of the criminal over that of the user of criminal services. The fact must be faced, however, that there is organized crime in America because people want what organized crime delivers: illicit goods and services. Say what you will about "the Mafia," mobsters did not create the demand for things like gambling dens and whorehouses. They have merely supplied the demand. But to admit that, of course, is to admit that *we* are to blame for organized crime and it is far pleasanter to think that *they* are to blame.

(It is worth noting, in this connection, that it would be a simple matter to get rid of organized crime if we wanted to. All we would need to do is make legal all of the illegal services that mobsters provide. That would not only eliminate—by definition—the "crimes," say of prostitution and gambling, but also the necessity of making the invidious payoffs that mobsters make to police and politicians, payoffs that corrupt the system. Organized crime only appeared in the United States when the big cities in the middle of the nineteenth century began establishing police departments. Before there were police departments there was no one to pay off. This removed an essential ingredient in the recipe for syndicated crime.)

That Italians in general and Sicilians in particular came to dominate organized crime is held to be a reflection on their native culture. It is thought that Italians imported to America criminal behavior they had perfected at home. But did they? Humbert S. Nelli, in his *The Business of Crime*, says that "most" of the men who joined Mafia gangs in the United States "had not belonged to *mafia* groups in the homeland." Nor is there any evidence that they had been engaged in any criminal behavior back home. When an Italian joined organized crime in the United States it was not because as an Italian he had an affinity for crime but because as an American he wanted to be a success. Like some of the Irish before them, some Italians resorted to crime as a means of social improvement. "In doing so," says Nelli, "they adjusted to the materialistic nature of American society, which preached honesty, virtue, and hard work, but placed major value on possession of money and power, with little concern evinced as to how that money and power were acquired."

We know that the Mafia existed in Sicily, but it was unlike our Mafia and could not have been transplanted to America. For the organizaion was embedded in the legitimate society and performed both legal and illegal services. The mafiosi were originally henchmen who had been employed by landowners for protection against marauding gangs and unruly serfs. But eventually the mafiosi them-selves became the landlords; using the tactics of violence they had employed against the serfs, they forced the landlords to sell off their property at rigged auctions attended solely by the mafiosi. As the new lords of the manor, the mafiosi established a patron-client relationship with the peasants, both protecting and exploiting them. Experts disagree about the details of the relationship, but it is clear that Sicily's mafiosi behaved far differently from the mafiosi in America and served a far different function.

There was an Italian organization that closely parallels the American Mafia: the *Camorra*, a secret Neapolitan society that operated exclusively outside the law. But the experts agree there's no evidence it was ever transferred to the United States.[10]

11
History

History cannot be discussed in this country without someone observing how little attention is paid to it here. It is the concern of pundits nationwide. But how much truth is there to the charge that Americans are "uninterested" in the past and what exactly is meant by it? Do the critics mean Americans hardly think about history or that they don't know much about it, which is quite different?

The evidence is there, if the critics would only look for it, that Americans do think about history. There are more books on Lincoln than on anybody but Jesus. And curious as Americans are about the future, it is the past that sells; any car buff knows that. A twenty-five-year-old Ford Mustang fetches a higher price than a ten-year-old model and a forty-year-old Hudson brings even more. Americans dote on the founding fathers and treat the Revolution, as Dave Barry has observed, with almost as much reverence as the Super Bowl. Though old Victorian buildings are torn down at an alarming rate, robbing cities of much of their nineteenth-century charm, the buildings that take their place are often designed to look just like the original ones. It's not that Americans don't like old things but they want them to appear the way they did when they were new. The fascination with things old, admittedly, often has more to do with the devotion to nostalgia than with the love of history. But say what you will about nostalgia, the feeling behind it is the same feeling behind much of formal history: the desire to put current events in some kind of perspective. The more things change, the more nostaglic people become.

All this doesn't mean Americans are in love with history. But neither can it be said, in light of these things, that they are indifferent to it. One hears all the time, of course, that "history is bunk." But the phrase is not meant to be taken seriously. Even Henry Ford, to whom the phrase is attributed (falsely), held strong views about the past. His objection was not to history per se; ahead of his time he held the belief that *social* history is eminently worthwhile. What he disliked was the history that emphasizes, to the exclusion of all else, the comings and goings of kings and presidents.[1]

No manner of argument, of course, can change the fact that Americans are grossly ignorant about history, Henry Ford especially. Asked once who Benedict Arnold was, Henry Ford guessed it was the name of one of his factory foremen. A recent test showed that two-thirds of American high school students don't know when the Civil War occurred. A third don't know when Pearl Harbor was bombed or the year Columbus landed. College seniors, when tested, do better but not much better. Nearly half don't know that Joseph Stalin ran the Soviet Union during World War II. Nearly two-thirds are unaware that the "shot heard round the world" was the shot fired at Concord at the opening of the Revolution. And Columbus's voyage still mystifies; by graduation a quarter remain unable to tell when he arrived.[2]

But incredible as these omissions in historical knowledge are, they are no more incredible than the omissions revealed by tests in other subjects. The fact must be faced that American students don't seem to know much about anything. This always seems to come as a shock, but then, most of their parents can't even name their own congressman.

And if people don't know much about history, it may not be

because they don't care for history but because they have simply never received much training in it. The very same professors who deplore the absence of historical knowledge in the electorate forget that few people were ever exposed to it in the first place. The problem is not with the students; it's with the schools. Since the 1920s, the schools have taught social studies. History has largely been considered a dead subject and has been taught, if at all, in connection mainly with civics. Grade-school students, who used to learn to read by reading stories about American heroes and history, now read stories about Dick and Jane.* [3]

A poll of students at a hundred schools nationwide showed that out of twenty-one subjects history was regarded as the most irrelevant. But given the dry way in which most history texts are written, who can blame them? When history is presented well, as it was in the 1990 PBS documentary on the Civil War produced by Ken Burns, interest soars. [4]

The great danger is not that Americans may make too little of history but that they will make too much of it. In politics, dubious policies have a far easier chance of winning public acceptance when they are defended on historical grounds. Support for the decision to go into Vietnam, for instance, was considerably strengthened when it was explained that fighting communism in Asia was analagous to fighting Nazism in Europe.

The problem, then, is not that Americans ignore history but that they misinterpret it. They do not know enough history to know that they need to know more. Some place too much faith in historical analogies. Others underestimate the role of accidents in history, as if everything in history is inevitable. And almost everybody thinks history is "predictable" and that "history repeats itself." The

---

* To a certain extent, John Dewey—and his disciples—are to blame for the abandonment of history as a subject worthy of independent study. It was Dewey who persuaded teachers to eliminate the formal teaching of history from public school. "The past is the past," he advised, "and the dead should be safely left to bury the dead." (John P. Diggins, *The Lost Soul of American Politics* [1984], p. 162.)

sophisticated insist history is governed by universal laws, like the law that "all civilizations rise and fall." All believe that "those who forget the past are condemned to repeat it." From time to time it becomes popular to say "History will judge."

The Munich analogy is not as popular now as it once was, but it remains a festering source of misinformation. There can be little doubt that Neville Chamberlain made a foolish and disastrous mistake in trying to appease Hitler at Munich, a mistake that was subsequently paid for in lost lives and plundered treasuries. But all Munich teaches is that it is a mistake to appease a dictator like Hitler in a place like Germany suffering from bad times. Applying it generally, as Lyndon Johnson did in Vietnam and as Ronald Reagan did in Nicaragua, is folly.

The Munich analogy may of course be credited with keeping American leaders alert to the danger of appeasement. But it has also had the frightening effect of freezing debate on the subject of aggression in such a way that policymakers may be leery of ever appeasing any dictator. And sometimes appeasement is just what's needed. The same president who believed it was wrong to appease Germany's Hitler believed it was right to appease Spain's Francisco Franco. And during the war years that is precisely what Franklin Roosevelt did, on the sensible assumption that it is sometimes better to appease a dictator than to fight him.[5]

Munich, in any case, is oversimplified. The thing worth emphasizing is not that appeasement led to war but that most people at the time thought it wouldn't. History is usually an exercise in irony —"how men's actions produce results other than those they intended"—and Munich is an excellent example of this. It is *that* people should remember.[6]

Even with hindsight it is not clear how the democracies should have responded to German, Italian, and Japanese aggression in the thirties. Some have argued that World War II wouldn't have happened if the democracies had acted earlier in the decade when Japan took over Manchuria, Italy invaded Ethiopia, and Hitler occupied the Rhineland. But as Bernard Weisberger has pointed out, "You can't know that for sure, or know what unintended consequences might have flowed from *those* decisions." It's possible decisive action earlier could have led to a Communist takeover in Germany or Italy, and a Great Power takeover in China.

And if taking decisive action would have been wise in the thirties, it need not always be so. It was decisive action in 1914 that led directly to World War I. After the Sarajevo assassination, Austria decided it had to punish Serbia. Russia decided it had to punish Austria. Germany decided it had to stand by Austria. France decided it had to stand by Russia. "And so," as Weinberger says, "everybody marched in lockstep to disaster."[7]

Vietnam did a lot to discredit the Munich analogy, but did nothing to improve the care with which historical analogies are employed. The very same people who pointed out the folly of using the Munich analogy to justify our intervention in Vietnam subsequently (mis)used the Vietnam analogy to defend a policy of nonintervention in other places. This led in the 1980s to the interesting War of Analogies over Nicaragua, Reagan insisting Nicaragua was "another Munich," his critics warning it might become "another Vietnam." Intervening in Nicaragua may of course have proved disastrous, but if it did, it would have done so in its own awful way. Vietnam was a separate case. All Vietnam proved, as one historian put it, only somewhat facetiously, was that America should never again "take on the job of trying to defeat a nationalist anticolonial movement under indigenous Communist control in former French Indochina."[8]

Historical analogies will hardly diminish merely because they have been shown to be fallacious. Every generation feels compelled to discover a new one based on its own experience as if the only history worth remembering is one's own. The generation that lived through Munich sees universal lessons in Munich. The Vietnam generation sees them in Vietnam. And so on and so on, in an unending and utterly arbitrary and unedifying process.

Nothing so captures people's imagination as the role of accidents in history, as attested by the popularity of the phrase, "For the want of a nail . . . ." But accidents in history are regarded as rare, which accounts in part for their fascination. Most of what happens, it is firmly thought, happens because it "had to." History, it is said, is inevitable.

In favor of the belief is simplicity, which no doubt partly explains its appeal. The world prefers simplicity and religion and science lead us to think simplicity in these matters is entirely sensible. Religion, though it's no longer the force it once was in the world, has left us with the strong conviction that things happen for a reason. Science leads us to believe that everything is explainable and that things happen in a rational manner.

Actually, though, religion and science mislead. Consider the effect Touissant L'Ouverture had on American history. Though few can identify him—or have ever even heard of him—he is responsible for Napoleon's decision to sell the Louisiana Purchase to the United States. But for L'Ouverture they all might be talking French in New Orleans. L'Ouverture started a slaves' revolt in Haiti, which in turn ended Haiti's role as an important economic anchor for the French empire, which in turn convinced Napoleon it was useless to hang on to the Louisiana territory—which, in sum, suggests our getting the Louisiana Purchase wasn't as inevitable as it's made out to be.[9]

Consider the War of 1812. Scholars report that the United States and Great Britain probably never would have gone to war but for the unexpected death of British Foreign Secretary Charles Fox. Fox, all agree, seemed well on the way to meeting the American demand for commercial freedom on the high seas. His replacement, however, took a hostile line, ending hope of a quick settlement of the conflict. In the end, the British backed down and repealed the much hated "Orders in Council," which had been used to seize American ships found trading with France. But the Congress didn't know it and two days later declared war. Had Parliament acted just a few weeks earlier, war probably would have been averted.[10]

In domestic politics there is the tantalizing possibility that U. S.

Grant might have ushered in a New Deal–style public works project three generations before Franklin Roosevelt did. The only thing that seems to have stopped him was the opposition of two advisers. What if . . . ?[11]

Actually, no sound basis exists for believing history is inevitable, predictable, or subject to universal laws. For history does not repeat itself. By definition every historical event is different fundamentally from every other. To quote from the polymath Bergen Evans, "The elements in any historical situation are always different: climates alter, empires dissolve, religions fade and merge, and new knowledge, new techniques, and new sources of power change the old equation. The world of steam and electricity is not the world of the slave and the water wheel. The airplane and the wireless have shrunk the globe and obliterated terra incognita. The control of infectious diseases has removed some of the most powerful forces that formerly shaped men's destinies. Nuclear fission has introduced 'riddles of death Thebes never knew.' Things cannot be the same again."[12]

There is less fascination with universal laws now than formerly, but it is still widely held that "all civilizations rise and fall," thanks no doubt to the continuing influence of Arnold Toynbee, one of those authors nobody reads but everybody cites. The assumption behind the idea, however, is that civilizations live and die like organisms. This is an understandable assumption and people as far back as the Greeks have made it. But it is nothing more than an analogy and as such it is utterly unprovable. Nothing supports the claim that societies are like organisms. It's pure supposition to think they are.[13]

The belief that "those who forget the past are condemned to repeat it" is misleading. The hard part is not remembering to consult history but figuring out how to interpret it. The confusion, as C. Vann Woodward has said, stems from the impression that history is "a record and historians are the keepers." In fact, the record is what historians make of it. Much as we may like to think historians merely compile "the facts," their choice of the facts is entirely subjective. Questions of bias intrude on history as they do in life. And no one can claim to be entirely impartial. It is no more possible to determine truth in history than it is to settle the question of who's right or wrong in a contentious divorce. A case can usually be made for either side (or, more usually, an equally damning case can be made *against* either side). Wisdom, however, lies in finding the little bit of truth in both. * [14]

It may be that the greater danger sometimes is not forgetting the past but remembering it. Professor Anne Scott has recalled how during World War II she foolishly underestimated Hitler's responsibility for the conflict because of books she had read about World War I. Rather than blame Hitler for the war, she blamed Georges Clemenceau and David Lloyd George, the European leaders who had masterminded the vengeful peace arranged at Versailles. [15]

No doubt, one is usually better off knowing history than not knowing it, but it's not as good a guide to current events as is thought. Not a historian in America, for example, predicted the liberation of eastern Europe in 1989. Some, indeed, had the misfortune of predicting it could not happen. The very year the Poles threw off Soviet despotism Professor William McNeill published an essay in which he said it was unlikely they could or would do it anytime in the foreseeable future. He explained that while the Poles hated the Soviets, they feared the Germans more and relied on the Red Army to protect them. His essay was titled "How History Helps Us to Understand Current Events." [16]

The belief that "history will judge" is held by millions, but is especially popular with failed politicians like Richard Nixon, and for understandable reasons. To those who have lost their reputations, it is reassuring to think that someday something known as

---

* Carl Becker, considered one of the deans of American history, wrote: "To establish the facts is always in order, and is indeed the first duty of the historian; but to suppose that the facts, once established in all their fullness, will 'speak for themselves' is an illusion." (Becker, *Everyman His Own Historian* [1966], p. 249.)

History will restore them. Actually, History doesn't judge; historians do. And while it's certainly possible historians in the future will, say, be less repulsed by Nixon's lies than people are today, they may be more repulsed. How they judge him will depend on *their* own feelings about lying (and, perhaps, on whether one of *their* presidents tells outrageous lies to them).

There are, of course, undeniable advantages in judging a man after he's dead. With distance comes perspective. But the belief that the judgments of the future are definitive is chimerical. There is no such thing as a "definitive" history. History isn't written in cement. Every generation rewrites history to its own tastes. No judgment stands forever. In several important cases, historians have come round to the view that the initial interpretation of an event was more accurate than those that subsequently replaced it. [17]

Consider the fascinating changes that have occurred in the interpretations of the Civil War. Immediately after the war it was regarded (in the North) as a fight over slavery. A little later it came to be seen as a fight between different cultures in which slavery played just a part. By the 1920s slavery hardly counted at all. Not until the 1950s did historians again return to the idea that slavery was central. [18]

Even the American Revolution has been subject to varying interpretations. Only the layman is under the illusion it has always been considered as it is today, a fight for freedom. At the start of the century, for instance, today's viewpoint would have been regarded as intolerably naive. Surely, it was reasoned, people did not bloody themselves in eight years of war merely to advance the highfalutin cause of liberty. Something more nitty-gritty must have been at stake: money, power, special interests. These are the "hard realities" behind the inflated rhetoric—or so it was thought. [19]

Even if it were possible for a historian to write a definitive interpretation of an event, the problem of how to think about the event would hardly be solved. For we have to interpret the interpretation, which is less easy than it seems. To this day Marx is remembered for saying, among other things, that the only thing that counts in history is economics. But Marx didn't say that. It was the opinion of Professor Allan Nevins, who was known for his conservatism, that Marx never excluded "noneconomic factors as contributing causes of events." Marx, Nevins conceded, "clearly perceived that society is molded by spirit and thought as well as material environment, and did not believe that history could be explained by a monistic materialism." Marx himself complained that he had been misunderstood. Near the end of his life he confessed that given the way Marxism had been construed, *he* was not a Marxist.[20]

Sometimes it is unclear even to the historians who have done the writing what they have written. Virtually every college student who reads Richard Hofstadter's seminal book[*] on the Populists, for instance, comes away thinking Hofstadter believes the source of their revolt was a loss of social status. It is safe to say that there is not a historian in the country who hasn't thought the exact same thing. Yet it has now been established from his private papers that Hofstadter himself thought the Populists revolted for economic reasons. When a fellow scholar, David Potter, listed the passages that pointed to the status interpretation, Hofstadter admitted Potter had "read the book with possibly more care on this point than I wrote it!" "I meant to offer," he added, "a straight economic interpretation of the origins of Populism, and I thought then as I do now that while there is an element of status concern in most social conflicts, it was not really very important in Populism."[21]

The average person might think that in general a historian can be trusted to know what he wrote. But there is enough ambiguity in history to guarantee confusion. History isn't clear. Indeed, if things seem clear it is often only because they are grossly oversimplified and misunderstood. No doubt the average person finds this frustrating. What people want from history is answers!

[*] *The Age of Reform,* first published in 1955.

12
So Many Myths

I love the story of Paul Revere,
whether he rode or not.
WARREN HARDING, 1923

In 1928 Herbert R. Mayes contributed to the fun and frolic of the Roaring Twenties with the publication of a whimsical and gossipy biography of Horatio Alger, Jr. The inside cover featured a silly map with a compass showing "up" for north and "down" for south. People in the book behaved like characters out of one of Alger's own Victorian rags-to-riches novels, always "bearing up bravely" in the face of adversity. Descriptions were humorous; Alger's father was said to have a mouth "that opened wide to let tiny words emerge, like a big gate opening for a poodle to trot through." And on almost every page there was adventure and tragedy. Alger's decision to adopt a Chinese boy ends when the child runs in front of a runaway horse and is killed. When Alger goes to sign up with the Union army during the Civil War, he breaks his arm. When he tries to sign up again, there is another mishap; the train he takes happens to stall and is hit by the train behind it. "From this Alger did not escape. Again he was hurt—again he broke his arm."

The gossip included the "revelation" that the moralistic Alger was a depraved sexual fanatic. On a trip to Paris he has an affair with a singing floozy. A trip across the United States is interrupted in Cincinnati (of all places), for a ménage à trois with two sisters. And so on and so on.

As Mayes eventually confessed, the biography was a "complete fabrication, with virtually no scintilla of basis in fact. Any word of truth in it got in unwittingly. I made it up out of nothing. Most of the few facts I uncovered were intentionally distorted." But it quickly was adopted by the nation's critics as definitive and for forty years remained a standard reference work. The *New Republic*'s Malcolm Cowley praised the book "as better than the average." Historian Allan Nevins, one-time president of the American Historical Association, commended the author for his collection of facts. Over the years the "facts" made their way into innumerable monographs and even formed the basis for a psychohistorian's analysis of Alger's oedipal complex. The august *Harvard Guide to American History* included the book in its list of reliable biographies. Subsequent Alger biographers, including the chairman of the Department of Journalism at New York University, freely borrowed from Mayes's book in writing their own.

Nothing seemed to undermine the book's credibility, not even the fact that critics couldn't locate the diary on which it purportedly was based. Not until Mayes himself confessed in the 1970s that it had been a hoax did the book finally come to be seen as a hoax. (And by then, ironically, it had become clear that Alger's sex life was in fact even more shocking than that portrayed in the biography. As revealed in an earlier chapter, he liked to have sex with young boys. But Mayes had been unaware of that.) [1]

Reviewing the Alger story, it begins to seem less astonishing that myths and lies flourish. Given the ease with which people can be fooled, the astonishing thing is that there are not more myths and lies. It has been said that there is a sucker born every minute. That, however, would appear an underestimation. Almost everybody plays the sucker sometime.

We may bemoan the frequency with which we are taken in by apocryphal stories, but there can be little doubt that we like them.

If we didn't, there wouldn't be so many. We are all suckers for the well-told tale, whether it is true or not. Countless persons—among them rank scoundrels—owe their elevation to the national pantheon because of their ability to spin a good yarn. Consider the trio Ethan Allen, Davy Crockett, and Joshua Barney. Allen and Crockett are esteemed national heroes, models for youth, paragons of virtue. Joshua Barney, on the other hand, is unknown; his only recognition consists of a small bust at the naval academy and a street named after him in Newport, Rhode Island. Yet among the three, only Barney is the genuine article.

Allen swindled land out of his neighbors in Vermont, and cavorted with the British during the Revolution; when he was captured he not only refused to try to escape but he prevented others from doing so, at one point stopping the captain of a privateer from taking over a lightly defended British ship. Crockett was a juvenile delinquent, wife-deserter, and braggart; after winning two terms to Congress from Tennessee, he lost a third and promptly left the state in disgrace. Though he was known as a crack shot, when he went west, in historian Horace Beck's vivid description, he "totally missed the target in a shooting match, then missed a buffalo, got himself lost, then lost his horse, was clawed by a cougar and captured by the Comanche." In short, "he acted very much as any Eastern greenhorn [would] in similar circumstances." At the Alamo he bravely stuck with William Travis, refusing to cross the famous line, but in the end he surrendered.

Barney was born with good looks and in two wars—the Revolution and the War of 1812—played the hero's role in twenty-some battles. At the outset of the Revolution, over the course of a month and a half, he helped capture three British ships, two of them virtually singlehandedly. Toward the end of the war, though commanding an inferior ship, he took on and defeated a British vessel in what has been described as the single "most outstanding" naval victory of the Revolution. During the battle he exposed himself to gunfire, his hat was shot off, and his uniform was "riddled with bullets." In the War of 1812 he delayed the British attack on Washington by six hours by seizing five naval guns with a commanding view of the British forces and firing ceaselessly. After other American troops had fled, the little force under his command continued firing, Barney atop a horse giving the orders. Several times in his career he was captured by British forces and escaped, once after dressing in a British officer's uniform. But despite his brilliant deployments and gallant actions, Barney remains unknown, whereas Allen and Crockett are heroes. More than anything, what seems to account for the difference in their reputations is that Allen and Crockett knew how to tell their own stories and Barney did not.[2]

The public takes special delight in stories that hint of a premonition, even if it takes the suppressison of essential details to put the stories across. Take the famous spooky dream Lincoln had just a few days before his assassination. In the dream, Lincoln told friends, he had been awakened in the White House by the aching cries of grieving mourners. Upon investigating, he discovered that the sounds were coming from the East Room. "There I met with a sickening surprise. Before me was a catafalque, on which rested a corpse wrapped in funeral vestments. Around it were stationed soldiers who were acting as guards; and there was a throng of people, some gazing mournfully upon the corpse, whose face was covered, others weeping pitifully. 'Who is dead in the White House?' I demanded of one of the soldiers. 'The President' was his answer; 'he was killed by an assassin.' "

As might be expected, when the story came out it took on mythical proportions, as it seemed Lincoln had somehow had a premonition of his own impending doom. But Lincoln never said it was he who was in the coffin; indeed, as the story was originally told in published form, Lincoln expressly denied it was he who had been killed. "In this dream," the president was quoted as saying, "it was not me, but some other fellow, that was killed. It seems that this ghostly assassin tried his hand on someone else." But of course people weren't satisfied with it being someone else in the coffin. It had to be Lincoln who was there. And so, in the popular imagination, it was. * [3]

Sentimentalism is another great source of error. Because we always want the good guys to win, we pretend they always do. But it's the powerful who usually win, whether they are good or bad. As the English historian A. J. P. Taylor has pointed out, the Romans didn't beat the Greeks because they were more civilized but because they "possessed a more efficient fighting machine. When Europeans established their authority throughout the world in the nineteenth century this was not because they were more civilised. It was because, in Hilaire Belloc's words: 'We have the Maxim gun, and they have not.' " Similarly, in this country, the North didn't triumph over the South in the Civil War because northerners were morally purer or because Abe Lincoln was a good man and Jefferson Davis was a bad one. The North won because it possessed more money and men. [4]

Worship of ancestors is an old and venerable custom with Americans as with other peoples. If it takes a little makeup to have our ancestors appear the way we like them to, so be it. Colonial Williamsburg discovered a few years ago, it does no good to try to be realistic. When the Williamsburg corporation began letting the paint chip on the village's reconstructed buildings, giving the place more of the run-down appearance it undoubtedly had in its heyday, visitors complained. Williamsburg, in consequence, resumed painting the buildings on a more regular basis. [5]

Of all our myths, we like best those that make us—and our nation—look best. As a nation we love collective self-flattery. All of the really famous myths—Plymouth Rock, the Liberty Bell,

---

* It is thought that historians can be relied on to keep matters straight, but even they are susceptible to the powerful appeal of myths. When historian and newspaperman Lloyd Lewis wrote about the Lincoln dream in a book designed to dispel myths about Lincoln, he told only the familiar half of the story, leaving out the part about it being someone else who got killed. (Lewis, *Myths After Lincoln* [1941], pp. 295–96.)

Washington and the cherry tree—tell us something pleasing about ourselves. Plymouth Rock celebrates the national commitment to religious freedom. The Liberty Bell reminds us of our Declaration of Independence. The cherry tree story shows how greatly we value truth.[6]

Those taken in by myths often assume they are the victims of a nefarious plot and in earnest go searching for the villain who has conspired to deceive them. This is understandable. For sometimes there are villains: self-promoting politicians, self-elected patriotic polemicists, filiopietists, and the like. If the Daughters of the American Revolution seem to have slipped into quiet obscurity of late as the makers of pseudohistory, other groups have stepped in with alacrity to take their place. Of these perhaps none has been as successful as the Iroquois. In the late eighties an Iroquois delegation persuaded New York State to teach students that the U.S. Constitution was influenced by the Iroquois, though of course there is no evidence of such influence.[7]

But almost always those who search for villains do so in vain. Most of our major nationalistic myths were manufactured by nineteenth-century poets and writers, who clearly were guilty of manipulating history (in C. Vann Woodward's choice phrase) to "sanctify the past," but who do not deserve to be remembered as villains. Following the Revolution, they simply reached the conclusion that it was no longer appropriate for American children to grow up on the myths of Great Britain. American children should have their own! With the help of the poets and writers, they would.[8]

For some myths we have no one to blame but ourselves. Thus, the better known an event is, the more pathetically confused people are about it, in part because their historical knowledge consists almost entirely of an arbitrary collection of generalizations made at different times and under widely different circumstances. Each generalization, standing on its own, may be plausible, if not entirely convincing. But taken together, the generalizations often amount to little more than a potpourri of nonsense. Victory in the American Revolution, for instance, is popularly attributed to the heroism of the minuteman and the inevitability of freedom. But these are two distinct interpretations. The first, that the Revolution was won by heroism, was offered immediately after the war by writers eager to celebrate it as a patriotic event that the British could well have won—if Americans hadn't worked so hard and so courageously to defeat them. The second, that the Revolution was inevitable, came a generation later, when Americans were concerned with proving that freedom (in the words of George Bancroft) "grew naturally and necessarily out of the series of past events" ordained in "the grand design of Providence." Quite clearly, it is inconsistent to hold both views (the Revolution cannot be both a near-miss and inevitable), but people do because (1) they haven't given the matter much thought, and (2) both views seem patriotic, and thus not manifestly in conflict. People, as a rule, do not supplant a new interpretation of an event with an old one; they simply adopt both.[9]

Sometimes, of course, the reason the truth is not told is that few know it. The story that Eli Whitney invented the cotton gin was disproven in a 1965 article by Daniel Thomas that was published in the *Journal of Southern History*. But how many historians read it? So many monographs appear each year that no historian can keep up with all of them. A few years ago the president of the Organization of American Historians, fed up with the widespread dissemination of misinformation, suggested his colleagues set up a computer network to keep track of it. But nobody has followed up on the suggestion.

That we have myths is thought to be something of a shock since Americans are supposed to be above that sort of thing. We are rational! That is yet another myth. Even the rational need myths. The only difference between us and primitive tribes is that we seem to have adopted our major myths in more of a hurry. Most of ours were produced in a frenzy of nationalism between the Revolution and the Civil War.

All people live by certain fictions to make life meaningful. But we may actually have been more in need of them than most others. We have little else that unites us. It may be absurd for the Italian boy on the plains of the Midwest to celebrate as his own the Pilgrim ancestors, but he will do so in the future as he has in the past. For it is one of the few things (other than football, TV, and video games) that ties him to the other American boys across this wide country.

The mistake is not creating myths but in pretending the myths are true, which breeds suspicion when it is discovered they are not. Actually, we can have our myths and truth, too. Myths serve as symbols of cultural unity even when their fictitiousness is well established. Just because Santa Claus is a fantasy doesn't mean we have to take him out and shoot him.

Acknowledgments

Among those who deserve mention are those who stood by me during the night-and-day writing of this book. First, of course, I want to thank Michael Reed, who has always been there when I needed him. I also want to thank Dennis Christopher, who helped me through a difficult period.

Stephen McAdoo, as he has in the past, proved to be both a fine and good friend and an expert wordsmith. He managed to read every chapter on deadline, often setting aside his own work to help me with mine.

Bernard Weisberger has been helping me understand American history for so long that I find it hard to believe he still has more to offer. But he always does. His notes on the manuscript—which he read in its entirety—are themselves so interesting I was tempted to include them in the book as an addendum.

I also want to thank Ed Victor, my agent, whose help in arranging for a publisher was extraordinary. There cannot be many agents like him.

Finally, I want to thank my editor, Cynthia Barrett, whom I value for her friendship as well as her editorial abilities.

Notes

Patriotism

1. Milo Milton Quaife, *The Flag of the United States* (1942), *passim*; Daniel Boorstin, *The Americans: The National Experience* (1965), p. 374; Wilbur Zelinsky, *Nation into State: The Shifting Symbolic Foundations of American Nationalism* (1988), pp. 201–02.

2. Zelinsky, *Nation into State*, pp. 202–03; David R. Manwaring, *Render unto Caesar: The Flag Salute Controversy* (1962), pp. 1–6; Bernard A. Weisberger, "The Flap over the Flag," *American Heritage* (Nov. 1990), pp. 24–26.

3. Quaife, *Flag*, pp. 53–61, 163, 184–89; on Betsy Ross see Shenkman, *Legends, Lies & Cherished Myths of American History* (1988), pp. 147–48.

4. Michael Kammen, *A Season of Youth* (1978), p. 40; Boorstin, *National Experience*, p. 383.

5. Philip F. Detweiler, "The Changing Reputation of the Declaration of Independence: The First Fifty Years," *William and Mary Quarterly*, XIX (October 1962), 557, 562, 566, 573.

6. Boorstin, *National Experience*, p. 386.

7. Walter Lord, *The Dawn's Early Light* (1972), pp. 274–75, 292–93, 365; Lord, "What Did Key See?" *American Heritage* (December 1990), p. 54. Interestingly, Lord indicated in 1972 that he thought Key could

have seen the small flag flying from the fort. In 1990, he said he doubted it.

8. Quaife, *Flag*, pp. 112–13; Boorstin, *National Experience*, p. 375; Edward S. Delaplaine, *Francis Scott Key* (1937), pp. 131, 137, 153, 173.

9. Kammen, *Youth*, pp. 120–23; Shenkman, *Legends, Lies & Cherished Myths of American History*, p. 156. And Nellie Wallington, ed., *American History by American Poets* (1911), for the Revere poetry excerpt.

10. Norman Gelb, *Less Than Glory* (1984), pp. 73–104.

11. Shelby Foote, *The Civil War: A Narrative* (1963), II, 151–52, 635–37.

12. Bernard Mayo, *Myths and Men* (1963), p. 15; Thomas A. Bailey, *Voices of America* (1976), p. 9.

13. Quaife, *Flag*, p. 102; Bailey, *Voices*, p. 36; Henry F. Woods, *American Sayings* (1949), pp. 12–13.

14. Quaife, *Flag*, p. 179.

15. Irvin Anthony, *Decatur* (1931), p. 265; Charles Lee Lewis, *The Romantic Decatur* (1937), p. 183.

Religion

1. Information on the Pilgrims is drawn, unless otherwise indicated, from George Willison, *Saints and Strangers* (1945).

2. Dr. Jeremy Dupertuis Bangs, curator of Plimoth Plantation, Plymouth, Massachusetts, in an oral communication with the author.

3. Mark L. Sargent, "The Conservative Covenant: The Rise of the Mayflower Compact in American Myth," *New England Quarterly* (June 1988), pp. 239, 251.

4. The *Concise Dictionary of American History* says the Pilgrims should be considered Puritans; Harvard's Perry Miller said they shouldn't. "The true Puritan," says Miller, "was a member of the Church of England." And of course Pilgrims weren't. Miller and Thomas Johnson, eds., *The Puritans* (rev. ed., 1963), I, 88.

5. All agree that a decline in churchgoing set in during the 1660s, but not everybody agrees the decline persisted. Robert G. Pope insists that in the 1690s, in response to the social and political crises of the previous fifteen years—King Philip's War, the smallpox epidemic, and the Boston fires—churchgoing ballooned. Pope, "The Myth of Declension," in

Religion in American History, eds. John Mulder and John Wilson (1978), p. 50.

6. The information in this chapter on Christianity, unless otherwise indicated, is drawn mainly from Jon Butler, *Awash in a Sea of Faith: Christianizing the American People* (1990).

7. David Hall, *Worlds of Wonder, Days of Judgment* (1978), pp. 16, 19, 98–99; Chadwick Hansen, *Witchcraft at Salem* (1969), pp. 32, 37, 48–49, 55, 99, 100, 106–07.

8. Hall, *Worlds of Wonder,* pp. 58, 101.

9. Clifford K. Shipton, "The Locus of Authority in Colonial Massachusetts," in *Myth and the American Experience,* eds. Nicholas Cords and Patrick Gerster (2d ed.; 1978), I, 64–73.

10. Darrett B. Rutman, "The Mirror of Puritan Authority," in *Selected Essays: Law and Authority in Colonial America,* ed. George Billias (1965), pp. 161–62.

11. Thomas A. Bailey, *The American Pageant* (1971), p. 26.

12. Jon Butler, "The Great Awakening as Interpretative Fiction," *Journal of American History,* (September 1982), pp. 305–23.

13. Kenneth Lockridge, *A New England Town* (1985), p. 162; Samuel Eliot Morison, *The Oxford History of the American People* (1965), pp. 150–51.

14. Alfred Owen Aldridge, *Benjamin Franklin and Nature's God* (1967), pp. 8–9, 25, 135, 193; Frank E. Manuel, *The Eighteenth Century Confronts the Gods* (1959), pp. 65, 277–79; Edwin S. Gaustad, *Faith of Our Fathers* (1987), pp. 100–06; Gaustad, *Religion in America: History and Historiography* (American Historical Association Pamphlet: 1973), pp. 14–15; Douglass Adair, *Fame and the Founding Fathers* (1974), pp. 145–59; Paul F. Boller, Jr., "George Washington and Religious Liberty," in *George Washington: A Profile,* ed. James Morton Smith (1969), p. 166.

15. Orrin Hatch, "Civic Virtue: Wellspring of Liberty," *National Forum: The Journal of the Honor Society of Phi Kappa Phi* (Special Issue: "Toward the Bicentennial of the Constitution," Fall 1984), p. 36; Thanksgiving Day Proclamation, *New York Times,* Nov. 21, 1987; George Will, *Statecraft as Soulcraft* (1983), p. 71.

16. On Madison, Adams, Hamilton, and Lincoln, see John Diggins, *The Lost Soul of American Politics* (1984), pp. 79–80, 303–33. On Reagan, see Garry Wills, *Reagan's America* (1987), p. 385.

17. Gaustad, *Faith of Our Fathers*, pp. 45, 53–54.

18. Gaustad, *Faith of Our Fathers*, pp. 41, 114–15.

19. Paul Boyer, *Urban Masses and Moral Order in America* (1978), pp. 35, 110.

20. Fawn M. Brodie, *No Man Knows My History* (1982), pp. 14–15.

21. Ernest Sandeen, *The Roots of Fundamentalism* (1970), pp. xi, 5, 106–08; Miller and Johnson, eds., *Puritans*, I, 4–5.

Work and Play

1. Daniel T. Rogers, *The Work Ethic in Industrial America* (1978), pp. 94–99.

2. Rogers, *Work Ethic*, p. 155.

3. Rogers, *Work Ethic*, p. 95; Foster Rhea Dulles, *A History of Recreation* (2nd ed.; 1965), pp. 195, 197, 203, 287; on the Gay Nineties, see Stuart Berg Flexner, *I Hear America Singing* (1976), pp. 162–63; on car racing, see Bernard A. Weisberger, *The Dream Maker* (1979), p. 63.

4. Benjamin Hunnicutt, *Work Without End* (1988), pp. 1–3, 18–19, 35, 156.

5. Rogers, *Work Ethic*, pp. 103–05.

6. Howard Feinstein, "The Use and Abuse of Illness in the James Family Circle," in *Our Selves/Our Past*, ed. Robert J. Brugger (1981), pp. 220–43.

7. Herbert Gutman, *Work, Culture and Society* (1976), p. 20; Roy Rosenzweig, *Eight Hours for What We Will* (1983), p. 36; Rogers, *Work Ethic*, p. 164.

8. Rosenzweig, *Eight Hours*, pp. 61–62; Hunnicutt, *Work Without End*, p. 13.

9. Gutman, *Work*, pp. 23, 36.

10. Richard Stivers, *A Hair of the Dog: Irish Drinking and American Stereotype* (1976), pp. 8–12, 129, 137–40.

11. Herbert Gutman, *Power and Culture*, ed. Ira Berlin (1987), p. 385.

12. Hunnicutt, *Work Without End*, p. 18; *New York Times*, June 3, 1990, section 4, p. 1. Stanley Lebergott, an economic historian, reports that between 1900 and 1970 the *average* worker reduced his work week from 66.8 to 45.0 hours, a substantial decline of about 33 percent. It is the hours of *union* workers that have declined only by ten hours a

week. Lebergott, *The American Economy: Income, Wealth and Want* (1976), p. 89.

13. Hunnicutt, *Work Without End*, pp. 151–56, 159.

14. Gutman, *Work*, p. 4.

15. Gutman, *Work*, pp. 5, 20.

16. Gutman, *Work*, pp. 27–28.

17. Rogers, *Work Ethic*, p. 18.

18. Gutman, *Work*, pp. 23, 36.

19. Rogers, *Work Ethic*, chapters 2, 3, and 6, especially pp. 67–68, 167.

20. Loren Baritz, *The Good Life* (1989), pp. 78–80.

21. Rogers, *Work Ethic*, chapter 4, especially pp. 99–100, 121; Hunnicutt, *Work Without End*, chapter 2, especially pp. 42–44.

22. Paul Boyer, *Urban Masses and Moral Order in America, 1820–1920* (1978), pp. 3, 236–37; Rosenzweig, *Eight Hours*, p. 127.

23. The Downing and Olmstead quotations are in Rosenzweig, *Eight Hours*, pp. 127–28; the Beecher and prostitution quotations are in Boyer, *Urban Masses*, pp. 237, 239.

24. Boyer, *Urban Masses*, p. 241.

25. Robert Caro, *The Power Broker: Robert Moses and the Fall of New York* (1974), pp. 318, 546–47, 951–54.

26. Rosenzweig, *Eight Hours*, p. 139.

27. All of the quotations on playgrounds are in Boyer, *Urban Masses*, pp. 242–51. For background information on the "playground movement," see Rosenzweig, *Eight Hours*, pp. 144, 150; and Hunnicutt, *Work Without End*, p. 109.

Business

1. Arthur Schlesinger, Jr., *The Cycles of American History* (1986), pp. 225–26; Douglass C. North et al., *Growth and Welfare in the American Past* (1983), p. 93.

2. Frank Bourgin, *The Great Challenge* (1989), p. 143.

3. E. A. J. Johnson, *The Foundations of American Economic Freedom* (1973), p. 153; Schlesinger, *Cycles*, p. 223.

4. W. W. Rostow, *The Stages of Economic Growth* (1967), p. 38, says the U.S. economy finally took off between 1843 and 1860.

5. Johnson, *Foundations*, p. 217; Schlesinger, *Cycles*, pp. 219, 224.

6. Schlesinger, *Cycles*, p. 221.

7. Bergen Evans, *Dictionary of Quotations* (1968), p. 285; Bourgin, *Great Challenge*, p. 124: "As long as the federal power was in the hands of those whom Jefferson believed were opposed to republicanism, he was suspicious of anything that accentuated the authority of government."

8. Bourgin, *Great Challenge*, chapter 8; Jefferson, Sixth Annual Message to Congress, December 2, 1806, in James D. Richardson, ed., *Messages and Papers of the Presidents* (1897), I, 397–98.

9. Bourgin, *Great Challenge*, p. 143; Johnson, *Foundations*, pp. 153, 202–03.

10. Garry Wills, *Nixon Agonistes* (1970), p. 467.

11. Pauline Maier, Review of *The Great Challenge*, by Frank Bourgin, *New York Times Book Review* (July 30, 1989), pp. 11–12; Schlesinger, *Cycles*, pp. 235–37.

12. Of the teenagers tested 51 percent could correctly define laissez-faire, while only 43 percent were able to identify Joe McCarthy and only 32 percent knew enough to place the Civil War within the last half of the nineteenth century. Diane Ravitch and Chester E. Finn, Jr., *What Do Our 17-Year-Olds Know?* (1988), pp. 49, 69, 83.

13. Edward Chase Kirkland, *Dream and Thought in the Business Community* (1964), pp. 7–9.

14. Richard B. Morris, *Government and Labor in Early America* (1946), pp. 92–96, 121–23, 134; Johnson, *Foundations*, pp. 162, 305; Schlesinger, *Cycles*, p. 229.

15. James W. Davidson and Mark H. Lytle, *After the Fact* (1982), p. 241.

16. William Greider, *Secrets of the Temple* (1987), pp. 304–10.

17. Thomas A. Bailey, *Probing America's Past* (1973), II, 537, 670–71.

18. Thomas C. Cochran, "Did the Civil War Retard Industrialization?" in *Essays in American Economic History*, ed. A. W. Coats (1969), p. 146.

19. John Kenneth Galbraith, *The Liberal Hour* (1960), p. 79. Galbraith describes the fifteen years it took the South to meet its prewar cotton-production levels as an encouraging development. It strikes me as evidence of an economic calamity.

20. These quotations are cited by Cochran, "Civil War," pp. 140–41.

21. Cochran, "Civil War," pp. 140–45.

22. On World War I, see Thomas A. Bailey, *Probing America's Past* (1973), II, 537, 670–71; on the Revolution, see Morris, *Government and Labor*, p. 529.

23. A recent statement of the Morgan myth, which depicts the banker as the leader of the affair, can be found in Harvey Wasserman's *History of the United States* (1988), p. 4. To see how his biographers have handled the matter, see Andrew Sinclair, *Corsair: The Life of J. Pierpont Morgan* (1981), pp. 18–21; George Wheeler, *Pierpont Morgan and Friends: The Anatomy of a Myth* (1973), pp. 74–78. The defense of Morgan is laid out in R. Gordon Wasson, *The Hall Carbine Affair: A Study in Contemporary Folklore* (rev. ed.; 1948), *passim.*

24. The quotation is from Allan Nevins, "Should American History Be Rewritten?" *Saturday Review* (Feb. 6, 1954), p. 10.

25. Allen Solganick, "The Robber Baron Concept and Its Revisionists," in *The Robber Barons Revisited,* ed. Peter d'A. Jones (1968), pp. 106–13.

26. W. Paul Strassmann, *Risk and Technological Innovation* (1959), pp. 43, 46, 48–49, 98–99, 209–26; W. E. Woodward, *The Way Our People Lived* (1944), pp. 299n, 326n.

27. See William Graham Sumner, *What the Social Classes Owe to Each Other* (1883; rpt. 1974), pp. 13, 114.

28. Quoted by Solganick, "Robber Baron Concept," p. 110. See also Kirkland, *Dream and Thought in the Business Community,* p. 27.

29. The first quotation, "excessive competition," is from the United States Industrial Commission that was appointed by Congress to report on the American economy. See Jones, *Robber Barons Revisited,* p. 67. The second quotation, "fallacious idea," is from Robert Harris, one-time president of Chicago, Burlington & Quincy. The quotation dismissing social Darwinism as a "pretty theory" is from Charles Perkins, president of the Chicago, Burlington & Quincy Railroad, January 19, 1888. See Thomas Cochran, *Railroad Leaders: 1845–1890* (1953), pp. 161, 447.

30. Cochran, *Railroad Leaders,* p. 182.

31. Albert Galoway Keller and Maurice R. Davie, *Essays of William Graham Sumner* (1934), II, 435–36.

32. On the income tax, see Lawrence M. Friedman, *A History of American Law* (1973), pp. 494–97; on Jefferson, see his Sixth Annual Message as reprinted in *Messages and Papers of the Presidents,* p. 397.

33. Herbert Gutman, *Power and Culture*, ed. Ira Berlin (1987), pp. 76–79.

Literature

1. Gene Tunney, "My Fights with Jack Dempsey," in *The Aspirin Age*, ed. Isabel Leighton (1949), pp. 158–59.

2. Lawrence Levine, *Highbrow/Lowbrow* (1989), pp. 4, 14–18, 25, 34, 37, 63–68, 86, 149, 221–22; David Hall, Review of *Highbrow/Lowbrow*, *Reviews in American History* (March 1990), pp. 10–13.

3. Richard M. Rollins, "Words as Social Control: Noah Webster and the Creation of the *American Dictionary*," *American Quarterly*, XXVIII (1976), 415–30; Rollins, *The Long Journey of Noah Webster* (1980), pp. 139–43.

4. James West Davidson and Mark Hamilton Lytle, *After the Fact* (1982), pp. 232–62.

5. Walter Harding, *The Days of Henry Thoreau* (1982), pp. xvii, 54, 179, 181–84, 189–90, 195.

6. Leo Marx, *The Pilot and the Passenger* (1988), pp. 83, 85, 90, 92, 96–97.

7. Harding, *Days*, p. 56.

8. Christopher Lehmann-Haupt, Review of *The Pencil*, by Henry Petroski, *New York Times* (Jan. 22, 1990), p. B-2.

9. Stanley Edgar Hyman, "Henry Thoreau in Our Time," in *Thoreau*, ed. Sherman Paul (1962), pp. 23–24.

10. Marx, *Pilot*, p. 99.

11. Kenneth S. Lynn, *Hemingway* (1987), pp. 9–10, 82–85.

12. Dixon Wecter, *The Hero in America* (1941), pp. 50–80.

13. Tom Burnam, *More Misinformation* (1980), pp. 148–49.

14. Marx, *Pilot*, pp. 103–04; Stanley Burnshaw, *Robert Frost Himself* (1986), pp. 210–40.

15. Gary Scharnhorst and Jack Bales, *The Lost Life of Horatio Alger, Jr.* (1985), pp. 1–3, 65–67, 86, 160.

16. Peggy Robbins, "The Defamation of Edgar Allan Poe," *American History Illustrated*, X (October 1975), 18–26.

17. Paul Johnson, *Intellectuals* (1988), pp. 1–2, 266–67.

18. Henry M. Littlefield, "The Wizard of Oz: Parable on Populism," *American Quarterly*, XVI (Spring 1964), 47–58.

19. The stories behind the quotes and misquotes covered in this chapter are told in Tom Burnam's *Dictionary of Misinformation* (1975); Paul Boller, Jr.'s *They Never Said It* (1989); Bergen Evans's *The Spoor of Spooks* (1954); and Evans's *Dictionary of Quotations* (1968).

20. *New York Times*, Nov. 7, 1989, p. A-10.

Politics

1. *Speeches and Addresses of Warren G. Harding, President of the United States: Delivered During the Course of His Tour from Washington, D.C., to Alaska and Return to San Francisco* (1923), pp. 256–57.

2. U.S. George Washington Bicentennial Commission, *Honor to George Washington* (n.d.) pp. ix, 140.

3. Garry Wills, *Explaining America* (1981), p. 266; Henry Steele Commager in an interview with John A. Garraty, ed., *Interpreting American History* (1970), I, 103.

4. Bernard Bailyn, *The Ideological Origins of the American Revolution* (1967), p. 60; Clinton Rossiter, ed., *Federalist Papers* (1961), pp. 54, 322.

5. Garry Wills takes the position that Hamilton and Madison really did not mean it when they expressed doubts about the goodness of man. As proof, he shows that the *Federalist Papers* are suffused with positive statements about man's nature. But even he concedes that as constitution-makers they had to act on the assumption that man is self-interested. For, as David Hume explained, "in contriving any system of government, and fixing the several checks and controls of the constitution, every man ought to be supposed a knave, and to have no other end, in all his actions, than private interest. By this interest we must govern him, and, by means of it, make him, notwithstanding his insatiable avarice and ambition, cooperate to public good." In making the assumption that man is self-interested, the founders were being far more realistic than their political heirs give them credit. Wills, *Explaining America* (1981), p. 190.

6. Wills, *Explaining America*, p. 266; Henry Steele Commager in an interview with John A. Garraty, *Interpreting American History*, I, 103.

7. Charles Beard, *The Republic* (1962), pp. 29–33; John Steele Gordon, "The Founding Wizard," *American Heritage* (July–August 1990), p. 44.

8. Orrin Hatch, "Civic Virtue: Wellspring of Liberty," *National Forum: The Phi Kappa Phi Journal* (Special Issue: "Toward the Bicentennial

of the Constitution," Fall 1989), pp. 34–38; Barry Goldwater, *The Conscience of a Conservative* (1960), p. 19.

9. John Diggins, "Comrades and Citizens: New Mythologies in American Historiography," *American Historical Review* (June 1985), pp. 630–31; Diggins, *The Lost Soul of American Politics* (1984), p. 39; J. G. A. Pocock, *The Machiavellian Moment* (1975), p. 526. Diggins has led the historians who believe the founders did not think virtue was indispensable, but for a whole review of the complicated literature, see Robert E. Shalhope, "Republicanism and Early American Historiography," *William and Mary Quarterly* (April 1982).

10. Douglass Adair, *Fame and the Founding Fathers*, (1974), pp. 8, 24.

11. Rossiter, *Federalist Papers*, pp. 82–83; Diggins, *Lost Soul of American Politics*, p. 51.

12. Ronald Reagan, *Speaking My Mind* (1989), pp. 296–300, 417; Michael Wallace, "Ronald Reagan and the Politics of History," *Tikkun*, (1987) 2, no. 1, 17.

13. Daniel Boorstin, ed., *An American Primer* (1966), pp. xiii, 8–25; Loren Baritz, *City on a Hill* (1964), pp. 14–17; Reagan, *Speaking My Mind*, p. 219.

14. Ronald Reagan, in his first inaugural address: "We are a nation under God, and I believe God intended for us to be free." Reagan, *Speaking My Mind*, p. 65.

15. Loren Baritz, *Backfire: A History of How American Culture Led Us into Vietnam and Made Us Fight the Way We Did* (1985), p. 31. Reagan, in his speech at the Statue of Liberty centennial celebration, 1986: "Our work can never be truly done until every man, woman, and child shares in our gift, in our hope, and stands with us in the light of liberty." (Reagan, *Speaking My Mind*, p. 300.) Lyndon Johnson, in 1966: "I want to leave the footprints of America in Vietnam. I want them to say when the Americans come, this is what they leave—schools, not long cigars. We're going to turn the Mekong into a Tennessee valley." (William Leuchtenburg, *In the Shadow of FDR* [1983], p. 151.) Nebraska Senator Kenneth Wherry, in 1940: "With God's help, we will lift Shanghai up and up, ever up, until it is just like Kansas City." Wendell Willkie, in 1943: "When you fly around the world in forty-nine days, you learn that the world has become small not only on the map, but also in the minds of men. All around the world, there are some ideas which millions and millions of men hold in common, almost as if they lived in the same [American?] town."

As *Life* magazine reported, before the onset of the Cold War, even Russians "look like Americans, dress like Americans and think like Americans." (The Wherry, Willkie, and *Life* quotes are from Robert Dallek, *The American Style of Foreign Policy* [1983], pp. 123, 138, 139.)

16. Richard Reeves, "The Class War Is Over, and the Rich Won," *Seattle Times*, January 25, 1990; *New York Times*, January 21, 1990, p. 4. Charles Beard believed Madison was a kind of pre-Marxist Marxist. That was undoubtedly an extreme judgment and says less about Madison than it does about Beard, who wanted to use Madison to show that economic determinism has deep American roots. But all agree the subject of class was a preoccupation of the founders. Richard Hofstadter, *The Progressive Historians* (1970), p. 223; Beard, *An Economic Interpretation of the Constitution* (1913; rpt. 1965), pp. 14–15.

17. Most of the polling numbers are from Hazel Erskine, "The Polls: Is War a Mistake?" *Public Opinion Quarterly* (1970), pp. 135–38; The numbers on Vietnam are in Alan D. Monroe, *Public Opinion in America* (1975), p. 210n; the Baritz quotation is in *Backfire*, p. 181. For background on isolationism in the thirties, see Thomas A. Bailey, *The Man in the Street* (1948), pp. 172–75, who makes the astute observation that opposition to World War I declined rapidly after 1937 as hatred for Germany and Hitler increased.

18. Arthur Schlesinger, Jr., *The Cycles of American History* (1986), p. 237.

19. Arthur Schlesinger, Jr., "Individualism and Apathy in Tocqueville's *Democracy,*" in *Reconsidering Tocqueville's Democracy in America*, ed. Abraham S. Eisenstadt (1988), pp. 96–97, 106–09; Raymond Aron, *Main Currents in Sociological Thought* (1968), I, 258; Diggins, *The Lost Soul of American Politics*, pp. 117, 232; Gordon Wood, *The Creation of the American Republic* (1969), pp. 63–64; Robert Shalhope, *The Roots of Democracy* (1990), pp. 44–46.

20. William Leuchtenburg, *In the Shadow of FDR* (1983), pp. 151, 181, 225; Thomas A. Bailey, "The Mythmakers of American History," *Journal of American History* (June 1968), pp. 5–21.

Alcohol and Drugs

1. Page Smith, *Dissenting Opinions* (1984), pp. 3–13.

2. W. J. Rorabaugh, *The Alcoholic Republic* (1979), pp. ix, 6, 10,

20–21, 26, 48, 55, 64, 84, 125, 151, 163, 169–70; Mark Edward Lender and James Kirby Martin, *Drinking in America: A History* (1982), pp. 2, 3, 7, 11, 30, 32–34.

3. Craig MacAndrew and Robert B. Edgerton, *Drunken Comportment* (1969), pp. 10, 14, 36, 100, 109, 111, 113–17, 122, 128–30, 133–34, 137, 144, 157, 173.

4. Lender, *Drinking*, p. 96; Bernard Weisberger, letter to the author, November 15, 1990.

5. Lender, *Dinking*, pp. 136–39, 147; Norman H. Clark, *Deliver Us from Evil* (1976), pp. 145–47.

6. The critic is Tom Dardis. See *The Thirsty Muse* (1989), p. 11. On Wolfe, see David Donald, *Look Homeward* (1987), pp. 75–76.

7. Dardis, *Thirsty Muse*, pp. 102–03, 105–07; Thomas B. Gilmore, *Equivocal Spirits* (1987), pp. 96, 99–100, 109–111.

8. Clark, *Deliver Us from Evil*, p. 148.

9. Clark, *Deliver Us from Evil*, pp. 145, 151.

10. Clark, *Deliver Us from Evil*, pp. 161–62.

11. Herbert Asbury, "The Noble Experiment of Izzie and Moe," in *The Aspirin Age*, ed. Isabel Leighton (1949), pp. 34–49; p. 46 for the statistics.

12. Lender, *Drinking*, pp. 146–47.

13. Lender, *Drinking*, pp. 125, 129, 134; Clark, *Deliver Us from Evil*, pp 179–30; James Timberlake, *Prohibition and the Progressive Movement* (1970), pp. 2, 83, 152, 168.

14. Bergen Evans, *The Natural History of Nonsense* (1946), p. 165; Evans, *The Spoor of Spooks* (1954), p. 234; Clark, *Deliver Us from Evil*, pp. 218–19.

15. Geoffrey Ward, " 'A Fair, Honorable, and Legitimate Trade,' " *American Heritage* (August–September 1986), pp. 49–64.

16. Brian Inglis, *The Forbidden Game* (1975), pp. 178–81; Clark, *Deliver Us from Evil*, pp. 218–26; H. Wayne Morgan, *Drugs in America: A Social History* (1980), p. 94.

17. Oscar E. Anderson, Jr., *The Health of a Nation* (1958), p. 315, n. 31.

Women

1. This viewpoint was advanced as recently as 1970. See Page Smith, *Daughters of the Promised Land* (1970), pp. 71–72, 275.

2. Carl Degler, *At Odds* (1980), p. 73.

3. Carol Ruth Berkin and Mary Beth Norton, *Women of America: A History* (1979), pp. 40–43; Linda Kerber, "Daughters of Columbia: Educating Women for the Republic," in *The Hofstadter Aegis*, ed. Stanley Elkins and Eric McKitrick (1974), p. 58; David Brion Davis, *From Homicide to Slavery* (1986), p. 177.

4. James B. McPherson, *Battle Cry of Freedom* (1988), pp. 34, 478; Barbara Welter, "The Cult of True Womanhood: 1820–1860," in *American Experiences*, eds. Randy Roberts and James Olson (1986), I, 163.

5. Frances B. Cogan, *All-American Girl* (1989), pp. 3, 27, *passim*.

6. Sarah M. Evans, *Born for Liberty* (1989), p. 61.

7. Maureen Honey, *Creating Rosie the Riveter* (1984), pp. 8–11, 19, 28–31, 117.

8. Steven Mintz and Susan Kellogg, *Domestic Revolutions* (1988), pp. 177–81.

9. Smith, *Daughters*, pp. 295–96.

10. Honey, *Rosie the Riveter*, p. 3.

11. Quoted by Degler, *At Odds*, p. 412.

12. Albie Sachs and Joan Hoff Wilson, *Sexism and the Law* (1978), pp. 74, 85–94.

13. Loren Baritz, *The Good Life* (1989), pp. 66–67.

14. Sachs and Wilson, *Sexism and the Law*, p. 149.

15. Ruth Schwartz Cowan, *More Work for Mother* (1983), pp. 51–53, 63–64, 100, 199–201, 208–09.

Freedom and Democracy

1. George Willison, *Saints and Strangers* (1945), pp. 143–44; Samuel Eliot Morison, *The Maritime History of Massachusetts* (1923), p. 23; Morison, *The Oxford History of the American People* (1965), p. 55.

2. William Bradford, *History of Plymouth Plantation*, ed. William T. Davis (1908), pp. 106–07.

3. Mark L. Sargent, "The Conservative Covenant: The Rise of the

Mayflower Compact in American Myth," *New England Quarterly* (June 1988), pp. 238–39.

4. Kenneth Lockridge, *A New England Town* (1985), pp. 4–5, 48–49, 105, 113–14, 121–38, 207; Perry Miller and Thomas Johnson, eds., *The Puritans* (rev. ed.; 1963), I, 182–85, 187.

5. Clifford K. Shipton, "The Locus of Authority in Colonial Massachusetts," in *Myth and the American Experience*, eds. Nicholas Cords and Patrick Gerster (2nd ed.; 1978), p. 67.

6. Lockridge, *A New England Town*, pp. 4–5.

7. David Syrett, "Town-Meeting Politics in Massachusetts, 1776–1786," *William and Mary Quarterly* (July 1964), pp. 352–66.

8. Estelle F. Feinstein, *Stamford in the Gilded Age: The Political Life of a Connecticut Town, 1868–1893* (1973), pp. 26–28, 31–34, 43–48.

9. Leonard W. Levy, "Did the Zenger Case Really Matter? Freedom of the Press in Colonial New York," *William and Mary Quarterly* (January 1960), pp. 35–50.

10. Thomas A. Bailey, *Probing America's Past* (1973), I, 79.

11. Hiller Zobel, "Law Under Pressure: Boston 1769–1771," in *Selected Essays: Law and Authority in Colonial America*, ed. George A. Billias (1965), pp. 202–05.

12. Page Smith, *John Adams* (1962), I, 124–26.

13. Robert E. Shalhope, *The Roots of Democracy* (1990), pp. 28–31; Benjamin W. Labaree, *The Boston Tea Party* (1964), pp. 7, 142–44, 147, 259.

14. Norman Gelb, *Less Than Glory* (1984), pp. 37, 41–42.

15. Barbara MacDonald Powell, "The Most Celebrated Encampment: Valley Forge in American Culture, 1777–1983," (unpublished Ph.D. dissertation, Cornell University, 1983), pp. 3, 7, 11–27, 220.

16. David Donald, *Lincoln Reconsidered* (1961), pp. 19–36.

17. Gilbert Hobbs Barnes, *The Antislavery Impulse* (1964), pp. 124–25.

18. David Donald, *Charles Sumner and the Coming of the Civil War* (1960), p. 336.

19. Thomas A. Bailey, *Probing the American Past* (1973), I, 240.

20. Stephan Thernstrom, "Urbanization, Migration, and Social Mobility in Late Nineteenth Century America," in *Towards a New Past*, ed. Barton J. Bernstein (1968), pp. 159–60; Clarence H. Danhof, "Economic Validity of the Safety-Valve Doctrine," in *Essays in American*

Economic History, eds. A. W. Coats and Ross M. Robertson (1969), pp. 219–27.

21. W. J. Rorabaugh, *The Alcoholic Republic* (1979), pp. 152–54.

Saints and Scalawags

1. Robert Shalhope, *The Roots of Democracy* (1990), pp. 23–25; the story of Allen's treason is told in my *Legends, Lies & Cherished Myths of American History* (1988), pp. 87–88.

2. Dixon Wecter, *The Hero in America* (1941), pp. 249–50; Allan Nevins, *The Emergence of Lincoln* (1950), II, 5–11.

3. Marcus Rediker, *Between the Devil and the Deep Blue Sea: Merchant Seamen, Pirates, and the Anglo-American Maritime World* (1987), chapter 6.

4. Charles W. Smith, *Roger B. Taney: Jacksonian Jurist* (1936), pp. 22, 141, 144, 156, 163; Carl Brent Swisher, *Roger B. Taney* (1961), p. 518. "Malevolent old man" quoting Swisher, who is summarizing the stereotype.

5. Leo Hershkowitz, *Tweed's New York: Another Look* (1977), *passim.* For the typical textbook treatment see Bernard Bailyn et al., *The Great Republic* (1977), pp. 803–04. The story of the cartoon that captured Tweed is related in all its glorious errors in Albert Bigelow Paine, *Th. Nast: His Period and His Pictures* (1904), pp. 318, 336.

6. Robert M. Utley, *Cavalier in Buckskin* (1988), chapters 1, 8, 9; Wayne Michael Sarf, Review of *Cavalier in Buckskin*, *American Scholar* (Autumn 1990), pp. 616, 618.

7. Tom Burnam, *The Dictionary of Misinformation* (1975), pp. 161–62.

8. Louis Koenig, *Bryan* (1971), pp. 12, 597–99, 606–09, 612–16, 629–33, 656.

9. Masayo Duus, *Tokyo Rose: Orphan of the Pacific* (1979), *passim.*

10. Joseph Albini, *The American Mafia: Genesis of a Legend* (1971), pp. 9, 37, 154, 178, 182–85, 248; Humbert S. Nelli, *The Business of Crime: Italians and Syndicate Crime in the United States* (1976), pp. 5–23, 255.

History

1. Robert Lacey, *Ford: The Men and the Machine* (1986), pp. 251–52.

2. Diane Ravitch and Chester E. Finn, Jr., *What Do Our 17-Year-Olds Know?* (1987), pp. 48–49; Gallup Organization, "A Survey of College Seniors: Knowledge of History and Literature" (October 1989), p. 7.

3. Hazel Hertzberg, "History and Progressivism: A Century of Reform Proposals," in *Historical Literacy*, ed. Paul Gagnon (1989), p. 89.

4. C. Vann Woodward, *The Future of the Past* (1989), p. 13.

5. Thomas A. Bailey, *The American Pageant Revisited* (1982), p. 201.

6. The quotation is from J. G. A. Pocock, as cited by Garry Wills, *The Kennedy Imprisonment* (1982), p. 217.

7. Bernard Weisberger, letter to the author, December 6, 1990. Weisberger added: "Reductionism is the enemy of common sense. History, with its complexity, should take us away from simplistic and reductive views of the past. Instead, it is appropriated to justify them. Its real usefulness, which seems to be to furnish perspective and perhaps reinforce the old Greek-tragedy notion that we cannot forsee what the gods have in store, is rarely recognized."

8. The quotation is from James C. Thomson, Jr., a member of President Johnson's National Security Council and later an academic. It is cited by Fox Butterfield, "The New Vietnam Scholarship," *New York Times Magazine* (February 13, 1983), p. 61.

9. Dumas Malone, *Jefferson the President: First Term, 1801–1805* (1970), p. 251.

10. Frank Bourgin, *The Great Challenge* (1989), p. 147.

11. Arthur Schlesinger, Jr., *The Cycles of American History* (1986), p. 235.

12. Bergen Evans, *The Spoor of Spooks* (1954), p. 33.

13. "People have to age and weaken, but societies may not need to. China has been powerful despite considerable ups and downs for thousands of years." James Fallows, *More Like Us* (1989), p. 11.

14. Woodward, *Future of the Past*, p. xi.

15. Anne Firor Scott, "One Woman's Experience of World War II," *Journal of American History* (September 1990), p. 557.

16. The McNeill essay is in Gagnon, *Historical Literacy*, p. 165.

17. Page Smith, *The Historian and History* (1964), p. 165.

18. Bert James Loewenberg, *American History in American Thought* (1972), pp. 311–12.

19. Gordon S. Wood, "Rhetoric and Reality in the American Revolution," *William and Mary Quarterly* (January 1965), p. 7.

20. Allan Nevins, *The Gateway to History* (rev. ed., 1962), p. 269.

21. Robert M. Collins, "The Originality Trap: Richard Hofstadter on Populism," *Journal of American History* (June 1989), pp. 150–67.

So Many Myths

1. Gary Scharnhorst and Jack Bales, *The Lost Life of Horatio Alger, Jr.* (1985), xiii, *passim*; Herbert Mayes, *Alger* (1928), *passim*.

2. Horace P. Beck, "The Making of the Popular Legendary Hero," in *American Folk Legend*, ed. Wayland Hand (1971), pp. 121–32.

3. The story is recounted in Gabor S. Boritt, ed., *The Historian's Lincoln* (1988), p. 253.

4. A. J. P. Taylor, *Politicians, Socialism, and Historians* (1982), p. 143.

5. Statement of a spokesman for Colonial Williamsburg, 1990.

6. Henry Steele Commager, "The Search for a Usable Past," *American Heritage* (February 1965).

7. *New York Times*, March 7, 1990, p. A-14.

8. Thomas A. Bailey, "Presidential Address [The Mythmakers of American History]," *Journal of American History* (June 1968), pp. 5–21; C. Vann Woodward, *The Future of the Past* (1989), p. viii.

9. Bernard Bailyn, *The Origins of American Politics* (1970), pp. 5–6.

Index

Adams, John
  Boston Massacre, 153–54
  death, 8
  and the flag, 2
  and religion 29
Adams, Sam, 100, 155
Alamo, 194
Albini, Joseph, 178–81
Alcott, Bronson, 85
Alcott, Louisa, 166
Alger, Horatio, 44n., 76, 90, 192–93
Algiers, 14
Allen, Ethan, 28, 165–66, 194–95
American Revolution, 17, 59, 65, 88,
    115–16, 142, 149, 152–58, 165,
    190, 194–95, 197–98
Anglican church, 25–26
Anthony, Susan B., 136
art, 3, 9–10
Astor Place Riot, 77–78
atheism, 21, 28
Attucks, Crispus, 152
Axis Sally, 177

Bailey, Thomas A., 161
Bailyn, Bernard, 100
balanced budgets, 102–3, 112n.
Bancroft, George, 198
Baptists, 31
Baritz, Loren, 105, 108
Barney, Joshua, 194–95
Barnum, P. T., 79

Barrett, Robert J., 9
Barry, Dave, 140, 182
Baum, L. Frank, 92
Bayer, 128
Beard, Charles, 91, 101, 163, 213 n. 16
Becker, Carl, 189n.
Beecher, Henry Ward, 34, 47
Belloc, Hillaire, 196
"benefit of clergy," 153n.
Bethlehem Steel, 71
Bible, 32–33, 81, 165
Bierce, Ambrose, 1, 34
Bloom, Sol, 99
Bonhomme Richard, 3
Borah, William, 124
Borden, Lizzie, 173
Boston Massacre, 140, 152–54
Boston Tea Party, 154–56
Boy Scout Handbook, 6
Bradford, William, 18, 141–42
Brazil, 105
British East India Company, 155–56
Brown, John, 166
Bryan, William Jennings, 173–74
Buell, Augustus C., 3
Burnam, Tom, 89, 96
Burnap, George, 48
Burns, Ken, 184
Bush, Barbara, 57–58n.
Bush, George, 106
Butler, Jon, 22
Byrd, William, 115

221

Capone, Al, 117, 120, 122n.
Carlyle, Thomas, 45
Carnegie, Andrew, 68, 69
Caro, Robert, 49n.
Cartier, Jacques, 118
Catholics, 31
Cavalry, U.S., 3
Central Pacific railroad, 118
Central Park, 47, 170
Chalmers, George, 142
Chamberlain, Neville, 185
Chicago, 126
China, 127
Chrysler, 52, 58
Church of England, 20n., 26, 142n.
Churchill, Winston, 112, 177
"City on a hill," 103–5
Civil War, 10, 64–65, 66–68, 69, 126,
    159–60, 166, 190, 196
Clark, Norman, 122n., 128
class warfare, 106
Clinton, George, 116
Coca-Cola, 120, 129
cocaine, 126
Cochran, Thomas, 64–65, 73
Cogan, Frances B., 132
Cold War, 63
Comstock, Anthony, 131
Congregationalism, 26
Congress, 29, 40, 82, 100, 106, 123, 157
Constitution, U.S., 2, 27, 30, 56, 197
Constitutional Convention, 29, 30
consumption ethic, 46
Cooke, Jay, 65
Coolidge, Calvin, 174
Cotton, John, 32n., 145n.
Cowan, Ruth, 137–38
crime, 122n., 123, 177–81
Crockett, Davy, 194–95
Cuba, 105, 171
Curti, Merle, 11
Cushman, H. B., 119
Custer, George Armstrong, 171–73

Danhof, Clarence, 162
Dark Ages, 31
Daughters of the American Revolution,
    5n.
Decatur, Stephen, 14–15
Declaration of Independence, 27, 88

Dedham, Massachusetts, 143n., 144–46,
    148
Defoe, Daniel, 167
Delano, Warren, 127
democracy, 141–42, 146–47, 148n., 148,
    161, 167
Democratic party, 106, 125
Dempsey, Jack, 76
depressions, economic, 69
Dewey, John, 184n.
Diem, Ngo Dinh, 112
Diggins, John, 28, 102
Donald, David, 159, 160
Downing, Andrew Jackson, 47
Dred Scott, 167–68
drinking, 38, 114–25
drugs, 125–29
Dunne, Finley Peter, 16
Dupuis, Charles, 27
Duus, Masayo, 177n.

Eccles, Marriner, 61
Edgerton, Robert, 118–19
education, and women, 134
Emerson, Ralph Waldo, 85–86, 94–95,
    166
Enlightenment, 30, 100
Erie Canal, 53
Evans, Bergen, 95, 126

farmers, 56
Feinstein, Estelle, 150–51
Fitzgerald, F. Scott, 96, 120–21
flag, 1–6
Flag Day, 5
Flexner, Eleanor, 136n.
Foote, Shelby, 12
Ford, Gerald, 175
Ford, Henry, 183
foreign affairs, 106–8
Fourth of July, 6–8
Fox, Charles, 187
Franco, Francisco, 185
Franklin, Benjamin, 2, 27, 40, 87–89,
    156
Frémont, John C., 67
French Revolution, 33
Fresh Air Fund, 50
Friedan, Betty, 135
Frietchie, Barbara, 95

frontier, 161–63
Frost, Robert, 89–90
Fundamentalism, 32–33

Gallup Poll, 108
Gandhi, Mahatma, 86
gangs, 179
Gilmore, Thomas, 121
Gimbel's, 130
Golden Spike, 118
Goldwater, Barry, 101
Grant, Ulysses S., 77, 188
Great Awakening, 26–27
Great Barbecue, 73n.
Great Britain, 106, 127, 152–53, 187, 197
Great Depression, 39
Griswold, Rufus, 91
Gusfield, Joseph, 120
Gutman, Herbert, 40, 74

Haiti, 187
Hall Carbine Affair, 66–68
Halsted, Stewart, 128
Hamilton, Alexander, 28, 40, 54, 102–3, 109, 211 n.5
Hancock, John, 155
Harding, Walter, 82–83
Harding, Warren, xi, 99, 192
Harland, Marion, 132
Harper, Robert Goodloe, 14
Harper's Ferry, 54
Harrison, William Henry, 163
Hatch, Orrin, 28, 101
Hayes, Rutherford B., 163
Hegel, 182
Hemingway, Ernest, 86–87, 96, 120
Henry, Patrick, 13–14
Herskowitz, Leo, 169–71
high brow literature, 79
history
    accidents in, 186–88
    danger of remembering, 189
    "history will judge," 189–91
    ignorance of, 183
    laws in, 188
    manipulated, 10, 18, 27, 89, 197
    misused by politicians, 108–12, 185–86
    popularity of, 84

Hitler, Adolf, 185
Hofstadter, Richard, 65, 191
Holland, 20–21
Homestead Act, 162
Hoover, Herbert, 125
Hopkinson, Francis, 6
housework, 137–38
human nature, 100
Hume, David, 211 n.5
Hunnicutt, Benjamin, 38–39

ice cream, 99n.
immigrants
    and city parks, 48
    and the flag, 5
    and the work ethic, 37–38, 43
India, 127
Indians, 118–19, 154, 172, 197
industrialism, 41–42, 137–38, 138n.
ington, 79n.
Irish, 38, 114–15, 119, 150, 170, 180
Iroquois, 197
Italians, 178–81
Izzie and Moe, 123

Jackson, Andrew, 60, 74, 111
Jacksonianism, 100
James, Henry, 36
James, William, 36
Jamestown, 46
Jay Treaty, 106
Jefferson, Thomas
    and balanced budgets, 111, 112n.
    death, 8
    and the Fourth of July, 7–8
    and laissez-faire, 55–56, 110
    and religion, 28–29
    on taxes, 74
Jews, 43, 119
Johnson, Samuel, 1
Johnson, E. A. J., 54, 59
Johnson, Paul, 92
Johnson, Lyndon, 112, 164, 212 n.15
Jones, John Paul, 3–4, 14
Jones Beach, 48–49

Kefauver Hearings, 178
Kennedy, John, 104, 104n., 111, 163
Key, Francis Scott, 8–9
Keynes, John Maynard, 61, 92n.

King, Martin Luther, Jr., 86
Korean War, 107, 108
Ky, Nguyen Cao, 112

L'Ouverture, Touissant, 187
labor
    conflicts, 36
    and industrialism, 41–42
    and Robber Barons, 74–75
LaFollette, Robert, 124
laissez-faire, 52–54, 58–59
League of Nations, 109, 174
Lebergott, Stanley, 138n.
Lender, Mark, 116
Leutze, Emanuel, 9
Levine, Lawrence, 77–78
Levy, Leonard, 151
Lewis and Clark expedition, 118
Lincoln, Abraham, views on
        abolitionism, 160
    books about, 182
    dream about assassination, 195–96,
        196n.
    allegedly given piece of John Paul
        Jones's flag, 4
    and religion, 29
    and Shakespeare, 77
Lincoln, Mary Todd, 32
Littlefield, Henry, 93
Locke, John, 7, 10
Lockheed, 58
Lockridge, Kenneth, 144–45
log cabin, 17
Longfellow, Henry Wadsworth, 10
Lord, Walter, 8–9
Louisiana Purchase, 112, 187
Lowell, Massachusetts, 37, 41
Lutherans, 31
Lynn, Kenneth, 86

MacAndrew, Craig, 118–19
Madison, James, 28, 100, 106, 211 n. 5
Mafia, 177–81
marijuana, 126
Martin, James, 116
Marx, Karl, 92, 106, 190–91
Mayes, Herbert R., 76, 192–93
Mayflower Compact, 18, 140–42
McCarthy, Joseph, 59
McNeill, William, 189

meat industry, 60, 81–82
Mecklenburg Declaration, 8
Mencken, H. L., 80, 125, 147
Methodists, 31
Mexican War, 85, 107
Miles, Nelson, 172–73
millenialism, 32n.
Miller, Perry, 33, 145n., 146
Millerites, 32, 32n.
minuteman, 12
Montesquieu, 30, 110
Morgan, J. P., 13, 66–68, 68n., 72
Morison, Samuel Eliot, 104n., 122
Mormons, 31, 31n., 61, 136n.
morphine, 126
Moses, Robert, 48, 49n.
Moynihan, Daniel Patrick, 106
Munich, 185
Myers, Gustavus, 67

Nash, Gerald, 163n.
Nast, Thomas, 169–71
National Park Service, 157
nature, 50
Nelli, Humbert S., 180
Nevins, Allan, 191
New Deal, 62, 111
New England Town Meeting, 140, 143–
    45
New York City, 168–71
New York Navy Yard, 3
Newton, Heber, 43
Nicaragua, 186
Nineteenth Amendment, 135
Nixon, Richard, 189
Noonan, Peggy, 98
North Carolina, 8
Nye Hearings, 63

Ohio Supreme Court, 136
Olmsted, Frederick Law, 47, 49
Oneida, 32
opium, 127–28

Paine, Thomas, 28
parks, 47–50
Parrington, Vernon Louis, 73n.
patriotism: in the Revolution, 5, 10–15
Pearl Harbor, 91
phrenology, 79

Pilgrims, 16–21, 115, 141–43, 142n.
Pinckney, Charles, 14
Pinkerton Detectives, 75
pirates, 14, 166–67
playgrounds, 50–51
pledge of allegiance, 4–5, 5n.
Plymouth Rock, 19n.
Poe, Edgar Allen, 91
Poland, 189
Pole, J. R., 145n.
polygamy, 31, 31n.
Populists, 93, 191
Potter, David, 191
Powell, Barbara MacDonald, 158
prayers, public, 29
Presbyterians, 31
Preston, Thomas, 153, 153n.
Prohibition, 119–22
prostitution, 79
Protestant Reformation, 46
Pullman cars, 37
Puritans, 20n., 21–26, 33, 103–4, 125,
    145–47

railroads, 52–53, 65, 118
Reagan, Ronald
    "city on a hill" speech, 103–4, 212
        nn. 14, 15
    and contras, 112, 106
    misuses history, 103–4, 185, 186
    use of myth, 98
    confused about Pilgrims, 19–20n.
    and religion, 28
    and idea of virtuousness, 111
Rediker, Marcus, 167
Reed, Michael, 201
Reischauer, Edwin O., 175
religion
    age of faith, 31
    doomsday beliefs, 32
    state support of, 24–25, 29–30
religiosity of Americans, 21–22
Republican party, 106, 163
Revere, Paul, 10
revivalism, 26–27
Riis, Jacob, 50
Robber Barons, 68–75
Rockefeller, John D., 68, 72
Rogers, Daniel, 42n., 44n., 69n.
Rollins, Richard, 80

Roosevelt, Theodore, 13, 57, 82, 124–
    25
Roosevelt, Franklin, 57, 57n., 61,
    61n., 91, 107, 127
Roosevelt, Eleanor, 58n., 124
Rorabaugh, W. J., 114
Rosenzweig, Roy, 48
Rosie the Riveter, 133–34
Ross, Betsy, 6, 9

Salem, Massachusetts, 21, 23–24
Sandeen, Ernest, 33
savings and loan scandal, 105
Schlesinger, Arthur, Jr., 54, 57n., 64,
    111
Schlesinger, Arthur, Sr., 153n.
Scopes Monkey Trial, 32
Scott, Anne, 189
self-government, 141–42
sex, 34, 90, 79, 87, 90, 131, 193
Shakers, 31
Shakespeare, William, 76–79, 79n.
Shaw, George Bernard, 182
Shays's Rebellion, 80
Shenkman, Richard: mistakes, 171n.
Shipton, Clifford, 24
Shipton, Clifford K., 144
Sicilians, 179–81
Sinclair, Upton, 81–82
slavery, 85, 159–60, 167–68
Smith, Adam, 55
Smith, Page, 134, 154
Smith College, 135
Smithsonian Institution, 4, 8
snobbery, 79
social Darwinism, 36, 72–73
Soviet Union, 46
Spanish-American War, 107
Spencer, Herbert, 36, 72
Stafford family, 4
Stamford, Connecticut, 150–51
Stamp Act, 13
"Star-Spangled Banner," 8
Stein, Gertrude, 91, 96
Strassmann, Paul W., 69–70
suffrage, 135–36, 157, 161
Sumner, William Graham, 72–73
Sumner, Charles, 158–59
Swedes, 114
Syrett, David, 149–50

Tammany Hall, 168–71
Taney, Roger, 166, 167–68
taxes, 10, 24, 74, 92, 106, 156
Taylor, John of Caroline, 56
Taylor, A. J. P., 196
Taylorism, 44
temperance, 37
Thanksgiving, 18
The Spirit of '76, 3
Thernstrom, Stephan, 162n.
Thompson, Lawrence, 89–90
Thoreau, Henry David, 34, 55, 82–86
Tilden, Samuel, 170n.
Timberlake, James, 124–25
Tocqueville, Alexis de, 111
Toguri, Iva, 175
Tojo, Hideki, 174
Tokyo Rose, 174–77
Tories, 18, 142
Tracy, Joseph, 26
Travis, William, 194
Triangular Trade, 117
Trumbull, John, 3
Tunney, Gene, 76
Turner, Frederick Jackson, 163n.
Twain, Mark, 77, 89, 95, 114
Tweed, William, 168–71

Union Pacific railroad, 119
Utley, Robert, 172–73

Valley Forge, 140, 157–58
Vandenberg, Arthur, 109
Vanderbilt, Cornelius, 70, 72
Vassar College, 132
Victoria, Queen, 34, 80
Victorians, 18, 34–36, 89, 130–33
Vietnam War, 107–8, 184, 186, 212 n.15
virtuousness, 10, 100–101, 110–11, 212 n.9
Volstead Act, 124

War of 1812, 8, 74, 81, 187
Ward, Geoffrey, 127
Warner, Charles Dudley, 95
Washington, George
  and alcohol, 116, 117–18, 164
  and the flag, 6
  and hemp, 129
  and Jay Treaty, 106
  and patriotism, 10
  and religion, 28
  his reputation, 99
  at Valley Forge, 158
  and virtuousness, 10, 102
Wasson, R. Gordon, 67
Webster, Noah, 80–81
Weisberger, Bernard, 6, 185–86, 201, 218 n.7
Welch Grape Juice, 120
Welter, Barbara, 132
West Point, 55
Westinghouse air brake, 70
Wherry, Kenneth, 212 n.15
Whiskey Rebellion, 117
Whitney, Eli, 198
Whittier, John Greenleaf, 95
Wilkie, Wendell, 212 n.15
Will, George, 28
Willard, Archibald, 3
Willard, Samuel, 147
Williams, Roger, 146
Williamsburg, Virginia, 196
Willison, George, 19
Wills, Garry, 52, 100, 211 n.5
Wilson, Edmund, 92
Wilson, Woodrow, 109n., 110, 124
Winthrop, John, 20n., 25, 103, 104n.
Witt, William, 13
witches, 23–24, 24n., 30, 32, 93
Wolfe, Thomas, 120
women's suffrage, 135–36, 161
Woodward, C. Vann, 188, 197
work
  absenteeism, 41
  long hours, 35–36, 38–39, 206 n.12
  work ethic, 38, 40, 42–46
World War I, 62, 64, 86–87, 101, 107, 109n., 122n., 124, 128, 186, 189
World War II, 62, 64, 91, 107, 108, 133–34, 174–77, 185–86
writers: and alcohol, 120–22

Yale Club, 124
YMCA, 31

Zenger, John Peter, 140, 151
Zobel, Hiller, 153